Praise for

Turning Points in Compassion

This collection of awakenings and acknowledgements of our innate compassion, sourced worldwide from many of the most eloquent, passionate and intellectually progressive voices in today's growing Animal Rights movement, then crafted into a beautiful tapestry by the editors, is bound to be the turning point for many to become, as Matthew Scully explains, "radically kind."

—Dr Craig Quarmby, A Gentle Place, Tasmania, Australia.

Our relationships with other animals and ourselves are complex. But this complexity and tension are arguably the greatest when it comes to discussions of how and who we eat. Drawing on reflections of diverse writers from around the world, Turning Points in Compassion *is a remarkable, inspirational exploration of plant-based (vegan) eating. The moving personal accounts comprising each chapter provide a rich philosophical and practical resource for any and everyone.*

—G A Bradshaw PhD PhD, Founder and Director, The Kerulos Center Oregon, U.S.A.

Giving voice to a diverse range of thought, and presented through a variety of contributing styles (articles, interviews, editorials and poetry), this ambitious volume offers a powerful, multi-vocal narrative across the spectrum of veganism. Covering a range of topics from politics and law, to spirituality and social change, Turning Points in Compassion *makes a compelling case for the recognition of the beauty, sentience and intelligence of all things – something sadly lost in the rampant consumerist-individualism of late modernity. This volume is essential reading for anyone interested in, or committed to, the ethics, politics and life of veganism.*

—Dr Shannon Brincat, Research Fellow at Griffith University, Queensland.

Turning Points in
Compassion
Personal Journeys of Animal Advocates

Edited by

Gypsy Wulff and Fran Chambers

Western Australia
www.turningpointsincompassion.info
www.spiritwingspubs.com.au

First published 2015 by SpiritWings Humane Education Inc.

National Library of Australia Cataloguing-in-Publication entry

Title: Turning points in compassion: personal journeys of animal advocates/editors: Gypsy Carmen Wulff, Frances Mary Chambers.

ISBN: 978-09871-92-967 (paperback)
ISBN: 978-09871-9-2974 (ebook)
ISBN: 97-809871-92-981 (hardback)

Subjects: Consciousness in animals.
Animal welfare—Moral and ethical aspects.
Animal rights activists.
Human-animal relationships.

Other Creators/Contributors:
Wulff, Gypsy (Gypsy Carmen), 1955- editor.
Chambers, Frances (Frances Mary), 1952- editor.

Dewey Number: 179.3

Cover design by Marion Duke.
Cover photo by Ariane Timmermans – Suraj and rescued calf at Animal Aid Unlimited, India.

Copyright photos are acknowledged where appropriate.

To

John and Pepe

The angels of light who opened my heart in a way no others could.

Contents

Acknowledgements

My heartfelt thanks to all the wonderful contributors who have made this book possible. Each one of you has been incredibly generous with your time, cooperation, support and goodwill. I have been deeply touched by the commitment and courage you display in your efforts to improve the lives of animals in this world, and the way in which each one of you has brought your own unique approach and humanity to bear. It truly has been a privilege and an honour to work with you.

A deep debt of gratitude also goes to the animals for whom this book was compiled. They are teaching us to move beyond ourselves into an understanding that all life is an interconnected web of co-existence. Their plight is challenging humankind to rethink its established perceptions of animals as commodities, rather than as feeling, sentient beings. They are proving to be potent teachers as we humans struggle to evolve beyond a relationship of exploitation, into one of deep care, appreciation and respect. As we look into the world we have created for them, we see reflected back a human value system that has strayed from an awareness of the sentience and interconnectedness of all life. It is only when their suffering and exploitation ceases, and we have found our way into harmonious cohabitation, we will have come of age.

And finally, to those unsung heroes in the background who have been there along the way, my appreciation knows no bounds. To Teena, your constant generosity in time and energy has been an ever-present reassurance. Thank you also to Pick-a-WooWoo Publishing Group for your guidance and hard work with the publishing details. You have been a dream to work with. To our friends and families – John, Mark, Grace, Colleen, Otis, Ella, Paddy, Missy, Cathryn and Jane and the many others – thank you for all your support and endurance during the very long journey this work has taken in coming to fruition. And to Fran Chambers, my incredible co-editor, you have made this possible by being there every step of the way. I couldn't have done it without you. My deepest thanks.

"If we could feel the pain of all that we destroy in the attainment of our desires our minds would drown in tears of sorrow and remorse. Then in the death of our denial we would be reborn."

—David Coles

Preface

It has been a great privilege to edit a book of this nature and we are deeply grateful to the many contributors who have made it possible.

Filled as it is with the personal journeys of people who have taken a stand for the things they really believe in, we are amazed to see how varied and unique their approaches have been. They have revealed to us both just how deep the well of human goodness and kindness can be when people learn the truth about the animals around them, and how desperately animals need a voice if they are ever to be heard.

Through the voice of each contributor we see both the animals and our relationship to them in a new light. Their words reveal a world of sentient beings who display intelligence and have the same desires to live lives without oppression and cruelty as we do ourselves but, lacking the means of protest, have been unable to do so. On the contrary, they have been forever victimised and used as food, clothing, entertainment and labour for thousands of years, in silent slavery. The pain and suffering of the animal kingdom has been well recorded, but with little compassion.

Habituated to the sights and sounds of such treatment for untold centuries, people accepted it all as normal, and never considered it as a misuse or abuse of creatures they little understood but regarded as inferior to themselves. Most of our own families like millions of others, were born into that same web of ignorance and taught to treat animals as objects, not as living creatures with cravings for love, care and consideration. There were few people around to tell them that animal hearts are broken for the same reasons ours so often are – cruelty, neglect, and pure indifference.

Is it not a wonderful thing that people like the contributors to this book have not only been awakened to the animal world around them but also so powerfully moved by the injustices being perpetrated upon those animals that they have seen fit to open their minds and hearts to a new understanding of them, and to take a stand for their actual liberation by sharing their experiences with others? We think it is.

In a hundred and one different ways the message contained in this book is reaching the world through conversations, encounters, films and a host of other mediums but nothing can ever replace the words of someone who has personally encountered all their doubts and fears, felt the rightness of what they were doing, and was openly prepared to let others know what prompted their decision to change their lives for the betterment of the entire animal kingdom and their own. The story of that turning point in their lives is a permanent treasure that thousands will read.

They know that they are challenged by the many myths that perpetuate the eating habits of most people when they live in a society that has an economic machinery primed and fuelled by the animal industry but despite the problems and difficulties both large and small, they know full well their persistence will win. Why? Because every day they are discovering more people who are not indifferent to the welfare of the animals, people who truly care, who are doing what they can to bring love, compassion and light into a world of darkness they once knew nothing about.

We feel very proud to walk beside every single person who contributes their time and energies to alleviating the plight of animals in this world. We are also grateful to have shared the incredible energy and determination of those who are educating people to understand that we really can have a different relationship with animals when we are no longer dependent on them as a food source. Plant-based food is more than sufficient for our needs, and once this is understood by more and more people, the demand for meat will decrease, and the slaughter of animals will one day be abolished. Only then will the animals be truly free. Their nightmare will have ceased.

DISCLAIMER

CHAPTER 1

Farmers As Visionaries: Stories of Emergence and Transition

■ FARMKIND
Harold Brown

Harold Brown is a former US cattle farmer who has spent most of his life in agriculture. He grew up on a cattle farm in Michigan and worked for three years in the dairy industry. He eventually left the farm and became a vegan/animal rights advocate and promoted plant-based agriculture and environmental sustainability. Harold has formed his own non-profit organisation called Farmkind and travels across North America talking to people about sustainability, veganism, kindness to animals and his experiences as a farmer. He has appeared in two documentaries by US director Jenny Stein: *Peaceable Kingdom*, released in 2004 and the remake in 2009, *Peaceable Kingdom, the Journey Home*. The films focus on farmers who were in the animal agriculture industry but ultimately rejected their profession because of the inhumane treatment and slaughter of animals and the severe damage to the earth as a result of livestock damage. Due to his heavy consumption of animal products Harold suffered a heart attack at the age of eighteen… ■

▶ Harold Brown.

Life happens, doesn't it? The more pertinent question though, is are we involved with the process? For the better part of my life I was not a conscious participant in what was happening. My observation has been that most human beings are not present enough to appreciate the awe and wonder of what is right in front of them.

I grew up on a small family farm in Michigan and worked for three years in the dairy industry. My great uncles who lived nearby raised sheep and dairy cattle. As on many family farms we raised different animals for food: Angus cattle, rabbits, pigs and dairy goats. I was also a hunter so my relationship and indoctrination to animals as food began on the farm.

As a farm boy, my indoctrination went beyond family to the rural community that surrounded us, which included our extended family, to 4-H, the world's largest youth organisation (The 4 Hs are head, hands, heart and health and the 4-H organisation is a driving force behind indoctrinating children into agriculture). Another influence was going to a land grant college, but more than anything the greatest impact was made by television. Nearly every TV commercial sold one or more animal products, so with all this reinforcement I truly believed I was doing good work, living a good life and being a good person.

Yet there were things I was expected to do or that I did of my own free will that deep down I found objectionable. Things such as castrating calves, killing rabbits with my bare hands, beating cows onto trailers; things that I did that are painful to share. Carl Jung talked about how we cast those things we find objectionable in ourselves upon our shadow selves, thereby allowing us to continue to feel good about ourselves. But if that shadow gets too big it consumes us.

A turning point came when I was working in the dairy industry and I injured myself. Blood tests revealed I had extremely high triglycerides, a problem that turned out to be the same one that had resulted in my father having bypass surgery and a stroke. The doctor gave me a warning: either change my ways or expect a bypass by the time I was thirty-five. Considering the amount of animal products I was eating, this now doesn't come as a surprise. I had already suffered a heart attack when I was only eighteen, so all this scared me. The doctor gave me a pamphlet on how to eat better. I took it to heart and made changes and within a couple of years I was on an entirely plant-based diet and had reversed my heart disease.

However, while I had made dramatic changes in my quality of life there was still something missing. I had become involved with an amazing community of people who practised veganism and while I intellectually understood what they were talking about in relation to animal issues, there was still a gap. The connection and next vital turning point came a few years later when I found out about animal sanctuaries, places where rescued farm animals are allowed to live out their lives in peace. I was intrigued and it was at one of these sanctuaries that I met and adopted a young steer called Snickers. One day, after meeting him only a few times, I thought I'd test him out to see if he remembered me. When I entered the barn he was standing over in the corner chewing his cud and I called out, "Snickers!"

He looked at me and immediately came running, planting his forehead into my chest with a thump. I wrapped my arms around his neck and gave him a hug and at that moment something amazing happened within me. It is hard to put into words but it was as if there was a torrent of emotion flooding through me and I immediately had some profound revelations. It was as if the last layer of my emotional armour had broken away.

I had the mental image of a light switch right over my heart. I call it my compassion switch. I realised I had developed the capacity to turn it on and off as circumstances dictated. Of course it was always my choice but at that moment I understood I had 'learnt' to turn it on for certain people and animals, and to turn it off for others.

Now I could clearly see that my coping mechanism had been the simple phrase, "I don't care." Whenever I was in a position of doing something that

wasn't in line with my core values I would say, "I don't care," and I was immediately in a place where I was disconnected psychologically, emotionally and
spiritually from the other and was capable of doing just about anything. I had
grown up in an environment where violence was commonplace and an accepted way of living and recreation. At that moment when Snickers nuzzled into my
heart, I knew I would never use that phrase again. I also knew the flip side of
that coin was that whenever I found myself in an objectionable situation I must
say, "I care."

When we say, "I care" we show up in the world in a very different and marvellous way. When we truly care, our intentions, words and deeds are acted out
with integrity and are consistent with our core desires of compassion, empathy
and love.

> *That day I truly became vegan. Being vegan is not just a way of eating. Sure, what we
> put in our mouths is very important but it is only one component of a vastly larger
> picture and way of being. It is a practice of selfless service, unconditional love, and a
> holistic understanding of the biota. It is non-cooperation and non-participation with
> anything that does not allow another being to live on their own terms. There was now a
> conscious connection between my heart and my head and I now had a moral and ethical
> foundation upon which to live my life. On that day I learnt to trust my heart.* ■

That day I truly became vegan. Being vegan is not just a way of eating. Sure,
what we put in our mouths is very important but it is only one component of a
vastly larger picture and way of being. It is a practice of selfless service, unconditional love, and a holistic understanding of the biota. It is non-cooperation and
non-participation with anything that does not allow another being to live on their
own terms. There was now a conscious connection between my heart and my head
and I now had a moral and ethical foundation upon which to live my life. On that
day I learnt to trust my heart.

As you will see in this book there are many people who have shared their stories of transformation. I don't believe we are extraordinary people; I know I am
not. In my interactions with those who have developed what I call animal consciousness, there are common themes found in everyone's story, yet no two are
alike. More than that, these folk are examples of how we can all be and do better,
and live lives where our core values are in line with words and actions; in other
words, to live lives of moral and ethical consistency. We are not perfect and we all
are works in progress but we have learnt to trust our intuition and our hearts and
I can say for me, it has never led me astray.

All people know they can do better. It is a question of having the emotional
courage and moral imagination to do so. By our choices we create and recreate our
reality and our world.

I invite you to take this journey. You won't be sorry. Besides, if this old farm
boy can do it, anyone can.

■ MAD COWBOY
Howard Lyman

▶ Howard Lyman.

Howard Lyman is a former Montana cattle rancher. He travels more than 100,000 miles every year as a speaker and lecturer and has been the subject of two documentary films, Mad Cowboy and Peaceable Kingdom. He is also the author of Mad Cowboy and No More Bull! He is the former director of the Beyond Beef Campaign and the Humane Society of the United States Eating With a Conscience Campaign as well as past president of both the International Vegetarian Union and EarthSave International. He is currently the president of Voice for a Viable Future. In 1997 he was awarded the Peace Abbey Courage of Conscience Award...   ■

Background

Every morning when I get up and put my feet on the floor, I realise I am one of the luckiest people alive. I have been able to walk since 1979, which at the time I didn't believe was ever going to be possible again.

I was a fourth generation farmer, rancher and feedlot operator from Montana who was raised during the Second World War. My parents had one of the largest dairy farms in the state and because they weren't able to hire any help, they milked the cows and my grandparents raised me. By the time I was four or five years of age I knew I also wanted to be a farmer.

Despite the fact I never paid much attention to school work or ever took a book home, I managed to graduate from high school and went back home to work on the family farm. I discovered that farming is a business and I didn't have the tools to run one. I decided to go to Montana State University and learn to be an agri-businessman. I graduated with a degree in agriculture and over a period of years I developed a small farm into an operation where I had seven thousand head of cattle, twelve hundred acres of crop and thirty employees.

A Wake Up Call

Just when I thought I was on top of the world, I woke up one morning to find I was paralysed from the waist down. Doctors discovered I had a spinal cord tumour. Prior to surgery to remove the tumour I was told I had less than one in a million chance of ever walking again. I can tell you I did a lot of thinking prior to that operation. I was convinced I would probably be in a wheelchair for the rest of my life and I started doing a real inventory of what I was doing to the planet. I made a decision there and then to never again in my life do anything I didn't think was right. I had to admit the way I worked the farm using chemical methods was doing harm. I had seen the birds die, the trees die and the soil change. I decided I was going to change.

It took twelve hours for the surgeons to remove the tumour from the inside of my spinal cord. I walked out of the hospital with that one in a million chance of doing so.

A New Direction

While I was recovering, I asked my doctor what had caused the tumour. He said adolescent cells were stimulated to grow by the chemicals I was using on the farm. I decided it was time to become an organic farmer.

I went and saw my banker and said, "I want to borrow some money. I want to start farming with nature."

My banker leaned back in his chair and said, "What in the world does that mean?"

I said, "Well, I want to become an organic farmer."

He looked at me and laughed. "You want me to lend you money but you are not going to spend it with my other customers – the chemical dealer and the pharmaceutical dealer and the fertiliser dealer?"

It was at that point I decided to sell the farm and pay my debts. It was 1983. I began working with other farmers, helping them not to make the mistakes I had made.

In 1987 a phone call came that turned me in a new direction. I was asked to go to Washington to work on Capitol Hill as a lobbyist for the National Farmer's Union. All I could think was "Geez…five hundred and thirty-five members of Congress!" I was absolutely convinced all they needed to know was the truth and we would have clear sledding on farming with nature.

I went to Washington DC and spent five years working on Capitol Hill and the first thing I learnt was the Golden Rule – "Them that got the gold, make the rules." There was no doubt after working there for five years that we were never going to achieve a solution. So I told my friends, "I'm going out to talk to the people."

My friends laughed and said, "You are never going to get half of the people to do anything."

I said, "We don't need half. Eighty per cent of the people are brain dead, they are part of the herd and they follow nose to tail and if you follow nose to tail there is only one thing you should see in front of you. Our job is to educate the twenty per cent who are still thinking and when the majority of those realises the solution, the herd will follow."

And that's what I did. After five years of working on Capitol Hill I went out and started talking to people about things like Mad Cow Disease and the environment and about what was happening to the birds, the trees, the soil and the water.

I've spent about twenty years travelling and speaking and at one time I was on the road for about three hundred days a year. I didn't have any money so I couldn't afford to fly and had to drive, sometimes up to a hundred thousand miles a year.

In Court with Oprah

In 1996 I ended up on the Oprah Winfrey show talking about Mad Cow Disease. Following my appearance on air I ended up getting sued along with Oprah by a group of Texas cattlemen. They had us in court for six years. We won four different cases before the judge threw out the case with prejudice in 2004, which meant they could not refile it. I ended up with a good deal of notoriety but my message is still the same. No matter how you do the inventory, there are fewer natural resources on Planet Earth today than there were the day *Homo sapiens* first inhabited the planet.

A Change of Diet

I was a three hundred pound football player and when I quit playing football I kept eating the same way I'd always eaten. I got much heavier than three hundred pounds. I would sit down and have lunch and my nose would bleed. You know, I'm not the sharpest knife in the drawer but I knew I wasn't going to live very long if I didn't change my bad habits. But I came from Montana and I'd rather be caught riding a stolen horse than admitting to someone that I was going to become a plant-eater. So I became a closet vegetarian. I didn't tell anyone about it. I lost some weight. My blood pressure went down, my cholesterol went down. I thought, "Gee, if I can do that being the world's worst vegetarian, just think what I could do if I became vegan."

I became a vegan in 1990. I lost a hundred and thirty pounds. My blood pressure went from sky high to normal. My cholesterol fell from three hundred to one hundred and thirty five. You know, at that time I was pretty cocky. I wanted to go out and tell everyone all they had to do was change their diet and we would save the world. But I found it is a little more difficult than that to educate people. When I went to my fiftieth class reunion in Great Falls, Montana, I found half of my graduating class had already died. Nobody wanted to talk to me about my diet unless it was some clown who would come along and say, "Do you ever sneak out and get a burger? Do you ever go to McDonalds?" The thing I have learnt is you cannot point at someone and say, "Let me tell you what you ought to eat." It is just too overwhelming for them. The thing you have to do is tell them, "You know I saved my own life by changing my diet." As long as you are talking about yourself they are willing to hear the message. They begin being convinced I am crazy but when I use myself as an example I open their minds and I can talk to them. Even in my hometown, Great Falls, Montana, there happens to be a vegan restaurant. Every supermarket in town is loaded with plant-based products so there must be a lot more vegans there now than there were before I started.

Getting the Message Across

I've spent twenty years on the road. I've been to all fifty states and ten or twelve overseas countries. My book, *Mad Cowboy*, is in its thirteenth printing. It is available in English, Polish, Korean, Japanese, Chinese and Serbian. So I think the message is being heard.

There is no doubt in my mind that before I die the majority of Americans will be plant-eaters. Now the bad part about that is that it may not be soon enough. We are going towards the cliff environmentally at two hundred miles an hour. Never have we had less topsoil, less clean water, less clean air, whatever natural resources you want to look at – we are putting ourselves in the same position as the dinosaurs. The dinosaurs didn't know they were going to become extinct. *Homo sapiens* should be smart enough to figure that out but it was the famous German philosopher Goethe who said, "We hide everything in plain sight."

Schopenhauer said, "Truth. First it is ridiculed, then it is violently opposed and then it is accepted as self-evident."

I believe it is extremely important to enjoy your life. I think it is mandatory that you have joy in your life and that you are able to laugh and that you are able to enjoy the small things. But when we look into the eyes of the children, we need to remember it is our responsibility to do everything we can to ensure they have a future.　▓

We're in a position right now that we are either going to change our habits as a species or we are going to disappear from the face of the Earth. That is the premise I work on. Every time I look in the eyes of my children or grandchildren, I want to be able to say to them, "I may be a crazy old dude but I have done everything I could in my life so that you would have an opportunity in the future of surviving as a species." Every time I talk to my grandson on the phone I realise he has no control yet over the world he has been brought into. It is up to me and the adults on the planet to find a solution for his future. We are not doing very well but I have great hopes.

Learning the Facts

You can't change anyone until they understand the magnitude of the issue or what you are talking about. I would say to any individual, "Educate yourself." If you take just the United States for example, one out of every two Americans is dying of heart disease, one out of three has cancer, one out of four is dying of cancer, sixty per cent of Americans are either overweight or obese, diabetes is growing astronomically. If you take a look at the largest dietary study that has ever been done in the history of the world, *The China Study* by Dr T Colin Campbell, you will find there is a direct relationship between our human health and the animal products in our diet. If we can get people to stop and assimilate the facts we have an opportunity of getting the majority of thinking people to change their diet. When ex-president Bill Clinton went on national TV and told Wolf Blitzer he was eating a near-vegan diet, a rocket went through the American people, so it's changing, but are we changing quickly enough?

I believe it is extremely important to enjoy your life. I think it is mandatory that you have joy in your life and that you are able to laugh and that you are able to enjoy the small things. But when we look into the eyes of the children, we need to remember it is our responsibility to do everything we can to ensure they have a future. I believe I have been marvellously blessed in my life. I just hope I do everything that I can, as well as I can for as long as I can.

■ A FARMER IN TRANSITION LEARNS A HEART LESSON
David Lay

▶ David Lay and Pooh Bear.

Born to parents who grew up on traditional depression era farms in the Midwest, USA, David was raised in a conservative family who lived in the suburbs of Chicago during the school year, and then spent much of his time on his Grandparents' farms in Kansas and Oklahoma. Despite going on to become a physics teacher, David also chose to follow in his Grandfather's footsteps to breed and raise Guernsey cows. Due to his mother's influence however, he found it difficult, and is now unwilling, to bring any of his animals to be killed.

David also raises free-range chickens who will never become 'dinner'. He also has three pigs who, because they were runts and would have died otherwise, were rescued and became pets who mingle with David's chickens and cows, but who mostly stand on the back door stoop begging for treats. David has rescued several older cows bound for slaughter, as well as two veal calves who are now rather large, gentle, pasture ornaments named Pooh Bear and Tigger... ■

The drought of 2012 came unexpectedly in the Midwest, USA, and its effect was like that of a house fire that was suddenly raging behind you while you read your morning paper. At first, surprise, almost an intellectual study, and then panic as the reality of its heat was felt upon the face of every farmer who stood overlooking their vast herds of cattle grazing in what only a few days before had been placid green fields now turned to dried wilted grass. I had just planted a field of buckwheat for ground cover and a field of sorghum/sudan grass hybrid as feed for my purebred Guernsey cows and bulls. There had been just enough moisture to allow the seeds to sprout into seedlings, and at a height of only a couple of inches it began to wilt and die in the unprecedented heat. The grass crunched when walked on and it was evident there would be little food for the animals who lived primarily on its sustenance.

I have always loved and cared about animals. My mother and father wanted my brothers and me to be 'animal husbands' and learn the responsibilities that came with that charge. As a child I had many different pets, from hamsters to rabbits and parakeets, and as an adult I always wanted to have my own farm to raise animals. When I retired from full-time teaching, this became a reality, and like my grandfather, I began to breed and raise Guernsey cattle. I have always seen animals as kindred spirits and though I knew the day would come when I would have to make the decision to send an animal for slaughter, the concept had always remained an academic exercise. In spite of a growing herd and limited pastures, I always found some good reason to put off any such act. I even went so far as to 'rescue' a few older cows from being taken to slaughter simply because I saw their beauty as living beings, and not as potential pet food. The drought of 2012 forced me to face the logic of animals as food, and to challenge seeing my cattle as sentient beings. If I did not reduce my herd of thirty-two animals, living on fifty-four acres of now dried and parched land, to a more manageable number of fifteen, I faced the very real possibility of watching them starve to death.

At the time it was still early summer and the total number of cattle being sold for slaughter was still relatively small. Most farmers wanted to try to wait out the dry weather until prices were higher. However, as the summer progressed, the drought became overbearing for everyone and panic set in. The market was glutted and prices dropped, so now selling an animal was done not to make money, but simply to avoid feeding it expensive feed. In the business world this was called 'cutting your losses'. Even though I was facing the same dilemma, there were no easy choices. All of my bulls were tame and every animal in my herd had a name and a personality. So I bought hay, very expensive hay at that. Because of the drought, the amount of hay available was low and prices were running about two hundred dollars a ton, and since my herd could eat a ton a day, it would not take a mathematical genius to know there was a limit on how much hay I would be able to afford. I advertised some of my young bulls for sale, and sold one young bull and traded another for a young heritage variety pig – the logic being a pig ate different things than cattle, and less – so better to trade a bull for a pig and give the bull a chance at life rather than have it slaughtered. The pig became a pet. I named him 'Bubby'.

I didn't want to cut my losses, I wanted these wonderful creatures to live out long and pleasant lives, so I continued to look for alternate ways of either reducing my herd or finding new ways to feed them. I continued to advertise, but I also contacted some farm sanctuaries around the country and found they were full. Even if there had been room, most sanctuaries tended to take in hopeless cases in need of rescue, not animals who came from loving farms.

I also looked into hydroponics to grow grass quickly, and even the possibility of feeding my cattle corn syrup, as one of my neighbours had started to do, if not for nutrition, at least they would have energy. For various reasons, none of these options was viable. With no hope that a solution would arise, such as a saviour who would show up at my doorstep and tell me there was a place not far from here where I could take my animals and keep them safe, I was back to the only option I could see: taking my animals to the sale barn to be sold for slaughter.

Earlier in the year, a neighbour told me, "You need to learn how to kill", and a friend told me, "You're a guy that never should have been a farmer." Those words seemed to be haunting me now. All I ever wanted was to raise these beautiful animals called Guernseys and sell them to other Guernsey breeders. There wasn't supposed to be any agony in it. This was my retirement dream, a way to spend my last years blissfully living in the country and enjoying fellowship with the spirits of such kind and gentle creatures. Now, with the final lesson my parents had tried to teach me years ago, I had to shun all of the love and caring I had given to these animals and send some of them off to a death I knew would not be easy or pleasant for them. I felt like a child being forced into adulthood, having to make 'adult' decisions – decisions of life and death.

In late August, I spent an evening going over the list of cattle I had, looking at pros and cons of keeping each or sending it away. With only names on paper, it seemed this was going to be easier than I had feared, and when I came down to the final choices, it would be easy, as my rational mind went, to load them onto the trailer and haul them away, 'away' being an abstraction that made the very real physical place I was taking them some ethereal shadow in the future that really didn't exist except in some horrid Grimm's fairy tale. I decided to take two yearling bulls – bulls because they had less 'value' to the herd than cows – and yearlings because they were actually about a year and a half old, big enough to not have to stand in a feed lot, and they would have less attachment to the farm and less trauma being removed, or so I thought. Bulls also tend to be very interested in cows, and they would be around many, many cows where they were going. Certainly this would be bliss for two young fellows with nothing but love-making on their minds. I could not have been more wrong.

My two fellows, two very handsome Guernsey bulls that surely all of the girls at the sale barn would swoon over, were named Valentino and Butternutts, and were easily lured to the trailer with sweet feed. My worry they would balk was unfounded. As they approached the trailer, I stepped into it holding the feed bucket in front of them, where they stood at the doorway, Valentino in front looking at the feed, and then around the inside of the trailer, and then back at the feed. I felt like the proverbial stalker who offers little children candy to lure them into his car, and the end result would be no better for these two. They were, in fact, children and what only a few hours before had been an abstraction for me, was now becoming reality and that's when the doubt started. Something didn't feel right about what I was doing. There was suddenly an underlying heaviness in my arms and seeing the innocence in their eyes was making this task increasingly difficult. Just when I was about to stop, to lower the feed bucket, give the feed to them and send them on their way, Valentino and then Butternutts stepped up into the trailer. I stepped back and closed the inner door to keep them toward the front of the trailer for balance, and then latched the outer door.

Up until now, the day had been calm, but suddenly a hot, dry wind came out of the south. This happened often in the late afternoon as the heat would build, but this time it was as if someone were pushing on me, to reinforce the dread that was building in my heart, and to tell me something just wasn't right.

When I've hauled animals before, they would tend to move from front to back as much as they could. This time was no different. These boys were going for a ride and for them it was an adventure, something new with new smells, and they vied for the best position to see a sight or smell a scent, just as I saw other cattle doing when riding in someone else's trailer. It's almost as if they were truly enjoying the experience, but time went fast, and I was soon pulling into the sale barn lot. I was surprised to see so many other trailers, with many more cattle than I had brought, and so we waited in a long line, waiting our turn. Having been to sale barns in the past, I was familiar with the bawling of cows, but as I turned off the engine of my truck while waiting I noticed a low hum. When I rolled down the window, the hum became louder, almost in a slow vibrato, in the key of low G, one octave below middle C, if my music training from high school had any credence. It then dawned on me this was the sound of more than a thousand cattle all bawling at the same time, with the occasional lone bawl from some animal with a distinguishable voice. I also noticed the motion in the trailer had lessened.

▶ Valentino.

▶ Butternutts.

It finally came the turn of the trailer in front of me, and I saw him pull to the left and reveal a long, red trailer full of young, black cattle. He backed up his trailer to the loading dock, got out and began to do some paper work with the attendant there. The back gate of the trailer was then opened, but the cattle would not come out. I saw a young boy, no older than six or seven years old, come out with a cattle prod, one that shocks the animals, and climb up onto the fender of his trailer. He began poking the cattle with the prod through the openings in the side of the trailer with the understandable result of the cattle in the back reluctantly pushing the animals in front of them and then all leaving the trailer. I could see the animals more closely, and saw they were young heifers, or young female cows, which are the animals a producer would normally keep back to replace his older cows. This could only mean that he was reducing his herd because of the drought. To get rid of his young females would mean that if he wanted to continue his business, he would have to buy new cows in the future in order to restore his herd. This is a drastic move for a farmer. These animals would be sold for slaughter, not for building someone else's herd, and this was an indicator of how serious this drought had become.

My turn came – or should I say our turn – as these two boys I had in the back of my trailer were as much a part of this as I was, but with a much deeper stake. I backed up to the loading dock. The little boy was already up on the fender and had unlatched the middle gate. The attendant opened the outer gate and both of my little boys were pushed up against the front of the trailer facing out the back gate staring at a wall of young, black calves in an open pen just inside the building, all bawling as loudly as they could.

The attendant looked in and said, "What 'a ya got? Guernseys?" It wasn't a question, this man knew his cattle. "Steers?" he asked.

"No, bulls," I said.

He nodded his head and took my information. While this was happening, I saw the little boy poke Valentino with the cattle prod and he came forward but halted at the door, then began to turn around when the little boy poked Butternutts, who then jumped forward and crashed into Valentino. The little boy was fast and had moved down to the end of the trailer, put the prod through the open part of the trailer, which was enough to get the two bulls moving into the area where the attendant stood. Their ears were back, their heads down and their tails were between their legs. The attendant drove them in with the young calves, trying to find someplace where it was least crowded. I took my receipt and drove away from the loading dock with a sinking feeling and my inner voice screaming that things just weren't right. I've learnt to listen to my inner voice over the years, as it's almost always been right, but this time I ignored it, and the voice became louder and louder.

That night, as I tried to sleep, I kept thinking of the sound coming from that sale barn, the sheer number of cattle needed to make such a woeful sound and the hell that Valentino and Butternutts must be enduring in the midst of so much bawling and crying, a sound that would not stop. I live near other farms that have beef cattle, and when they wean the calves off the mommas, their woeful crying can be heard for three days before it begins to wane and then silence. It would seem these farmers had entirely bypassed the weaning process. Added to this is the fear of being taken out of their familiar, peaceful pasture, surroundings and family of cows, and dumped into a living sea of fear, smell of manure and urine, which could only add to the volume of the bawling. At times I would wake from briefly falling asleep to the sense I was seeing what they were seeing, hearing what they were hearing, and feeling the fear they were feeling. I agonised all night long and knew I had to go back and get them before they were sold.

I figured if I could get up early enough, I could get my chores done and run to get them in the morning before I had to go in to teach. I was up extra early, but by the time I'd finished the farm chores, it was time to leave to teach.

Stellar teaching was not what you would have witnessed in my classroom that day, and if you chose the word 'distracted' then you would have been close. But it was worse than that; my mind was with Valentino and Butternutts, and hoping they were going to be all right, wanting them to not suffer but knowing that was what they were going to do. At lunch, the agony ceased, as if a small voice said, "They're going to be fine, they're not sold yet." I relaxed, finished my last class and was on the road by 2pm, arriving at the sale barn in what was probably record time. I went to the front desk and asked if they had been sold and the receptionist typed some things into the computer and said, "No, they won't be sold until later this evening." Fortunately for the bulls, as it turns out, because they were Guernseys and weren't black, they were less preferred animals and would have sold as slaughter cows, or 'junk cows', which means these beautiful, purebred bulls would have brought the lowest possible price. The fact is, this facility which was made to hold a maximum of fifteen hundred animals, and normally only handled seven or eight hundred on a typical sale day, was handling more than two thousand five hundred head of cattle, and so the sale would go on late into the evening.

I said, "I want them back."

She looked at me and replied, rather stunned, "I've never heard of anyone wanting their animals back before."

When I got to the loading dock, it was the same attendant who had been there the previous evening. I gave him the ticket and explained what I wanted. He looked at the ticket and then gave me a sideways glance, like, "This guy is nuts," and then he asked when I would be back to pick them up, because he left at five o'clock and there would be someone else there. I told him I'd be back before five and so I jumped into my car and raced home to get my truck and trailer.

Notably, when I got back to the saleyards, there was no waiting line. I backed up to the loading dock and the attendant told another worker to get my bulls. It seemed like an eternity, but actually was only a few minutes before they were brought up. What I saw when they came to the alley into the loading area broke my heart. My two beautiful bulls were smeared with manure and dirt, had snot running out of their noses, were hunched up in total fear, and seemed not to want to move. Up came the same little boy from the previous evening, but this time with a stick with a large plastic 'hand' filled with marbles on the end. He raised the stick up and with a swift, rattling 'whack' came down on Butternutts's hind quarter and they started to move, though not seeming to know in what direction to go, until they saw the trailer.

"I used to eat meat, eat eggs from cruel farms, and drink milk from cruel dairies. I've fished and even hunted until I killed my first deer, when I cried afterward and have never picked up any of my guns to kill since then, and I've thrown away my fishing rods. I am in the middle of evolution, and have 'seen the light', but for those who know me as I used to be – it's kind of like when a good friend announces he's become a 'born again Christian' and everyone cringes."

I can only describe their motion toward and into the trailer as 'flying', because it seemed their feet hardly touched the ground. They ran to the very front of the trailer, even trying to get up into the storage compartment, trying to get as far away from that place as they could. When they couldn't get up there they cowered against the front wall of the trailer, each trying to push the other out of the way, vying for front-most position. I could almost smell their fear. I closed the back door on the trailer without closing the middle door; I just wanted to get them out of there.

As I drove home, I was not in as much of a rush, wanting more to give them a gentle ride. I could feel them moving in the trailer; the difference this time, however, was they were not moving front to back and front again, but from side to side, and always at the front. As I drove, in my silent voice I kept saying, "I'm sorry" over and over. When I pulled into the driveway of my farm it seemed they recognised the sights and smells and they began to bawl, and continued to do so as I went through the gate and up to the field where I was going to release them. I stopped the truck, opened the gate to the field and then opened the trailer door. At first they seemed hesitant, but then stepped out, bawling the whole time, walked only a few steps and stopped, just bawling out to seemingly no one. The other cows and bulls began coming up to them, but they still continued to bawl. It took a few moments before I realised what they were doing.

A friend of mine had fought through some of the most highly pitched battles of the Korean War, and had witnessed many of his young comrades' deaths.

"Almost every one, when death was imminent, would call out for their mothers," he said.

My bulls, my little boys who had long since been weaned, were calling for their mothers.

Doctors as Activists

INTERVIEW WITH

Dr Neal Barnard

Founder, Physicians' Committee for Responsible Medicine

> *"If a man aspires towards a righteous life, his first act of abstinence is from injury to animals."* ■

> —Albert Einstein.

Neal Barnard, MD, is a clinical researcher, author and health advocate. He has been the principal investigator or co-investigator on several clinical trials investigating the effects of diet on health. Most recently, he was the principal investigator of a study on dietary interventions in diabetes, funded by the National Institute of Health and conducted under the auspices of the George Washington University School of Medicine in association with the University of Toronto.

▶ Dr Neal Barnard.

He is the author of dozens of publications in scientific and medical journals as well as numerous nutrition books for lay readers and is frequently called on by news programs to discuss issues related to nutrition, research and other controversial areas in modern medicine. He is a frequent lecturer at scientific and lay conferences and has made presentations for the American Diabetes Association, the American Public Health Association, the World Bank, the National Library of Medicine and many other medical and scientific organisations.

Dr Barnard grew up in Fargo, North Dakota. He received his MD degree at the George Washington University School of Medicine in Washington, DC, and completed his residency at the same institution. He practised at St Vincent's Hospital in New York before returning to Washington to found the Physicians' Committee for Responsible Medicine (PCRM) in 1985. PCRM has since grown into a nationwide group of physicians and lay supporters, which promotes preventive medicine and addresses controversies in modern medicine.

Dr Barnard is an Adjunct Associate Professor of Medicine at the George Washington University School of Medicine and Health Sciences, a Life Member of the American Medical Association, and a member of the American Diabetes Association...   ■

Having been trained in conventional medical practices why have you chosen a dietary approach instead of the standard medical treatments for disease?

In my first year of medical practice it occurred to me that the great bulk of problems affecting people, not only in America but worldwide, is largely responsive to dietary changes. In other words, heart attacks are caused mostly by our bad diets. The same is true of cancer, diabetes, hypertension and many other problems. It doesn't mean there is not a role for medical treatment, but that we've got to look at the causes first, and the causes are typically right on our own plate.

This might seem a fairly obvious question, but what do you consider a bad diet?

A bad diet is animal based. A bad diet is what I grew up on in Fargo, North Dakota. I come from a long range of cattle ranchers. What we had was a bad diet. A good diet is based on plants.

What happened to change your direction to a diet based on plants given that you came from a cattle ranching family?

I give some credit to my father for this because even though he grew up in the cattle business, he took a great dislike to it and left and went to medical school. I still grew up eating a lot of meat, but like him I chose medicine and the year before I went to medical school I had an epiphany.

I had a job as a morgue attendant in a hospital and I was assisting at autopsies. One day a person in the hospital died of a massive heart attack. In order to examine the heart we had to remove a section of ribs from the chest and the pathologist pointed out the blocked coronary arteries and the blocked carotid arteries. This was quite an eye opener for me. At the end of the examination I went up to the cafeteria where, as fate would have it, they were serving ribs for lunch and the ribs they were encouraging people to eat looked just like the ribs on the dead body. They smelled the same and I just couldn't eat them. That was the beginning of the end of my meat-eating life.

And that's where you made the connection?

That was the beginning of it and as time went on I learnt more and more about how a meaty diet causes heart disease. That it played a role in causing common forms of cancer was shocking to me. Then of course our own research eventually showed how diseases like diabetes and other ailments were exquisitely responsive to dietary changes.

Along the way I've come to recognise that animals are not particularly interested in being eaten; that farms are almost universally abusive, far beyond what any civilised person would consider acceptable if they really understood what goes on, and that the effects on the environment are grotesque.

So what are the problems generally associated with consuming meat?

Meat products have a lot of fat, particularly the bad, saturated fat. They also contain cholesterol. As a result these products tend to raise the amount of cholesterol in our blood and that leads to heart disease, stroke and other problems. But meats are also deficient; they are very low in protective vitamins like vitamin C and other antioxidants. They tend to squeeze off the plate the foods that will protect us. Beyond that they have hormonal effects. I am not speaking about the hormones that are fed to cows and chickens. I am talking about changes that occur in the human body when we eat these foods; our hormone levels are altered by consumption of these products. For example, oestrogen and testosterone activity tend to rise, which in turn increases the risk of certain forms of cancer. As animal fat packs into the cells of our bodies, particularly the muscle cells, they become resistant to insulin's efforts to escort glucose into our cells and that leads to diabetes. When a person switches to a plant-based diet, the animal fat is one hundred percent gone as is the cholesterol. All the foods are rich in fibre so it is very easy to slim down. Cholesterol levels plummet, blood pressure returns to normal in most cases, and diabetes improves. There is even some evidence that Alzheimer's disease might be less frequent in people who consume plant-based diets. You get a few extra years of life too.

It sounds like a good deal then.

Yes it certainly is. You also have a long line of cows and chickens waving white handkerchiefs at you saying thank you.

So the high protein diets that have been the fad for many years really don't have a lot of science behind them?

More and more researchers are studying low carbohydrate diets, and diets of all kinds, and it's pretty clear that as long as animal products are part of the diet, cholesterol levels will not fall to where they should be, sometimes with disastrous results. We published a case study of a man who adopted a low carbohydrate diet who was just trying to lose a few pounds. He ended up with crushing chest pain and massive heart disease very, very rapidly. So that is not the way to go.

What about dairy products?

Dairy products share many of the problems that meat has and actually accentuate some. Keep in mind that milk's natural function is to nourish a growing bovine infant so it is very high in certain things the calf would not consume later in life such as saturated fat, lactose and sugar. Unfortunately, milk and milk products are so high in saturated fat that they have a major link with heart disease, diabetes and certain forms of cancer. Cheese is seventy percent fat; from a nutritional standpoint this is absurd.

Are there any particular cancers that you see dominating as a result of this type of diet?

The digestive cancers, especially colon cancer, are linked to animal products. The most obvious examples are bacon, hot dogs, deli slices, the so-called 'processed' meats on which dozens and dozens of research studies have been done. The World Cancer Research Fund and American Institute for Cancer Research issued a report published in 2007 which said the evidence linking processed meats to colorectal cancer was convincing. It's pretty clear that people should never ever consume those foods. But unfortunately not only do they consume them, they give them to their children. Hormone-related cancers such as breast cancer, uterine cancer and prostate cancer are also linked to animal product consumption. If you add these dietary cancers to lung cancer, which is primarily linked to smoking, the great bulk of cancers can be prevented.

People should take dietary steps early in life to prevent cancer later, but it is never too late. Studies show that when people move toward a plant-based diet, even after cancer diagnosis their survival is improved.

What about chicken and fish?

Chicken is essentially the same as red meat. People think it is lower in fat but if you strip the skin off chicken the numbers are something like this: compared with lean beef which is about twenty eight or twenty nine percent fat, lean chicken is about twenty three percent fat. It is really not much lower. Compare that to a bean, which is all of four percent fat. Fish vary a lot. Some such as Chinook Salmon are over fifty percent fat; Atlantic Salmon are approximately forty percent, and some types are lower.

Some people excuse fish because the fat in it is supposedly good fat. What they are referring to is Omega-three fatty acids, which are the good fats. But we have to disappoint these people by reminding them that seventy percent of the fat in fish is not Omega-three. It's a mixture of saturated fat and various forms of completely unnecessary unsaturated fats. And there are mercury and other toxins sprinkled into the mix, so fish is not health food by any stretch of the imagination. You are also eating an animal who lives, in many circumstances, in what has become the human sewer. I'm talking about our rivers and waterways and some of the intentionally set up breeding facilities, which are concentrated and not clean. If they are wild fish they are migratory so you don't know where they've been. The smaller fish are eaten by larger fish and we now have a genuine food chain where toxins are concentrated, which is why we have mercury warnings all the time for pregnant women not to eat this or that fish. If you look at the Omega-three fatty acids there are certain fats that you need but what really counts is the proportion of them. Beans, vegetables and fruits don't have very much fat in them but the traces of fat they have are proportionally quite high in Omega-three. And that's really all we need.

Recent evidence suggests diabetes is more common among fish eaters. Certainly when compared to people who avoid fish and all other meats, the fish eaters don't really do very well.

You mentioned that going onto a plant-based diet could bring improvements to various diseases and that it's never too late. What are some of the results you've seen in patients who have adopted a plant-based diet?

In 2003 we launched a large diabetes study, which was really very exciting. We brought in a group of people with Type II diabetes. Half of them, the control group, began a more conventional diabetes diet, which involved restricting carbohydrates and eliminating calories. The experimental group followed a totally vegan diet. We asked the experimental group to keep oils low and to favour what I'm going to call 'good' carbohydrates, so instead of white bread they might favour rye bread or pumpernickel bread. It was not a low carbohydrate diet, in fact it was quite generous in carbohydrate-containing foods, with lots of beans, vegetables, fruit and whole grains.

The vegans did terrifically well. Their improvements in blood sugar, weight, cholesterol and blood pressure were quite remarkable. They exceeded the changes we saw with the conventional group, and individuals in this group were thrilled. I remember a man in his late thirties who told me about his own father being dead by age thirty. He himself was thirty-one when he was diagnosed. He came in to see us several years later and his diabetes had completely disappeared in the course of this trial. Not everybody had their diabetes absolutely go away but it improved for almost everybody. We saw people with arthritis improve and over the years we have seen so many improvements in people's health beyond what they had expected. This research has been now recognised by the American Diabetes Association in their clinical practice guidelines. In other words it is a healthy way to go if you've got diabetes and from an individual standpoint it is absolutely life changing.

Many doctors are still ignoring these facts and our job is to make sure they become aware of it. We have a huge pharmaceutical industry that unfortunately has been a first stop for doctors addressing diabetes but our results show that a vegan diet is stronger in its glucose lowering effects than typical oral diabetes medication and all the side effects are good. People lose weight and diabetes drugs often do the opposite, they cause people to gain weight. If I could wave a magic wand I would have people not wait until diabetes is diagnosed. People should be raised on a vegan diet. We would revolutionise the health of the world if we did that.

That leads beautifully to the next question, is a vegan diet safe for everyone and does that include children and pregnant women?

Yes. Not only is a vegan diet safe, but it is not safe to add animal products to the diet to the extent that most people do. Two things happen. The first is that children acquire a taste for foods that could kill them in later life. The second thing is that they start paying a price quite early on. About twenty percent of children in the United States now have an abnormal cholesterol level and one-third of them are overweight. One-third of children born since 2000 will develop diabetes and this is not just due to physical inactivity. Studies show it is clearly diet related, including the increase of cheese and meat into the American diet. We have found the average American now eats seventy-five pounds (thirty-four kilograms) more meat per person per year compared to a century ago and thirty pounds (thirteen kilograms) more cheese. These are huge amounts.

How old are the children when they are developing diabetes? Is it at a young age or is it in adulthood?

In most of them it does not become manifest until adulthood. As you know there are two kinds of diabetes; Type I used to be called childhood onset, and Type II, the more common form, used to be called adult onset but we are seeing it at earlier and earlier ages. The seeds of Type II diabetes are sown in childhood; children start to gain weight and then as adults they are overweight or obese and their risk of diabetes escalates dramatically.

Are you saying that one doesn't suffer deficiencies on a vegan diet?

We study the nutritional profile of people beginning vegan diets and their nutrition improves quite dramatically in two directions. The first is that the bad things are reduced: they ingest less fat and very little or no cholesterol. The good things are increased: they get more fibre, more vitamins, more folic acid, more vitamin C and so forth. This doesn't mean you don't have to do some planning but it's easier than anyone could have guessed. Protein is effectively a no-brainer. There is so much protein in beans and grains and vegetables that you don't have to do anything special to get adequate protein. Calcium is good to think about – it's in green leafy vegetables and beans so it's very easy to find. Vitamin B12 is something I encourage people to take notice of, because it's needed for healthy nerves and healthy blood. B12 is not made by animals or plants, but by bacteria, and the theory, at least historically, is that the traces of bacteria in the soil or on plants might give us the traces we need, which as we know is an unreliable source these days. I encourage people to take a supplement and B12 is in every multiple vitamin you take. That's all you really need. People should not neglect B12 but neither should they worry about it very much, just take a multiple vitamin or another source.

To summarise, a healthy diet consists of four groups: vegetables, fruits, whole grains, and legumes or beans, then make sure you have a source of B12 and you are set.

If a person reading this interview says, "OK, I buy into all this but I've been eating meat heavily. Do I just switch to a vegan diet immediately or is there a plan of action that I should take?"

I split it into two steps.

Step 1: Check out your options and see what you like. If right now you are having eggs and sausage for breakfast then now is the time to check out the veggie sausage or make a big plate of pancakes. If you want to flavour them up have blueberry pancakes, or oatmeal with cinnamon and raisins or whatever your preference may be. What are you having for lunch? What are you having for dinner? Find a low-fat vegan healthy lunch and dinner that really works for you and it may take you a week or so to sort out the ones you like the most. We have lots of recipes which you can access on our website and we also have many suggestions for when people eat at restaurants. After you know the foods you like for breakfast, lunch, dinner and snacks, then I encourage people to go to the second step.

Step 2: Take three weeks, twenty-one days, and do it all vegan, all the time. At the end of that time you will be healthier, you will feel better, you'll have more energy, your weight will be trimming away and your tastes will be starting to change. When you put all that together it's really a very easy transition to make.

You founded the Physicians' Committee for Responsible Medicine in 1985. How exactly did that come about and what is PCRM's aim?

I was in my first year of practice after medical school and I felt it was important for doctors to not simply treat one patient at a time. I thought doctors really needed to speak out about the issues of the day – prevention, nutrition, diet, human and animal ethics. We have published a number of research studies where we have put diets to the test. When it comes to research we also need to speak out on ethical issues because humans are sometimes abused, although it's much better regulated today than it was a few decades ago. Animal experimentation is still not well regulated and doctors need to raise their voice here as well. We've been tackling all of those things and we are bigger and more vigorous now than we have ever been.

I know you've been involved in a lot of campaigns in this area and also with your government. What are the campaigns involved and how effective has PCRM been in achieving results?

When it comes to nutrition the US government has had dietary guidelines that mix good scientific evidence with the mandates for promoting industry. In other words, on the one hand they are making some sensible suggestions about what people should eat. On the other hand they are busily trying to hawk meat and dairy products, so we ended up with a hybrid. PCRM had a pyramid for approximately twenty years that said you should base your diet on whole grains, vegetables and fruits. But the US Department of Agriculture (USDA) included a meat group and a dairy group, which was entirely in conflict with the

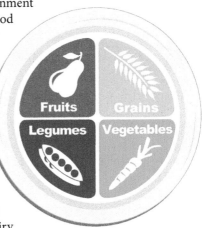

▶ PCRM Nutrition Plate.

science that showed people who avoided meat and dairy products were healthier than other people. The pyramid was finally scrapped in favour of a new plate shaped diagram. We lobbied hard and in 2009 we sent a plate to the Department of Agriculture and suggested they adopt it. In 2011 the USDA did adopt a plate that looks a lot like ours, but it was not exactly as we had suggested. They added a dairy group, which we think is a mistake. They included the vegetables, fruits and whole grains but they changed the bean/legume group to a "protein" group so that meat could be part of it. We are currently litigating against the US Government to rectify this, and I think it's safe to say we've been successful. The dietary guidelines for Americans now include vegetarian and vegan diets and lots of ideas on how to adopt them. But we are not where we need to be because there is still too much promotion of meat and dairy products and that has to change.

What is the litigation based on?

The current litigation against the US Government is a result of their complete lack of response when we originally sent them our plate diagram. We had to sue them to respond, after which they released the dietary guidelines for Americans, which were the best guidelines we've ever had. They lay out pages and pages on vegetarian and vegan diets and sing their praises. However, as good as that is, it's not good enough. We continue to lobby against the promotion of meat and dairy products and so litigation on those fronts continues. And we are also suing seven or eight fast food chains because they misrepresent their products and hide some things from the consumer.

How much of your motivation for promoting a vegan diet had to do with alleviating animal suffering? Is part of your mission to work against animal cruelty?

Happily all of these things go in exactly the same direction. The diet that makes people healthier is a diet that excludes animals and a diet that lets the earth breathe more easily. People come to veganism from various directions and often with more than one motivation occurring simultaneously. I sometimes wonder what would happen if you were, maybe a century ago, in a part of the world where people consumed blood and they offered you a glass of blood to drink. Would the objection be an ethical one, an aesthetic one, or a health one? Or would it be all of those things mixed at the same time? It is perhaps a peculiar analogy but it's not so different to when a person offers you a piece of skeletal muscle.

Would you say the use of animals for medical purposes is ever justified?

Animal research is cruel. It is fundamentally extremely taxing for the animals even before the experiment begins and it is almost always fatal. I've recently been reading about what is referred to as developing animal 'models' for Type I diabetes. This research has consumed an enormous amount of money and time and something like one hundred and ninety-five treatments have been shown to be effective in improving or reversing Type I diabetes in animals but not a single one of these has proven effective in human beings. When one thinks about the waste of time and money and animals' lives, as well as the fact we have failed to do what science really needs to do which is to stand back and look at who is getting Type I diabetes. What do the people have in common? How can we intervene? Science has an unfortunate tendency to try to tease apart details with crude copies of diseases in animals. Just as John Bailar, editor and chief of the *Journal of the National Cancer Institute*, said, we have got to change course in cancer research. He wasn't specifically talking about animal research but he was talking about the current headlong commitment to try to tease apart cancer processes so we can make better and better treatments. He finally said we have got to stand back and focus more on preventing cancer, rather than focusing so much on cancer treatments. Unfortunately that is a message scientists don't want to hear in many cases, but it is an essential one if we are going to conquer these diseases.

In your journey so far what do you consider some of the your biggest accomplishments?

We have a very long way to go and any time I look back I think it's important to not over-blow any particular accomplishment because the task ahead remains very large.

When we started we felt it was important to end the use of animals in medical education because as long as doctors trained in laboratories where they were using and killing animals they would never come to see the problems of animal use. We have been largely successful in eliminating the use of animals in medical schools in the USA and Canada in particular, as well as in trauma training, paediatrics and much of nursing training. We are now turning our attention to the use of animals in research per se which is a bigger target but even more important. It has certainly been gratifying to have a number of research teams who have influenced medical practice and helped to mainstream vegetarian and vegan diets. We have television programs and books and many people now are either adopting vegetarian or vegan diets or at least feeling validated and supported based on the work that we and others have done. I hasten to say that everything achieved is always part of a team effort. There are many individuals, groups, scientists, teachers and laypeople from different countries and all walks of life working in the same direction and no one candle is as bright as all.

Neal, your work is very clearly purposed. That comes across strongly. What's the bigger vision associated with it?

My hope is that if we are successful the world will be more compassionate and that the toll currently being exacted on animals, on human health and on the environment will reduce to as close to zero as we can make it. Then we can all retire and go out and play golf and party and do what we want. Maybe even take Wednesdays off.

I think it's important to remember that life is very, very short. Each and every one of us has a very short window of time in which we can have any effect on the world around us and I don't wish to squander that time with unimportant pursuits. It is my hope that we can inspire as many people as we can to work together to make our world kinder for ourselves and for future generations.

Links:

http://www.pcrm.org/health/diets/

http://www.nutritionmd.org/nutrition_tips/nutrition_tips_understand_foods/
fattyacids_omega3.html

http://www.pcrm.org/health/diets/vegdiets/dont-vegetarians-have-trouble-get-
ting-enough-vitamin B12.

■ ACTIVIST. PHYSICIAN. EDUCATOR. HEALER.
Holly Wilson MD

*"I am awake in a world that is sleeping. I am aware of the horrors that have been
carefully sheltered from my sight, and will never see food the same. I hear cows crying
for their babies when I see cartons of milk. I see a pig being boiled alive in the de-hairing
tank when I smell bacon. I see marine animals entangled and drowning in nets when I
smell seafood. I see a cow hung by his back leg, fighting for his life as he is dismembered
when I smell a barbecue. I see miserable, diseased birds when I see a carton of eggs. I
can't turn it off, and am compelled to speak to anyone that will listen."* ■

—Dr Holly Wilson.

▶ Dr Holly Wilson and friend.

Dr Holly Wilson is board certified in Emergency
Medicine and works in various hospitals
as a travelling physician. In the Emergency
Department, she educates her patients as
well as staff members about the benefits
of compassionate food choices. She is an
outspoken, dedicated activist. In South Beach,
Miami, she established her own vegan education
table, airing undercover videos and distributing
literature. While living in Fort Lauderdale, she
volunteered with Sea Turtle Oversight Protection
during sea turtle nesting season. She ensured
the hatchlings made their way into the ocean,
as the artificial lights along the beach routinely
disorient them. She also enlightened the curious
tourists and local residents about the hardships
sea turtles face – in particular, the commercial
fishing industry. From 2011 to 2013, In Defense
of Animals featured a monthly 'Ask Dr Wilson'
column, which allowed her to answer health and diet questions, while simultaneously
incorporating the ethics of veganism. She served as the ship's doctor with Sea Shepherd
Conservation Society during the 2011 Blue Rage II bluefin tuna campaign in the Mediterranean
Sea on the MY Steve Irwin and on the second half of Operation Divine Wind in the Southern

Ocean in 2012 on the MV Bob Barker. When the rodeo or circus comes to town, she protests in full costume and hands out leaflets. At present, she is a contributing writer for Free from Harm. She is always ready to discuss her vegan lifestyle and serve as a mentor for those ready to embark upon their journey... ■

I grew up in a working middle class neighbourhood in Long Island, New York, USA. There were sidewalks and lush trees, and I rode my bicycle everywhere. My childhood was as rich as it was ordinary. I had many friends who lived close by, my parents were nurturing and supportive, and I enjoyed four seasons of weather. An early yet distinct memory of mine is relocating the wayward earthworms after the rain fell. They would make their way onto the concrete sidewalks, and if they remained there once the sun began to shine – they would die. I felt responsible for them. I'd place them back onto the soil, to continue doing whatever it is earthworms do. I enjoyed watching them wriggle with excitement. I was also that sensitive kid others laughed at, because of how much I loved my guinea pigs and rabbits. Then something went tragically awry. I had always loved animals, but became unconscious to the suffering of those sheltered from my sight. This was not an active process, but one merely of indoctrination.

Well into my adulthood, I was able to maintain the dichotomy of loving animals and eating any food form whatsoever. I would often say, "Put it in front of me and give me a fork." I was proud of the fact that I would try anything at least once. I felt adventurous. I never saw fit to question who I was eating, whether or not my cosmetics were tested on animals, whose skin I was wearing, or any other such aspects behind the enjoyment and routines of my life. Brutality and exploitation had become the norm, hidden behind clever advertising and convenient packaging.

I attended medical school at Tel Aviv University in Israel. I was often asked about the difficulties of living abroad, and my response was always the same. They did not entail the language barrier, the cultural differences, or even the threat of a suicide bomber. The greatest challenge that I encountered was witnessing the suffering of the feral cats; they were everywhere. It is impossible to walk through Tel Aviv and not see their struggle. There are individuals who take action and trap for sterilisation, and who also leave food and water outside. My apartment was often a foster home for a sick or injured cat or kitten. Turning my back on them was never an option.

During my time in Israel, I saw a TV program on sea turtles. Horrified to learn that they drown in fishing gear, I immediately gave up seafood. This was truly an epiphany; the first bolt in my blinders had been removed. I remember thinking, "How can I eat fish, knowing that I killed a sea turtle?" Sadly, I valued the life of the sea turtle more than the animal I saw only as food, yet this is how my journey began. For the first time in my life, I had thought about the impact of my choices. I started asking questions, and the more I learnt, the more I changed.

In June 2011 I served as the ship's doctor for Sea Shepherd's Blue Rage II campaign. I was becoming increasingly frustrated at my job, and was ready for change and adventure. The timing was perfect. When interviewed, I was asked if I had any food allergies. I replied, "I am allergic to cruelty. I am vegan." I was informed that the ships only serve vegan fare. In addition to performing my medical duties, I would also be working in the galley, preparing meals for the crew.

We headed out on 1 June 2011. I heard the motors start. I heard the dense clanging thud of the anchor chains being drawn. I was still in my medical room arranging everything. I stepped outside and saw the deck hands furiously buzzing about. Then we actually started to move slowly away from the harbour. The sky was bright blue with thick white clouds. The sun shone on the side of the ship. We picked up speed, and small white crests began forming on the side of the boat. I started to cry. It still did not feel real to me. It was like living on a movie set, or being a character in an action novel. Each page turned brought new adventures and new emotions. It was profoundly thrilling.

Being on campaign with Sea Shepherd has made me a better activist. The oceans are grossly overlooked, even by fellow vegans. People have difficulty feeling empathy for those they can't relate to. Marine animals breathe underwater, have gills, fins, hard shells, tentacles- yet contrary to popular belief, have an exquisite ability to feel pain. Furthermore, we have brought many species to extinction or on the brink thereof simply because we won't stop eating them. Others that we do not consume are also being pushed to extinction as by-catch. Fishing gear indiscriminately catches and kills approximately twenty-five million tons of non-target animals annually, worldwide. Non-target animals include dolphins, sharks, sea turtles, juvenile fish, sea lions, whales, and albatrosses as well as other endangered seabirds. Seabirds grab the bait on longlines, then become ensnared on the hooks. When the lines get lowered into the water, they drown. They also become entangled in nets when they are hunting their prey. When challenged with questions about animals eating other animals, I explain that true predators only utilize the weapons that they were born with. One of the highlights of the campaign was giving tours of the MY Steve Irwin in Barcelona with another crew-member who is well known by Whale Wars fans. People are captivated by endangered animals. It was a unique opportunity to engage people about the horrors of the commercial fishing industry and the state of our oceans, and I am fortunate to have had this experience.

I will always treasure the time I spent with Sea Shepherd Conservation Society serving as the ship's doctor. Most crewmembers are vegan, and being surrounded by like-minded activists from around the globe was incredibly unique and inspiring. I am also now a better advocate for the ocean's treasures.

Veganism is a wave of compassion. I am but a single molecule in the ocean. Sometimes I ride the wave and it keeps me afloat when I am weak. Other times I am the driving force creating movement. And when I am feeling utter despair and devastation, I feel like I am being swallowed alive by this wave. I am acutely aware of my vulnerability, and my strength. The two compliment each other well, and continuously inspire me to do more. Although it is abundantly clear that I should have been vegan my whole life, I am powerless to rewrite my past. It does however serve to inspire me to help others.

The following excerpts are from Holly's journal while at sea with the Sea Shepherd Conservation Society.

4 June 2011: Apparently we are very close to Libya. Some fishing boats have been spotted, and a tuna cage. After capture, the cages are towed to a tuna farm to be fattened up as they are sold by weight. Quotas established by the EU (in tonnes) are magically not exceeded by various countries,

▶ Holly Wilson during Operation Divine Wind.

even though each year more and more fishing permits are distributed – and there are less and less fish.

23 February 2012: Wellington Harbour, New Zealand. We are finally moving, and it is windy and raining. I can hear the rhythmic rattle of the motors. The on-shore crewmembers got smaller and smaller as we rolled gently into the dark ocean. It felt good to leave civilisation behind. I looked up and saw thin puffs of white clouds with bright stars in between, dotting the nighttime sky. It was stunning. I stared into the ocean, wondering what was lurking below. As I type this, I am seated in the mess hall. The surge of the ocean gnawing at the ship is making typing interesting.

27 February 2012: Humans are just not meant to be here. Last night the ocean tossed our vessel around with an impressive force. My bunk has become an amusement park ride, and the movements became incorporated into my dreams. Several times I was awoken. We were rolling hard, and I could feel my organs lift and shake in tune with the ship.

5 March 2012: I have seen photos of the Japanese whaling fleet, and it was absolutely surreal having two 'research' vessels on either side of us. Frantic messages could be overheard on their loudspeaker system in Japanese. The manoeuvrability of their vessels is far superior to ours, as is their speed. They cut directly in front of our bow several times and we avoided them by changing course. It was snowing, and soon dark after the confrontation began. Icicles hung from the aft deck's covering, and a slippery, lumpy mash covered our decks. Floodlights were shining from all directions on our frosty ship and illuminated the snow that was falling. It appeared as though rhinestones were gently twinkling down from the black sky, juxtaposed with the demonic roar of the harpoon vessels' motors. Their rapid manoeuvres and episodic lunges towards our bow perpendicular to our path of travel created a tension-filled, high pitched whir that was unnerving. Amid the spectacle of lights and the whaling fleet tailing us, I was acutely aware of how cold it was. My fingers and toes protested being subjected to such temperatures through vasoconstriction, leaving my digits numb and almost immobile.

Although the Nisshin Maru and third harpoon vessel are now off our radar, they have clearly shut down whaling for the rest of the season. The other two harpoon vessels are tailing us, instead of killing whales. Today the weather is calm and perfect for hunting, but they are dealing with Sea Shepherd's irritating and steadfast presence. This is a huge blow to the Japanese whaling fleet.

■ MAKING A POWERFUL CONNECTION
Dr Aryan Tavakkoli

"When I can nurture my body and soul with Nature's abundant supply, what reason have I to maim and to hurt? What possible reason have I?" Excerpt from the song "The Way of Compassion".   ■

▶ Dr Aryan Tavakkoli.

Dr Aryan Tavakkoli MBBS, MRCP, FRACP, practises as a specialist in Respiratory Medicine. She qualified from St Bartholomew's Hospital Medical School, London in 1991, and achieved her specialty in General Internal Medicine and Respiratory Medicine after postgraduate training in South-East England.

She developed an interest in complementary medicine at an early stage in her career as a conventional doctor, obtaining qualifications in Traditional Chinese Acupuncture from the British College of Acupuncture in 1996, and in herbal medicine from the College of Phytotherapy, UK in 2002. Aryan is also interested in the manifold and far-reaching effects of our diets, particularly how our diet affects the environment. She has written and spoken widely about this topic and has presented her talk, *Our Diet – Leading to a Sustainable Future, Or Killing Our Planet?* in many venues around New Zealand and Australia. She has been interviewed on national radio about the link between diet and climate change. Aryan is passionate about spreading the message regarding the benefits of a vegan lifestyle, with the aim of empowering individuals to make well-informed choices about their diet that not only result in a healthy body but also help to prevent the enormous environmental destruction caused by our current choices...   ■

They say the closest experience of Divine love on Earth is that of a mother's love towards her child. I can truthfully say there have been few events in my life leading to such a profound influence that they caused the direction of my life to change to a different, and in many ways better, path. Motherhood was one of those events.

Like many mothers, I was emotional in the early days after giving birth. Perhaps 'emotional' isn't quite the right word to use. It was more like a deep empathy had awoken within me, connecting me with everyone around me. I experienced others' feelings as if they were my own. I shared their joys and their pains just as if I were in their shoes, even if I barely knew them. I remember how difficult it was to hold back tears when we passed the scene of a car accident with an injured person being carried into an ambulance. I felt that person's distress and wished I could comfort them somehow. Returning to work as a hospital doctor was difficult. I could understand my patients' distress on a much deeper and more personal level than I could before. It didn't make my job easy.

Looking back, I think what I was experiencing during those first few months of motherhood, was an extension of my newly discovered gift of maternal love, not only towards my newborn baby but to everyone around me. The maternal bond was very strong and, unknowingly, I felt like a mother to everyone I met.

And so it was with this heightened sense of compassion and connection with others that I was to experience a life-changing event a few weeks after having my baby.

My mother was visiting and had just cooked dinner for us. I remember walking into the kitchen – same kitchen, same smells – but then my eyes fell on what was to be our dinner, and something felt very, very different. I saw a row of bodies, headless, charred, and so small – roast chicks. And then it hit me like a ton of bricks. I remember thinking, "Oh my God. Those are *babies*. I've just had a baby. How can I eat another mother's babies?"

Suddenly I felt disgust at the thought of eating flesh. Previously I had thought of meat as a food item like any other, I had not really *seen* the connection to any living being. But now I was seeing meat for what it truly was – a dead body. The thought of eating the corpses of animals, especially babies, was too much for me to bear. It was simply too barbaric an act for me to be able to do it anymore. From then onwards, I didn't eat animal flesh – meat, fowl or fish. Anything that had a face and parents was not meant to end up on my dinner plate. They had their own lives and their own purpose, and I was no longer prepared to be responsible for their deaths. *Not in my name.* I would find another way of nourishing myself that didn't involve killing.

It was easy being vegetarian. I continued for about six years as a vegetarian and whilst it was a good step forward, I was still unwittingly participating in many violent acts towards animals. I just didn't realise it then, but with time, I became more aware of the dark side of dairy and egg production. I learnt how male chicks were sliced or ground up alive after birth, and the misery of the dairy cow, forcibly impregnated year after year in order to produce milk for human consumption, only to have her calves torn from her side a few hours or days after birth, causing great distress to both mother and calf.

The more I learnt about the animal food industry, the more I realised I could not be a part of the brutality anymore. After all, aren't we all against violence and rape and slavery, and of course the ultimate inhumanity, the act of killing? Yet these violent acts are part of the daily lives of billions of animals that are incarcerated, mutilated, mentally and physically tortured and then killed – so that we can eat their bodies and their body secretions.

I could no longer ignore the shocking facts about our 'food' industry. The burden on my conscience became too much to bear, and I made the transition to vegan. It was a natural progression, an obvious one. For me it was simply no longer an option to partake in the killing and eating of animals.

My decision to become vegan was an ethical issue, one of compassion. But I also learnt of the strong environmental reasons for making a wide-scale transition to the vegan lifestyle. I have one person to thank for this – Supreme Master Ching Hai, a spiritual teacher and humanitarian who works tirelessly to awaken the world's population to the imminent dangers of climate change and the solution that is already in our hands. The wide-scale adoption of an organic vegan diet is the answer to most of the critical issues facing us today, including food and water shortages, biodiversity loss and species extinctions, desertification and oceanic dead zones. It is also the one lifeline we have to avert the ominous 'tipping point' that is fast approaching, threatening to catapult us into a frightening era of abrupt climate change, over which we will have lost control. The organic vegan lifestyle is not just a diet, it is a choice that will save countless lives (animal *and* human) and ensure a bright future for planet Earth. If you are not aware of the chaos caused by animal farming and the solution that lies in your hands, now is the time to inform yourselves. The websites below offer valuable information.

There is only one winner in the whole animal food industry – and that is the animal food industry. We, the consumers, have been brainwashed since birth, by mass advertising, and misinformed by our education systems, even by our own parents. God bless them, they were brainwashed too. When you grow up being told by everyone that meat is good for you, why wouldn't you believe it?

The truth is that eating animals is making us fat and sick. Many of the diseases we take for granted are preventable and treatable just by changing to a healthy vegan diet, preferably organic. Anatomically, the human body is designed for a plant-based diet. The vegan diet is our original natural diet. Unprocessed, whole foods are always healthier, but being vegan doesn't mean you have to give up anything you love, like cheese, chocolate, ice-cream or even sausages. You just learn to make, or buy, the vegan version instead. It is so easy, especially these days when you can find every kind of vegan food readily available in many stores, and there are so many websites offering easy recipes and information on how to make the transition to vegan.

By doing so, not only do we protect our own health and reduce our risk of developing cancer, heart disease and many other diseases, but we also prevent immense cruelty to billions of animals who experience the same emotions as we do, who feel the same pain as we do, and who want to love and nurture their offspring just as we do ours. The added bonus is that the lifestyle that is best for our health turns out to be the best for our environment and our children's future too.

The organic vegan lifestyle means LIFE in every sense of the word. It is a win-win choice. Don't miss this treasure. Grab it with both hands and don't let go!

Links:

Website: www.vegsense.net

Youtube channel: aryan tavakkoli

The Way of Compassion: http://www.youtube.com/watch?v=S93yyorDEDo

Photo credit David Lay.

▶ Rosie and her calf Mary.

"The very saddest sound in my memory was burned into my awareness at age five on my uncle's dairy farm in Wisconsin. A cow had given birth to a beautiful male calf. On the second day after birth, my uncle took the calf from the mother and placed him in the veal pen in the barn – only ten yards away, in plain view of his mother. The mother cow could see her infant, smell him, hear him, but could not touch him, comfort him, or nurse him. The heartrending bellows that she poured forth – minute after minute, hour after hour, for five long days, were excruciating to listen to. They are the most poignant and painful auditory memories I carry in my brain."

—**Dr Michael Klaper** is a practitioner of preventative and nutritional medicine in California and Hawaii.

For further information on Dairy Cows, a downloadable Fact Sheet is available from: http://www.animalsaustralia.org/factsheets/dairy_cows.php

■ INTERVIEW WITH
Dr Andrew Knight, Veterinarian

"Ask the experimenters why they experiment on animals, and the answer is, 'Because the animals are like us.' Ask the experimenters why it is morally OK to experiment on animals, and the answer is, 'Because the animals are not like us.' Animal experimentation rests on a logical contradiction."   ■

—Dr. Charles Magel, Professor of Ethics, Moorhead State University, California.

▶ Dr Andrew Knight.

Australian-British animal ethicist, Dr Andrew Knight, has published over fifty academic publications on animal issues, many of which formed the basis of his PhD and his 2011 book, *The Costs and Benefits of Animal Experiments.* Andrew's other publications have examined the contributions of the livestock sector to climate change, vegetarian companion animal diets, animal welfare standards of veterinarians, and the latest evidence about animal cognitive and related abilities and the resultant moral implications.

Andrew is a European Veterinary Specialist in Welfare Science, Ethics and Law, a Fellow of the Oxford Centre for Animal Ethics, and an Associate Professor of Welfare and Ethics at Ross University School of Veterinary Medicine in the Caribbean. He was a spokesperson for the Animals Count from 2007-2012, a British political party for people and animals (now the Animal Welfare Party), and was the director of Animal Consultants International from 2004-2103. He is also the founder of the Extreme Vegan Sporting Association, which is dedicated to vegan fitness and adventures…   ■

Your activism began when you were a vet student at Murdoch University in Western Australia. Can you share what happened and how that impacted on your studies?

In 1998 Murdoch University became the first Australian university to formally allow conscientious objection by students to its teaching or assessment activities. This followed a year-long struggle for humane teaching methods when I was a veterinary student.

My main battles began when Murdoch refused to allow alternatives and tried (unsuccessfully) to penalise me for boycotting several physiology laboratories in which animals were subjected to extremely invasive experiments ending in death. After I initiated legal action and started to facilitate media exposure of the curricular animal killing my marks were restored. My alternative submission to the university's ethics committee also resulted in the cancellation of nearly all of these laboratories in 1999.

In 2000 a classmate and I became Murdoch's first alternative surgical students, gaining approximately five times as much surgical and anaesthetic experience as our classmates who practised surgical procedures on healthy animals and then killed them. Instead we assisted with beneficial surgeries on real patients under close supervision, similar to the training of human surgeons. We particularly assisted with the neutering of homeless cats and dogs from shelters, thereby increasing their adoption chances and decreasing pet overpopulation.

The precedents set at Murdoch have since helped bring about changes at other campuses within Australia and overseas. These have included the establishment of conscientious objection policies at a few campuses and the introduction of humane teaching methods at many more. I am very proud to report that by 2005 the first students had graduated from every established Australian veterinary school without harming animals in their surgical training, overcoming the strong opposition of many of their faculty members in almost every case.

Are vets associated with slaughterhouses concerned about cruelty to the animals?

In general, yes. However, all who work in those environments become desensitised to death and suffering, and veterinarians working there would, I believe, be considerably less moved by cases that would evoke strong emotional reactions in the average member of society. To a lesser degree I believe such desensitisation affects most veterinarians and indeed, published studies have demonstrated that the positions of veterinary associations on animal welfare issues are sometimes behind those of the general public.

Personal variation exists but unfortunately, concern about animal welfare is minor in a small minority of veterinarians. The majority are in the middle, and I'm aware of at least one slaughterhouse veterinarian who actually became a whistle-blower, doubtless ruining his slaughterhouse career, because he was so concerned about the animal abuse he saw.

Nevertheless, most slaughterhouse veterinarians would aim to ensure that at least basic animal welfare standards are upheld. Indeed, they are probably the major figures in slaughterhouses advocating for such standards.

Is animal experimentation ever justified?

My PhD examined this question in detail, as did my subsequent book *The Costs and Benefits of Animal Experiments*, published in 2011 by Palgrave Macmillan. It is part of an advanced series of at least fifteen texts on animal ethics being produced by the Oxford Centre for Animal Ethics. My book provides the most science-based examination of the ethics of animal experimentation yet published in book form. It also comprehensively reviews alternative research, testing and educational strategies.

When considering costs and benefits overall, and particularly the published studies examining the human clinical or toxicological utility of animal research, one cannot reasonably conclude the benefits accruing to human patients or consumers, or to those motivated by scientific curiosity or profit, exceed the costs incurred by animals subjected to scientific procedures. On the contrary, the evidence indicates that actual human benefit is rarely, if ever, sufficient to justify such costs.

Yet, as described in my book, a small minority of animal-based research and teaching is ethically sound. Clear-cut examples include non-invasive observational or behavioural studies of domesticated species, or of non-domesticated species in sanctuaries or the wild; the education of veterinary students via participation in beneficial clinical or surgical procedures on genuine animal patients; and experimental treatment of animal patients genuinely suffering from severe, naturally occurring disease or injury, when conventional treatment is ineffective.

Limiting animal experimentation to such cases would inevitably restrict the range of scientific questions that could be investigated. It would, however, strike the correct ethical balance between satisfying the interests of animals and satisfying those of human beings.

As a vet do you treat your animals with standard drugs?

Yes, I most certainly do. I am interested in whatever approach is likely to most benefit my patients, particularly when based on good quality evidence. This includes studies examining the efficacy of clinical interventions of good methodological quality that have successfully achieved publication in peer-reviewed journals. It does not mean limiting oneself to personal experience and opinion, which can vary considerably, even between experts.

Evidence-based medicine (EBM) bases clinical decisions on methodologically sound, prospective, randomised, blinded, controlled clinical trials. Genuine animal patients can be, and are, enrolled in such clinical trials, although laboratory animals are more commonly used, which is ethically much more problematic. The gold standard for EBM is the large prospective epidemiological (ie population) study, or the combination and analysis of multiple randomised and blinded, controlled clinical trials.

One of the areas you have been promoting is that of vegan diets for dogs and cats. What is wrong with them eating commercial pet food and why is a vegan diet better for them?

The health hazards to dogs and cats, and of course, to all 'food' animals, that are inherent in commercial meat-based companion animal diets are numerous and difficult to avoid. These diets provide an industrial dumping ground for slaughterhouse waste products – Four-D meat (from dead, dying, diseased or disabled animals), old or spoiled supermarket meat, large numbers of rendered dogs and cats from animal shelters in countries such as the US, old restaurant grease, complete with high concentrations of dangerous free radicals and *trans* fatty acids, and damaged or spoiled fish, complete with dangerous levels of mercury, PCBs and other toxins.

These diets may contain pathogenic bacteria, protozoa, fungi, viruses and even prions, and their associated endotoxins and mycotoxins. And, particularly in countries such as the US, they may contain hormone and antibiotic residues and hazardous preservatives.

Diseases described in the scientific literature following long-term maintenance of cats and dogs on meat-based diets include kidney, liver, heart, neurologic, visual, neuromuscular and skin diseases, bleeding disorders, birth defects, immunocompromisation and infectious diseases (DiBartola *et al* 1993, Dow *et al* 1989, Freytag *et al* 2003 and Strieker *et al* 1996).

My veterinary experience leads me to believe so-called degenerative diseases such as cancer, kidney, liver and heart failure are far more common than would be likely to occur naturally, and that many cases are probably exacerbated, if not directly caused by, the hazardous ingredients of meat-based diets.

Vegan diets aim to meet all the nutritional needs of cats or dogs using only plant, mineral and synthetically based ingredients. There is absolutely no scientific reason why such diets cannot be formulated to meet all of the palatability, nutritional and bioavailability – which primarily refers to digestibility – needs of cats, dogs, humans, or virtually any species. Crucially, vegan diets also avoid most of the hazards found in meat-based diets.

Many people who have tried to transition their dogs and cats to a vegan diet have been unsuccessful. How should they approach that transition and how do they need to manage the change so their animals remain healthy?

Considerable patience and persistence may be required when altering diets, particularly of fussy cats. In difficult cases it may first be necessary to withhold food, but obviously not water, perhaps for a day. This will stimulate the appetite without causing harm. It may be necessary to gradually transition to the new diet over weeks, or even months if necessary. A gradual change is more acceptable behaviourally in difficult cases, and also allows an appropriate transition of digestive enzymes (to the extent possible) and intestinal flora (bacteria), thereby minimising the chance of gastrointestinal reactions such as diarrhoea.

Guardians should demonstrate by their behaviour that they consider the new diet just as edible as the old, without possibly warning or alarming their pet by making a fuss. They should not be concerned if their pet eats around the vegan food at first; just having it in close proximity to the other food will help the pet make the necessary mental association. Mixing the food thoroughly may help, as may the addition of odiforous – the sense of smell is very important – and tasty additives, such as nutritional yeast, vegetable oil, nori flakes and spirulina. Gently warming the food may also help. Guardians should remove uneaten food and offer only fresh food.

The most important factors for transitioning difficult pets onto a vegetarian diet are gradual change and persistence. Using these principles, the most stubborn of cats and dogs have been successfully weaned onto healthy vegetarian diets.

Use of a complete and balanced nutritional supplement with a home-made diet, or a nutritionally complete commercial vegan diet is essential to safeguard health. Supplements and diets may be obtained from the suppliers listed at our VegePets website.

Regular urine pH monitoring is also important to detect the urinary alkalinisation, with its consequent potential for urinary stones and life-threatening blockages, that may result from a vegan diet in a small minority of cases (most commonly, male cats). Advice on monitoring and correcting alkalinisation using dietary additives is also available at our VegePets website.

What are the aims of the Animal Welfare Party?

The Animal Welfare Party, initially called Animals Count, is a British political party for animals. I was spokesperson for the party between 2007 and 2012. Although broad concern for animals is a mainstream priority, this is poorly reflected in the policies of most political parties. Often animal protection ends up near the bottom of the political agenda and millions of animals continue to suffer. We aim to emphasise to politicians in other parties through direct dialogue and particularly by contesting key seats, that voters care about animal issues. We hope this will influence their own policies and actions.

Has it achieved any success so far?

We've encouraged other political parties in the UK, notably the Green Party, to consider the adoption of more animal-friendly policies, particularly for companion animals. Our 2006 launch was reported by the BBC and other media outlets internationally, and we've helped inspire and assist with the establishment of similar parties in countries such as Israel and Australia, which now has the Animal Justice Party. Our own parent organisation, the Dutch Party for the Animals, had twenty-three elected representatives from national to local level by late 2011, and their elected MPs have been more active in influencing government policy than virtually any others, when corrected for the numbers in each party.

Does your party differ significantly from the Green Party in their manifesto on animal rights?

Some Green leaders and elected members have excellent track records when it comes to animal protection, and some Green policies are good for animals. However, this is far from uniform. Whilst these inconsistencies remain, we feel we still have a duty to exist and provide a consistent voice for the hundreds of thousands of animals who suffer daily.

You are also the Founder of the Extreme Vegan Sporting Association. What does the organisation do and what does it promote?

The association exists to showcase vegan fitness and to demonstrate how much fun the vegan lifestyle can be. We occasionally hold events such as mountaineering challenges, but mostly we simply showcase pictures of extremely fit or fun-loving vegans in our ExtremeVeganSports web galleries. We also provide a review of the scientific evidence about vegan diets for athletes, and links to a bunch of amazing adventure challenges around the world.

You were also the Director of Animal Consultants International until recently. In what way does this organisation support your animal advocacy work?

Animal Consultants International exists to maximise the accessibility of people with key skills or qualifications to animal advocacy campaigns worldwide. Such international skill-sharing has the potential to significantly increase the professionalism and effectiveness of the animal protection movement. We currently include veterinarians, scientists, educators and graphic designers, all of whom are keen to assist animal advocacy campaigns.

What are your priorities at the moment, Andrew?

I am very keen for students, scientists, policy-makers and others to become aware of my recent book *The Costs and Benefits of Animal Experiments*. I continue to speak at appropriate academic conferences internationally, including laboratory animal science conferences, and I publish short pieces such as editorials in popular media. I make virtually no money from this, but am very keen to widely outreach the controversial information in this book.

This advocacy costs me a great deal financially, so I also have to work as a veterinarian for a large part of each year. As soon as I've saved enough to take another long period of leave, I'd like to research and write my next book. I'm very interested in both the contributions of the livestock sector to climate change, and vegan companion animal diets. Climate change is likely to be the greatest contributor to biodiversity loss since the extinction of the dinosaurs. It will bring suffering and death to greater numbers of animals and people than virtually any other cause. The production of animal products and their consumption by humans and to a lesser degree our companion animals, is one of the greatest contributors to climate change, although one of the least acknowledged.

I'm also interested in taking on some more extreme vegan challenges before too long and in moving somewhere a lot sunnier than England!

What do you recommend as the best way forward for animal rights activists who want to see significant change for animals as soon as possible?

It is essential such activists present cases that will be seen by their target audiences as reasonable and rational. Unfortunately, the animal rights movement is generally perceived as extreme and out of touch with mainstream culture. This is worst in countries such as Britain and the US, where militant activism has been strongest.

Such activism does indeed win individual battles. It also gives the activists involved a sense of achievement, and a sense of belonging to a subculture. However, it alienates the mainstream population and media outlets, thereby losing the overall war.

One of the most important requirements when seeking social change is for activists to have a realistic viewpoint of both human society and psychology. They must choose strategies that are truly likely to achieve their aims. Common mistakes made by a very small proportion of activists include abusive language, which is almost certain to harden, rather than weaken, the resolve of opponents; radical dress or appearance, which is likely to further alienate those one is seeking to connect with and persuade; and actions that our opponents can use to falsely portray us as violent.

Direct action can publicise an issue, but to have a positive impact the action and resultant publicity must generate mainstream sympathy for, rather than opposition to, the cause. Mistakes include images of balaclavas, bolt-cutters or anything suggesting property destruction. Positive examples include humorous actions and those that clearly highlight the plight of the animals.

Being realistic also means recognising that in many cases, relatively small, incremental changes are the best that may be achieved. This can be deeply frustrating, but there is no excuse for letting personal frustration interfere with implementation of the strategy most likely to yield the best results for animals. Realism also means focusing on perhaps one or two issues in which one's time, energy and money are likely to yield the greatest positive change, rather than picking less winnable issues, or spreading oneself too thin.

If activists wish to achieve a greater impact, and the possibility exists, then it may be worth pursuing a career that will offer increased power to advocate for animals, such as medicine, veterinary medicine, law, dietetics, or environmental science. The movement also needs support skills such as IT, graphic design, photography and videography, management, marketing and fundraising.

Links:

www.AnimalExperiments.info

www.HumaneLearning.info

www.ExtremeVeganSports.org

www.VegePets.info

www.vegan15peaks.info

www.vegan3peaks.info

Reference:

Knight A (2011). *The Costs and Benefits of Animal Experiments*, Palgrave Macmillan.

■ MAKING THE CONNECTION IN MEDICAL EXPERIMENTATION

Helen Marston

"I shall pass through this world but once; any good thing therefore I can do, or any kindness I can show to any fellow creature, let me do it now; let me not defer or neglect it, for I shall not pass this way again." ■

—Stephen Grellet

Helen Marston is employed by Humane Research Australia Inc, as their chief executive officer. HRA is an information service attempting to bring to the attention of the public the ethical and scientific arguments against the continued use of animals in research, and to promote the more humane and scientifically valid alternatives. Helen's role involves planning campaign strategies, writing government submissions, and she is media spokesperson for the association.

Animal experimentation has always been the issue she has felt most strongly about, and her current role enables her to fulfil her dream of opposing what she believes is the worst injustice toward both human and non-human animals… ■

▶ Helen Marston.

I've never considered myself to be an 'animal-lover'. In fact, it was my younger sister Joanne who was renowned in the family for bringing home injured birds, lost dogs and any other animal she found in distress. I have always had a strong sense of justice however, and I believe the ways in which our society treats animals are reflective of an unjust society.

I first became aware all was not just in the world when I quizzed my mum about my (then) favourite meal – heart and chips. Why was this little meaty morsel called heart – the same name as the thing that beats inside our own chests? Whilst my parents spared me the graphic details, they were always truthful to me and explained that it was the heart of a lamb. I was confused. It led to more questions, like what were the ham slices, sausage rolls and other meaty foods made from? While I wasn't familiar with the actual word, I understood injustice for the first time. If meat was from animals then I assumed the animals had to be dead – and that didn't seem right. Surely a pig, a sheep or a cow didn't need to die for me to enjoy the taste of a sausage roll.

That was before I was even aware of factory farming, crude transportations to abattoirs and offshore 'processing plants' and the eventual murder of sensitive creatures. Becoming a vegetarian was an obvious choice, which later led to becoming vegan after realising the consumption of eggs and dairy products inflicted even more unimaginable cruelty than the meat industry.

It was in high school however, that I learnt of the worst animal cruelty of all – animal experimentation. A senior year project about cosmetic testing taught me about the Draize Test (applying chemicals to the eyes of restrained rabbits) and the LD50 Test (chemicals force-fed to animals until fifty percent died) and I was horrified. So much so that this quiet, shy girl stood up in front of her classmates with no qualms to let them all know about the horrors we were all financially supporting through our purchase of cosmetics.

Today, that knowledge has grown into a strong understanding of the wide range of animal experiments – including medical research – that is carried out today. I have learnt that not only is the practice extremely unethical; it's scientifically flawed and does the human population absolutely no benefit. I am therefore committed to spending my life exposing the cruelty and advocating for more compassionate and, just as importantly, scientifically-sound research for human advancement.

In my current role at Humane Research Australia, we have uncovered experiments that should never have been approved, including implanting silicone breasts onto pigs[1], feeding alcohol to pregnant sheep[2], marijuana to rats[3] and shaking baby lambs to death[4] to prove 'shaking baby syndrome'. How could any Animal 'Ethics' Committee approve such unscrupulous acts? We've also exposed the importation of primates for research purposes – despite Australia already having three government-funded primate breeding facilities, which few people are even aware of. This issue was highlighted in a feature article in Melbourne's Sunday Age newspaper[5]. It still amazes me that such atrocities are inflicted upon our closest living relatives.

Professor Charles R Magel has said *"Ask the experimenters why they experiment on animals, and the answer is: 'Because the animals are like us.' Ask the experimenters why it is morally OK to experiment on animals, and the answer is: 'Because the animals are not like us.'"*

Ironically, the opposite is true. Genetically, metabolically and anatomically, animals differ from us, meaning that data obtained from animal tests are misleading. Morally, animals have the same capacity to suffer pain, fear and distress as humans and should not be subject to cruel and useless experiments.

My strong opposition to animal experimentation was brought into question in late 2011 when I was diagnosed with breast cancer. Did my treatment – if I was to accept it – mean that I would need to compromise my core values? Would it be hypocritical to expose my body to drugs that I knew involved animal testing at some stage before they came onto the market? Or in fact would I be of better use to refuse such a treatment? Despite my own fear, I felt so very sorry that my disease, and that of others in my situation, was the reason so many animals are routinely subjected to cruel procedures and then merely discarded.

Following my diagnosis and subsequent surgery, I was scheduled to undergo chemotherapy. Knowing that enormous funding is pumped into cancer research each year, I conducted my own investigations and discovered that each of the drugs that I was to be given was discovered more than forty years ago – almost before I was born.

It didn't make sense. We've all seen countless news headlines over the past few decades heralding cures of cancer – all based on animal trials. Where was that miracle cure now that I needed it? And what have all the millions of animal lives lost and billions of dollars pumped into cancer research in the interim achieved? And there I was, being treated with the generation-old cut/poison/burn technique that's been used for years.

The USA's Federal Drug Administration – which guides Australian research – tells us that nine out of ten drugs 'successfully' tested on animals don't work when translated to humans[6]. Some even cause significant harm to humans. Considering the intricate yet critical differences between species, what else can we expect?

Frustratingly, I also asked myself about all the thousands of drugs that were tested on animals but thrown out when they were found to be 'unsuccessful' – surely if there was some hope of those drugs working in the first place, to the extent they were good enough to be tested on animals, they were worth pursuing via other means? Could we have inadvertently discarded a potential cure for cancer?

I eventually elected to proceed with the conventional course of treatment. Ultimately, what really convinced me is that I strongly believe that those 1960s' drugs were developed not *because* of animal experiments but *despite* them.

Now that I am personally affected by cancer I can confirm that my position on animal experimentation has strengthened. Animal experiments are extremely cruel and scientifically flawed. If we are to find genuine cures for cancer and other ailments, we must focus on species-specific research – not antiquated methods that are erroneously extrapolated from a species that differs from us genetically, metabolically and anatomically.

I will continue to use my experience and to focus my efforts on opposing the injustice that is animal experimentation. I'm not that quiet, shy girl I was in high school, because some things are far too important to shy away from. People need to know what is happening behind closed doors. They need to know animal experiments are not a 'necessary evil'; they are unjust, most certainly unnecessary and slow the medical advancement of our own species on this planet.

Current figures show Australia uses more than seven million animals in research every year[7], making us the forth-highest user behind the United States, Japan and China. When we consider our smaller population this makes our per capita use embarrassingly high. Whilst animal experiments must be approved by an animal ethics committee before they may proceed, the system is far from flawless. It is self regulated and hidden in secrecy due to members having to sign confidentiality agreements. Furthermore, there is no requirement for the animal welfare representatives on these committees to be suitably qualified to challenge the justification of the research on a scientific basis. There is also no government incentive – as there are in other nations – for the development and validation of alternative testing methods, despite there being numerous systematic reviews illustrating that non-animal methodologies are more predictive of human outcomes than data obtained from a different species[8].

Despite animal experimentation being a vast industry with huge vested interests, there are ways in which everyone can help bring an end to this antiquated practice:

- Only purchase cosmetics that have been accredited as Cruelty-Free (refer to www.choosecrueltyfree.org.au),
- Refuse to donate to any medical or health charity that funds animal experiments (those who do not fund animal experiments can be found at www.humanecharities.org.au),
- Become knowledgeable about the issue so you can help dispel the myth that it is a 'necessary evil',
- Use that knowledge to write letters to newspapers and to charities explaining you will not support them until they cease funding animal experiments,
- Become a member of Humane Research Australia to add your voice and to learn about our campaigns at www.humaneresearch.org.au.

Endnotes:

[1] Subclinical (Biofilm) Infection Causes Capsular Contracture in a Porcine Model following Augmentation Mammoplasty. Tamboto, Vickery and Deva (2010).

[2] Acute ethanol exposure in pregnancy alters the insulin-like growth factor axis of foetal and maternal sheep. Gatford, KL, Dalitz, PA, Cock, ML, Harding R, Owens, JA (2007).

[3] *Cannabinoids increase conditioned ultrasonic vocalisations and cat odour avoidance in rats: Strain differences in drug-induced anxiety.* Jonathon C. Arnold, Robert A. Dielenberg, Iain S. McGrego (2010).

[4] Neurological changes in a lamb model of non-accidental head injury (the shaken baby syndrome) JW Finnie, PC Blumbergs, J Manavis, RJ Turner, S Helps, R Vink, RW Byard, G Chidlow, B Sandoz, J Dutschke and RWG. Anderson (2012).

[5] http://www.theage.com.au/victoria/the-monkey-farm-primates-being-bred-for-experiments-20121124-2a0gz.html#ixzz2DbesfVHb.

[6] Source: FDA Issues Advice to Make Earliest Stages Of Clinical Drug Development More Efficient. Press release / FDA 12jan2006.

[7] Statistics collated from state departments by Humane Research Australia Inc. http://www.humaneresearch.org.au/statistics/.

[8] *The Costs and Benefits of Animal Experiments.* Andrew Knight, Palgrave MacMillan.

Compassion in Action: Rescue and Giving Sanctuary

INDIA

"I continue to be amazed at the almost mystical quality of the emotional connection I feel for animals. I feel blessed to be in their midst and I am in awe of my fellow defenders who are paving the way with love and compassion to an entirely new world." ■

—Claire Abrams.

■ LEARNING AND GROWING WITH ANIMALS

Claire Abrams Myers
Co-Founder, Animal Aid Unlimited in Udaipur, Rajasthan, India

I've been so lucky to have had not just animals, but thousands of ill and injured rescued animals be an integral part of my life since my early teens. My parents, Erika and Jim, founded Animal Aid when I was twelve and so my coming of age took place amidst a grassroots, bustling animal rescue centre in India. I have been fully involved in

▶ Claire Abrams Myers and Teddy Bear.

43

the enterprise of animal protection outreach and advocacy ever since in the form of humane education, shelter management, social media outreach, volunteer coordination, public relations and fundraising. Today, at age twenty-three and more passionate about animal protection than ever, I'm beginning to be able to understand with more clarity why it is I feel I am exactly where I want to be in life.

My happiness is achieved through the art of learning how to engage with the world, in observation with *participation*. My pursuit of happiness is through learning how to be an agent of inspiration. I see people all around me struggling to find meaning in their life, lacking energy and motivation, unenthused or even depressed. I want to invite anyone feeling uninspired to join in the incredible phenomenon which takes place in the expansion of our circle of compassion to include animals and their homes: jungles, oceans, mountains and the sky.

We're in a terribly exciting time in the history of man in which millions of people around the world are evolving right before our eyes in what seems like almost quantum leaps. Left and right, people's levels of other-awareness and compassion in the form of animal and environmental protection are increasing exponentially. It's exciting to fathom that perhaps those of us in animal and environmental protection are in an evolutionary sense similar to the tadpole who climbed out of the water or the bird who grew wings.

On a more emotional level, I have found that while empathising with suffering animals on a daily basis can be painful, it has vitally enhanced my sensitivity and appreciation of beauty, grace and joy. I've heard a few activists say that sometimes they miss the days of their ignorance, because the knowledge of animal suffering is such a heavy burden to carry. However, I feel the love I have given, received and been witness to in animals and the people who care for them has been so inspiring and energising that I could never even imagine what my life would be like without it.

I continue to be amazed at the almost mystical quality of the emotional connection I feel for animals. I feel blessed to be in their midst and I am in awe of my fellow defenders who are paving the way with love and compassion to an entirely new world.

Link:

www.animalaidunlimited.com

■ FREEDOM THROUGH LOOKING

Erika Abrams
Co-founder, Animal Aid Unlimited, Udaipur, Rajasthan, India

> *"I am one of the luckiest people on earth because by a wondrous miracle I figured out how much fun it is to give."* ■
>
> —Erika Abrams.

It was the greatest liberation of my life to discover that if I looked at suffering with a determination to do what I could to eliminate it to the very borders of my personal capacity, I found I could cope with the daily knowledge of all I can NOT do.

I wake up each day and within minutes I am surrounded by three hundred and fifty animals, belonging to many of the species I longed to touch and snuggle and understand as a child. Dogs run to me, donkeys amble toward me. I can find a little bull who loves having his neck scratched, or a pig with bad hind feet learning to walk again. They are injured, ill or disabled, but what happy beings they are despite their infirmities.

This is the joy of Animal Aid in Udaipur, Rajasthan, India – a shelter, hospital and sanctuary for street animals located in the lap of rolling ancient hills, but close to a mid-sized Indian city.

I am one of the luckiest people on earth because by a wondrous miracle I figured out how much fun it is to give. How easy it is to figure out ways of giving

▶ The Abrams Myers family – Erika, Jim, Kheli, Claire and Lilly.

intelligently, generously, quickly, strategically. Anybody can do it. All it takes is the wish to be creative with whatever little bit extra you have, and after discovering how good it can feel, to give it away to help others who really need it, convincing first yourself and then others that your strategy works.

I am fifty-eight and I feel I learnt about giving somewhat late (in my early forties.) How it has changed my life! Realising I could make my own lifestyle much more modest was the first step. What *don't* I need? What do I have, or do, that doesn't give me pleasure? How can I stop buying that useless object and start doing more of the activities that give my life meaning?

I had reached a point in life where I was sick of simply 'yearning' and I could see that if I re-imagined what I thought I wanted, if I could get to the essence of these and package them in perhaps a different form, I could literally make a life where all my dreams came true. *Anyone* can do it.

How I prayed for a horse as a child. I would draw them. Any proximity and I would literally refuse to wash my hands after touching them so I could smell 'horse' on my hands just a little longer. When I was ten, my cat was killed by a car and I became hysterical. My father held me close on his lap and I remember screaming, "No! No!" – it was not a child crying in me, it was the full raging disbelief that who I loved so dearly could be taken. It was my first experience of true grief.

In my twenties I sought out chances to take care of animals, including wildlife, and lived for a few years in a beautiful rural area on the Washington State coast, where I could marvel at hawks, coyotes, seals and even otters.

These were some of the clues about animals as my destiny but I really did not recognise them. I lived every day wishing for more contact with animals but not taking myself or the pull of animals seriously enough to do anything about it. I lived in increasing fear about facing animal suffering. I thought I would perish from considering what happens to the animals in our oceans, or other hunted animals. I would switch off the TV as soon as an animal appeared.

It was the greatest liberation of my life to discover that if I looked at suffering with a determination to do what I could to eliminate it to the very borders of my personal capacity, I found I could cope with the daily knowledge of all I can NOT do. To say it again, by doing what I could, however limited and small, I have found the courage to face what I cannot do. And with that burden thrown off, the burden of frustration about the magnitude of the problems of animal suffering, I have more energy and vitality to do what I can do with immeasurable joy.

My personal 'turning point in compassion' may have come when I came across a puppy who had been critically injured on a busy Delhi street. I was on my way to the airport. My daughter was seven. The puppy's back was torn open. Its mother was trying to pull her off the road. I had never seen an injury like this up close. My head became light and I wanted to run away.

"Oh God, Claire, what can we do?" I said. We were late; I had absolutely no knowledge that there could possibly be practical help for this puppy. The streets were full of roaming stray dogs. Summoning all my courage I took my scarf off and lifted the puppy to the side of the road, under the shade of a tree, where she could die without being hit again by another car.

"Hold my hand tight," I said to Claire, and I was trembling. "I did it! I did it!" For me this was one of the most difficult moments of my life. I faced the pain up close. I couldn't do a fraction of what was ultimately needed, but I could do *something*, and I did.

I think most of us already have compassion. The turning points are important because they are the places where we learn how to use our compassion as the fuel for practical action, however seemingly small. These small acts are like seeds and the compassion you already have is like water.

Rescue Story...

Hurt to Healed. Amber recovers at Animal Aid Unlimited, India.

What a delight to see an animal who for weeks has been trapped in the confines of her disability finally stand on her own and make wobbly but determined steps towards a friend. Known for her playful love-bites, Amber had been hit by a car and had lost the use of her hind legs. For millions of street dogs across India who live in cities that have no rescue service or shelter, unable to get out of harm's way or find food and water, a back injury means a slow and painful death. But in Udaipur, at Animal Aid, road accident victims like Amber are given a second chance. Rest, painkillers, physical therapy, and of course, love, helped Amber recover and slowly learn to walk again.

▶ Amber recovers at Animal Aid Unlimited, India.

U.S.A

◼ LOOKING FROM THE INSIDE OUT

Jenny Brown

Co-founder and Director, Woodstock Farm Animal Sanctuary

"Non-violence leads to the highest ethics, which is the goal of all evolution. Until we stop harming all other living beings, we are still savages."   ◼

—Thomas Edison.

Jenny Brown is the co-founder and director of the Woodstock Farm Animal Sanctuary, a not-for-profit organisation and farm-animal shelter located in the Catskill Mountains of New York. Jenny is an outspoken vegan animal rights activist who previously worked as a television producer until 2002 when she went undercover in Texas to film farmed animal abuse. That experience led her to dedicate her life to helping farm animals and raising awareness of their plight. Jenny's story and the work of her sanctuary has been featured in the *New York Times, Cosmopolitan Magazine, New York Magazine, New York Daily News, NPR's Weekend America.* Her book, *The Lucky Ones: My Passionate Fight for Farm Animals,* was published in 2012…   ◼

▶ Jenny Brown, Dylan and Doug Abel.

When talking about the suffering of animals, I have usually tried to keep my own tough break out of it. However, my first step toward becoming an animal rights activist and eventually, to starting Woodstock Farm Animal Sanctuary, is tied in to my childhood illness. I lost my right leg, just below the knee, to cancer when I was ten years old. If the amputation was all I had to deal with, I would have been lucky. Two and a half years of debilitating chemotherapy was by far the worst part of it – the hair loss (all of it), the nausea, the countless days spent in the children's cancer ward at the hospital, my mother's grief – these things almost killed me.

Because of my illness, I had to sit out of my fifth and sixth grade years of school. As well as the longer stays for surgery, I was typically in the hospital for four days of the week. The other three days I spent at home mostly alone while my sister went to school and my mother slept from working the nightshift to make ends meet as a nurse and single mother. It wasn't until this time that I was allowed to adopt a pet, something I had wanted since my earliest memories. Cancer was the ultimate opportunity for a kid to get what she wanted so I took advantage of it and the result was adopting Boogie. She was a calico kitten, the runt of the litter, and she became my muse and best friend for eighteen years. It was Boogie who helped me begin to see animals as true individuals. She made me look at them in a different light. She is the catalyst for my dedication to animal rights. If I had a soul and would go to Heaven, wouldn't Boogie be granted the same opportunity? Surely she had a soul, I would ponder, and in my young mind, the brewing of justice for animals began.

I was eighteen, and still living in my hometown of Louisville, Kentucky, when I learnt the truth about the miserable lives of animals used for food. Before that time, like most people, I had imagined farmed animals lived good lives in spacious pastures and straw-filled barns until they served their purpose, and that this was the natural order of things. It was something I hadn't really questioned before.

It was college orientation week at the University of Louisville when I picked up some animal rights literature about how animals live and die to become our food, and that's all it took. I became a vegetarian. That was in 1989. I grew up in a fairly conservative, right wing, religious household, and growing up in the South there was never a meal without meat served in our house and hardly a vegetable that wasn't stewed to death with a ham hock.

It was during college that life took a turn and I landed in Chicago where I finished my undergraduate degree studying film and television production. There, I learnt how to use film and video cameras and began making short films for school assignments. I relished my newfound big-city life and career decision to pursue an exciting job in film but a chance meeting with a campaign coordinator who worked for People for the Ethical Treatment of Animals (PETA) would eventually change everything.

While still in film school and because of this chance meeting, I began going on occasional assignments undercover, shooting video around the country in places I had never dreamed, doing things I had never imagined, like breaking and entering to film animal abuse. The acts of cruelty and suffering I witnessed on those assignments still haunt me today. Almost a decade later, after establishing a career in film and television, I went undercover again. This time it was for Farm Sanctuary, an organisation that focuses specifically on farmed animals. My assignment was to capture video of 'downers', as they are known, animals too weak, sick or injured to stand, who are eventually dragged on to the trucks headed to slaughter or left to die without food, water or veterinary care. That week sealed my fate. I left my career and concluded that I wanted to dedicate my life to help farmed animals, the most exploited and abused beings on this planet. And from that day I have never looked back.

Each year in the United States alone, a staggering ten billion animals are killed for human consumption – and that doesn't include aquatic animals. *Ten billion!* Almost sixty billion worldwide. It's hard to wrap your head around a number like this, let alone stop to consider that each was a *someone* – someone who had a personality, likes and dislikes, a mother and father they never got to know – a personal story and history unique to them. On factory farms, which house nine-ty-nine percent of animals raised and slaughtered in the US, they suffer beyond my comprehension – deprivation, isolation, confinement, physical mutilation and misery day in, day out[1]. Most never experience fresh air, freedom to move around or any semblance of kindness during their entire stressed out lives.

Today, as a society, we are utterly disconnected from how these animals live and die. Gone are the days of *Little House on the Prairie* where Pa would cry before going out to slaughter an animal to feed the family. Most people never see the animals raised for food, much less slaughter an animal themselves. To do so is anathema for many. The bacon, bologna, hamburger, steak and many other products not only don't resemble animals by name but also don't resemble a once-living animal at all. We are out of touch with what is happening and sadly, purposefully so. The meat and dairy industries are big business with powerful and influential lobbyists who line our politicians' pockets and pour dollars into clever and persuasive advertising. Animal products come at us in every direction – on TV, in the paper, in slick magazine ads with happy people chomping down on the appendages and cuts of nameless, faceless animals.

It's time to pay attention if we are to progress as a moral society or as a sustainable planet. The ethical questioning of the treatment of farmed animals has lagged far behind other animal issues. A giant void exists in the public mind when it comes to the reality of today's farming practices. Thankfully, in the past few decades, some sympathetic awareness of animal suffering is taking hold. People are becoming increasingly aware that animals raised today for food are terribly mistreated. Awareness campaigns, films and news stories are finally helping to fuel some dissent against the most egregious forms of intensive farming – showing us not only the cruel, systematic deaths of billions of animals but also the lifelong deprivation of absolutely everything that makes life worth living or even tolerable for these thinking, feeling beings.

Animal cruelty is just one issue. Environmental devastation, public health concerns, world hunger, obesity, heart disease and cancer rates are some others. And, as I have learnt, becoming a vegan is the most powerful step anyone can take to stop this madness. That, and for me personally, starting a sanctuary where I could rescue victims of the meat and dairy industries and advocate on their behalf. Here people meet Beatrice the turkey, Elvis the steer, Judy the pig and the other animals who live here with us. They see their individual personalities and learn how they came to us. They also learn how all the other farmed animals across the country live and die before making their way to America's plates. We don't point fingers, chastise or proselytise, as we were once hamburger and milkshake lovers too. We strive to teach, not preach, in the gentlest way we can. These animals deserve our attention and the mass killing of them is literally killing us, morally, physically and environmentally.

In 2004 my devoted husband, Doug, and I bought twenty-three acres in the town of Woodstock, New York. Yes *that* Woodstock. Here we started Woodstock

Farm Animal Sanctuary – a bustling refuge for roughly three hundred rescued farmed animals who live out their lives in peace and comfort in an environment set up for their wellbeing. All who come through our gates are the lucky ones. Their numbers, combined with all the rescued farmed animals around the world living at sanctuaries and loving homes, are the tiny fraction who know the joys of freedom and compassion.

Once they become accustomed to human kindness, many of our animals are as interactive, attention seeking and loving as a family dog. We hope not even the most ardent meat-eater can leave here thinking these animals aren't sentient individuals. A lick from Dylan, our youngest steer, or a nuzzle from Louise, a sheep who *always* wants a scratch, will often do the trick. And once people clear that hurdle, it's easier to convey that these animals are deserving of our moral consideration. No one wants to think they are contributing to animal cruelty but sadly, if you are eating meat, including fish and dairy, you are.

Each time you sit down to a meal you have the power to stop your participation in the institutionalised cruelty and exploitation that is animal agriculture. As a vegan, by not eating animals you have the power to save lives (approximately two hundred per year for the average person and half that as a vegetarian[2]). These are animals who won't be torn out of their ocean homes or confined to cramped, filthy buildings, cages and pens before meeting their untimely deaths.

In eight short years, we have helped hundreds of farm animals find their way to freedom, either at our sanctuary or at loving, forever homes where they can live out their lives in peace. And we have helped countless others by inspiring people to leave animals off their plates and adopt a healthy and compassionate diet. We want to inspire people to open their eyes and question the system. Could it be that animals are here *with* us and not *for* us?

It's always a beautiful thing to see a chicken who has never

▶ Sisters Judy and Patsy at Woodstock Farm Sanctuary.

Photo credit: Rebecca Moore.

▶ Felix at Woodstock.

Photo credit: Bob Esposito.

known life outside of a tiny, cramped cage walk outdoors for the first time. To watch them spread their wings, feel the sun on their back and grass underfoot is to watch their rebirth from a life of misery to one of freedom. It's a sight to behold and one that makes me realise every day that I was put on this earth to do this work. I consider myself a voice for the voiceless and through me, and the others who make up Woodstock Farm Animal Sanctuary, the animals shall be heard.

Excerpt taken from: The Lucky Ones: My Passionate Fight For Farm Animals.

Link:

www.WoodstockSanctuary.org

Endnotes:

1. Farm Forward calculation based on US Department of Agriculture, 2002 *Census of Agriculture*, June 2004; and *ibid*.

2. http://www.peta.org/b/thepetafiles/archive/2010/12/13/vegans-save-185-animals-a-year.aspx

 TURKEY LIKE ME
Dr Gay Bradshaw

"Plant-based eating is a simple, straightforward step toward solving a lot of the mess that modern humans have created on this planet."

—Gay Bradshaw.

Whatever we inherit from the fortunate

We have taken from the defeated

What they had to leave us – a symbol:

A symbol perfected in death.

And all shall be well and

All manner of thing shall be well

By the purification of the motive

In the ground of our beseeching.

T S Eliot

G A Bradshaw, PhD, PhD, is Executive Director of The Kerulos Center in Oregon, USA. She holds doctorate degrees in ecology and psychology and has published, taught and lectured widely in these fields both in the US and internationally. She is the author of *Elephants on the Edge: What Animals Teach Us about Humanity*, published by Yale University Press, an in-depth psychological portrait of elephants in captivity and in the wild, and *The Elephant Letters*, a children's book seen through the lens of Elephant experience in the wild and captivity. Dr Bradshaw's work focuses on trans-species psychology, the theory and methods for the study and care of human and non-human animal psychological wellbeing and multi-species cultures. Her research expertise includes the effects of violence on, and trauma recovery of, elephants, grizzly bears, chimpanzees, parrots and other species in captivity...   ■

▶ Gay and Panama Bradshaw.

I am a plant-based eater. I use this expression in lieu of 'vegan' because it directly communicates what I do without any reference to humans. While we live with others in a shared culture, each of us is responsible for ourselves. Ultimately, individual ethics and actions have nothing to do with what others think. What we do and think is our responsibility alone. How we live and whom we eat comprises an individual contract with nature, the universe, and soul.

I became plant-based because I wanted to refrain from harming other animals who, unlike most of humanity today, are willing and able to tread lightly on the planet's tender skin. My decision lessens the angst associated with being a human in this day and age, and provides hope that humanity will soon learn again how to live peacefully with animal kin and other life. I am inspired to be a 'votary of *ahimsa*', someone whom Gandhi describes as one who "...remains true to his faith if the spring of all his actions is compassion, if he shuns to the best of his ability the destruction of the tiniest creature, tries to save it, and thus incessantly strives to be free from the deadly coil of *himsa*" (*An Autobiography, or The Story of My Experiments*, 2001, p319).

I am fortunate to have the extra pleasure in eating the same food as other herbivores with whom I share the land – Rabbits, Deer, Sparrows, Parrots, Quail and Wild Turkeys. This commonality in sustenance and restraint brings deeper connection and a heightened sense of kinship. Plant-based eating is a simple, straightforward step toward solving much of the mess that modern humans have created on this planet. It also helps us move from the practice of domestication. While the joy of getting to know Cats, Rabbits, Sheep, Pigs, Horses, Chickens and other farmed animals cannot be surpassed, domestication causes immense suffering.

It is true that many domesticated animals live rich and happy lives, but, as psychologists remind us, because they are forced to depend on humans, domesticated animals are denied an essential elemental core to wellbeing – the ability to act on one's own, independent of the wishes of another.

Most live under greatly compromised conditions that bring enormous psychological, emotional and physical pain and loss. It has been only very recently that psychological trauma and stress have been recognised as real and pernicious to non-human animal wellbeing. Neuroscience concurs with intuition which tells us all animals are vulnerable to abuse and imprisonment just as we are. Most causes of this suffering derive from what is regarded as acceptable cultural practices. For example, the majority of birds in captivity live in cages. Confinement and loss of freedom affects avian minds and bodies just as it does human prisoners who are subjected to similar deprivations.

The differential between captive and free-living conditions is enormous. A bird taken from her or his flock in the wild, or deprived of one when captive-bred, suffers multiple traumas – loss of family, isolation, nutritional compromise, and dramatic decreases in natural movement. By definition, even the 'best' captive situation falls short of basic bird needs – free living in a flock with hundreds of miles to explore and with the right of choice and agency. Notably, a flock is not 'just' a collection of individuals, but an emergent entity. Contained within the beautifully feathered bodies of a Wild Turkey or Parrot is a self-similar fractal of consciousness drawn from generation after generation and flock after flock. A Turkey flock is a dynamic, pulsing field of consciousness and life. When a bird is taken from the flock, the group and the individual experience profound rupture.

Despite well-accepted science showing the profound suffering that captivity causes, illegal poaching, selling and captive breeding continue. In Mexico alone, it is estimated that sixty-five to seventy-eight thousand Parrots are captured each year and more than seventy-five percent of these individuals die even before reaching the purchaser. This means that in one year in one country alone, fifty to sixty thousand birds are brutally torn from their families, packed into crates so tightly that they suffocate and die. Multiply these numbers by the tens of countries that capture, buy and sell Parrots, let alone other birds, and the resultant statistics are mind numbing. Even more birds die in 'pet' stores, while others succumb in private homes from abuse and neglect.

The wildlife captive trade, domestication and captive 'breeding' persist because they are socially accepted practices that give pleasure and money to humans. Further, the practice is actively defended by veterinarians, conservationists, researchers and others who directly profit from the institution of captivity. Wildlife captivity is culturally engrained. Cultural habits are just that, habits, things we do without thinking. Chicken soup, the quintessential and iconic symbol of care and nourishment, involves the brutal treatment of sentient beings who have the same kinds of aspirations, desires, loves, dreams and emotions that we have. Chickens reared for eggs and meat live a true Treblinka. Their suffering translates to our own. How can chicken soup heal when it is composed of agonised minds and bodies of suffering souls? Animal symptoms of despair become our own. We are what we eat. Our human minds, bodies and souls are not separate from other animals.

Change to plant-based eating can be hard because our dualistic culture represents human and other animal welfare as conflicting goals. In so doing, there is an implied demand that an individual make a choice between allegiance to humans or other animals. I experienced this artificial Sophie's choice myself.

Let me be clear. The conflict was my own. It did not generate from my human family. It had to do with ego and self-identity. I knew myself through a cultural identity. Unconsciously, I felt that becoming plant-based comprised a break from my familial customs, which meant a loss of connection with those I loved. The cultural rituals associated with my family life were integral to self-identity. Giving up these rituals seemed like a betrayal with my Danish heritage.

When I became a plant-based eater, however, my sense of self changed – for the better. I realised that there was no loss, only gain. Love doesn't take sides. Love isn't a pie that, when sliced up, may leave someone without. I was as close and part of my human family as before without having to cause harm to other animals. Self-honesty in mind and action is exhilaratingly liberating! I believe I would have become plant-based well before if I had looked into the eyes of an animal who was sacrificed for food. All you have to do is look into a Turkey's eyes, see beyond their beautiful form and know they have a zest for life, a soul, aspirations, loves and dreams. Try it. Look into the beautiful face and eyes of a Turkey and your opening heart will open your mind. You will be privileged to experience a glimpse into the exquisite Turkey universe, their goodness and ascendant natures.

My personal experience is a microcosm of the deep psychological schism and dissociative states in which modern humans live. I chose the passage from T S Eliot for the epigraph because it reminds me of my own journey that is part of a profound paradigm shift taking place today – humanity's transformation from an embrace of *himsa* to *ahimsa* as the guiding principle of life on earth. "*Whatever we inherit from the fortunate*" – these were the blessings that I inherited when growing up – "*We have taken from the defeated*" – were the trees hewn to build the home in which I lived, glass windows made from the boiled bones of stones, and land taken from American Indians and wildlife. I now understand that in some small way, by the work that I do and being a plant-based eater, I am undoing what my ancestors wrought. The choices I make, the actions I take and those I do not, are steps of atonement to heal who has been harmed.

I have given myself over to an open social identity that does not exclude or partition non-human animals from humans – a trans-species identity of self. When I became plant-based, an inner psychic wall, of which I was not consciously aware, dissolved. This shift had other effects. I do not reject other humans, but I don't privilege someone just because she or he is human. I simply don't see myself as that important anymore, someone worth more than anyone else. My pleasure is not worth the suffering of others.

When people argue that, "Animals eat animals so why can't humans eat animals", I reply that most of us have a choice to do otherwise. We do not have to eat animals whereas Cougars and some Sharks and other Animals need to eat other Animals. Further, these animals do not create obliterating warehouses of agony that not only kill, but torture individuals whom, neuroscientists proclaim, possess brain structures and functions comparable to our own that underlie the capacity to think, feel and experience consciousness. Disabling the 'meat' industry is plain logical given what is known about their associated effects of pollution, deforestation and other harmful effects on the planet. Being plant-based is more than a change in diet. To restore this beautiful world to the way it was before colonialism, agentic and burgeoning with health, our species is called upon to change the fundaments of culture from exploitation to subsistence.

It is critical to remember that we live in a time of contradictions by force of where we are now. This relates to our philosophy and work at The Kerulos Center. We seek to provide the science and other information about animal sentience, their capacity to feel, think and be conscious and then provide ways that support and facilitate a move toward *ahimsa, nature-based* consciousness – a return to ways of living that benefit all species. The task before each of us is to learn, reflect deeply and honestly and then act and live according to what we truly believe inside.

Living is a privilege. The decision to eat *someone* is an act with profound moral implications and responsibilities. Since I have decided to live, I try and take comfort that the material world is only a tiny fraction of life and that we all live on together in other dimensions. It is my vision that humanity sets its sights on becoming subsistence plant eaters. This may seem more difficult than the present fast food, ready-access elective lifestyle, but there is an infinite gain – the cessation of animal subjugation. We are kin under skin, fin, feather and fur and lucky to be alive in their brilliant, compassionate company. Take a page from the ethics of Wild Turkeys and you can't go wrong.

"Only when the power of love is greater than the love for power, will the world change." Pim van Lommel.

Link:

www.kerulos.org

■ YOUR WAY BUT MY DECISION
Louie Gedo

Louie Gedo was born in Manhasset, New York, in 1965, and several years and many relocations later, settled in Flushing, NY. In his mid twenties he became an environmental advocate. At age twenty-six, he turned his focus to advocacy on behalf of animals and would later be involved with and spearhead educational outreach campaigns on the streets of New York City. Today, Louie continues his animal advocacy in a variety of ways, including writing letters, engaging in online discussions and rescuing rats from glue traps in garbage bins and rehabilitating them…   ■

Allow me to start my story by telling you something about my childhood. More than any other kid I knew whilst growing up, my rocky upbringing was made up of constant instability, ridicule and punishment. Feelings of distrust, inadequacy,

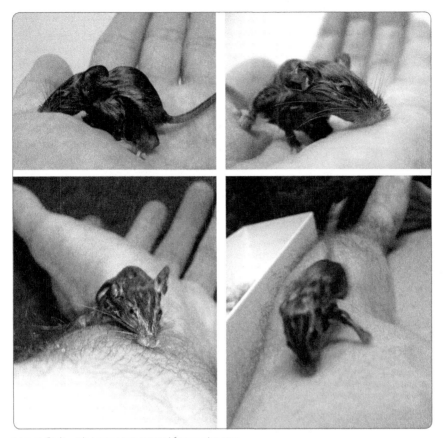

▶ Louie Gedo with Jumpy, just rescued from a glue trap.

shame, fear and a great degree of self-worthlessness resulted from oppressive and repressive domination by my father. I grew up at the hands of an exceptionally abusive father and I would come to learn that not even the cute, innocent family pets were safe from the abuse and full, brutal physical violence my father unapologetically executed upon us.

In my home, my father dictated practically everything, from what second-hand, or third-hand clothing I was told to wear, when to speak, what to do with myself when not at school or doing homework, how I was allowed to feel when he took me on one of his many hunting trips, and whether or not I could bathe today or this week. Obviously, what to eat was always dictated to me as well. For all practical purposes, making decisions for myself was verboten in the worst kind of way. If my home were a small country, my father would be labelled an authoritarian despot.

Of course, every child is influenced to some level by their parents, figures of authority, their peers, and society's traditions, laws and expectations as a whole. But these mild forms of inculcation are entirely normal in every society.

The experience of my childhood was so frightening and hurtful that I recall a moment of thinking to myself that in a heartbeat I would trade places with a boy I saw one afternoon who had no legs. For at least standing behind him pushing his wheelchair was a dad (or at least that's who I assumed the man was) who was asking him at that moment, "Where would you like to go next?"

Feathers or fur, what's the difference?

One day, after getting home from school, my parents took me to the window at the back of our first-floor apartment, which overlooked a small patch of dirt and grass. There I saw three chickens pecking around in the dirt. A couple of days later, again after rushing home from grade school, I heard chicken chatter and shuffling noises coming from the bathroom. My father gave me permission to go in, and in the tub, there were the three chickens, with curious eyes fixed upon me as soon as I entered. I don't recall us ever having pets in the house before and I was surprised my father seemed to finally find it in his heart to do this.

Now the chickens were up close, it took no time for me to become very interested in them. I learnt that two chickens were girls and one was a boy, a rooster. After a couple of days I could pet each bird and we named them. Finally, there was something to look forward to at home. Sure my pets were unusual, because friends at school had cats and dogs but I didn't feel envious. I had a bond with my chickens in just the same way my friends did with their animals.

I don't recall now how long it was after we got the chickens, but one day after getting home from school I noticed the chickens were no longer in the bathroom. I was worried but my parents were always too busy with 'very serious stuff' so I dared not ask them something as 'unimportant' as where the chickens might be. I would simply have to wait for my father to let me know. I just wanted to pet them and not knowing was dreadful. After dinner and helping to put the leftovers away in the refrigerator, my curiosity got the better of me and I decided to ask my mom where the chickens were hidden. My mom, after getting the nod of okay from my father, told me some of the chickens were now in the refrigerator and some were in my stomach. More than revolted in that moment, I was in utter disbelief because that meant the chickens I ate for dinner were my chickens. That just couldn't be possible! Nobody eats their pets.

I grew up being fed meat at every single meal and usually big portions of it. At the same time I also came to like the taste of meat. (Do we come to like meat because we eat it out of habit or do we eat meat because we like it? I'm not sure. Maybe a little bit of both.) But in any case, the result was the same. Chicken was among my favourite foods growing up. The vegetables we were given depended on the meat and the meal; potatoes, chopped spinach, canned corn, carrots, canned beans and overcooked broccoli.

I can vividly remember times when my mom took me shopping and going through the meat aisle, I would even help her pick out the shiny cellophane-wrapped, sterilised-looking trays of chopped meat or drumsticks that were for dinner that night. But in that moment as a child, I understood and recognised without any ambiguity or uncertainty at all, that chicken comes from killed chickens.

The lessons I learnt that day were seared into my memory. Chickens really only had one obvious purpose. My pets got treated differently from my friends' pet cats and dogs because that's just the way it is. It was also reinforced upon me that I had no choice in the matter and my feelings were inconsequential. I would carry these lessons with me for many years to come.

I think it was the following year when we moved to a new apartment in a different part of the city that my father found a hungry stray cat out by the back of the building near the garbage cans when he was cleaning up late one night. He brought the cat up into the apartment and that was my family's first cat, Cica. She was a small female striped tabby and I think her playfulness was what got my family to really like her. Even my father at times seemed to care about her.

We moved about every eighteen months because my father kept losing his superintendent's jobs; and as the apartment usually came with the job we'd have to go. We had three other cats during our moves, not at the same time though because my father would punish cats who annoyed him. He knew I loved the kitties and to cruelly manipulate my emotions he would do bad things to them.

The value of being honest with myself.

Fast-forward to the spring of 1992 when I was twenty-six and managed somehow to stumble my way into a committed relationship with an attractive Asian woman named Yoko. A few months later, wanting to look better and impress her, I asked her about her beautiful hair and radiant skin. Her answer was, "a vegetarian diet." Oh right, I thought. Not what I was expecting. I imagined she'd tell me the name of some exotic lotion or beauty care product from Japan – something I could do too, without difficulty. But give up my meat? Ha ha, that wasn't happening in this lifetime. After all I'd grown up believing I needed to eat plenty of meat to get protein and sufficient nutrition. In school I learnt from the Four Food Groups posters, and later from television. In my early twenties, I couldn't get enough of Bill Bixby and Lou Ferrigno starring as the Incredible Hulk on TV. You just knew the Hulk didn't eat Brussels sprouts, cauliflower and lettuce – that's pretty much what vegetarians eat, isn't it? I needed to defend my way of life because this was who I was and that was that. No cauliflower for me!

But wanting to look good and keep my relationship with Yoko led to the beginning of my research into vegetarian diets. I read articles, studies and books on the subject and realised much of this information was already out there. But now instead of paying no mind to it I began to pay attention.

I learnt farmed animals suffer and are killed in terrible ways and within three weeks I reluctantly gave up eating beef. Within a few more weeks I could not only do fine without meat, but a healthy plant-based diet was helping me to feel healthier and look better. And importantly, this meant I no longer played a part in the slaughter of farmed animals.

It was during these few weeks that I had the first "Aha!" moment. I realised the human body has no requirement for animal flesh. This immediately led to the next and most revolutionary "Aha!" moment I have ever experienced. That moment gave me the first true taste of what self empowerment is and feels like because in that moment I made a choice – not for my father, not because television advertising told me so, not because others were habituated into doing something I also had to do to fit in and not feel like an outcast, but because it was the right thing to do for me and for animals who shouldn't be harmed in the first place. That moment was the beginning of my liberation from an oppressive and repressive past.

Keeping it to myself is selfish.

I knew I was doing the right thing, because I knew I was sparing the lives of many animals. But in spite of my new, compassionate way of living, I knew billions of farmed animals were still being purpose bred, exploited, treated inhumanely, and ultimately met the most severe form of violence – being killed. This was unacceptable to me now but what could I possibly do?

Remember, I had been socially neutered as a child and I am still shy, socially very awkward (but getting better), and while I found the power to make my own personal choices, who was I to suggest or tell someone else what to do? I knew raising my voice was the answer, because in doing so, I could alert other people to what was happening and to how, together, we could make a difference for the animals.

I found out about some local animal advocacy organisations that conducted public protests against terrible things such as factory farming, killing furbearing animals for vanity, seal hunts and captive animal circuses. Despite my shyness, I knew the public had to find out so I nervously joined.

When I was out there protesting, yes I felt uncomfortable, but not as uncomfortable as I assumed I would. It seems speaking out on behalf of someone else wasn't nearly as difficult or stressful as speaking out for myself.

Tharz ah muus luus in tha huus!

"*Tharz ah muus luus in tha huus!*"…a Scottish friend once told me. "There's a mouse loose in the house!" These days, when I'm not working, sleeping or eating I am an animal rights activist. Every opportunity I get I speak out on behalf of the rights animals deserve.

I now work in a complex of residential buildings in Queens, New York City, managing the garbage and the trash compactors and maintaining the grounds.

What do most of the tenants in my buildings do if they find themselves with a rodent problem in their apartment? They put out glue traps. Glue traps are inexpensive, effective, require no maintenance and no baiting or re-baiting, and are treated just like any other inconsequential piece of garbage with their unwilling victims virtually welded to them. They are hideous and diabolical and always result in cruel suffering when they have effectively trapped their victim. The first time I came upon a mouse was the one I found stuck to a glue trap. The little mouse was frantically struggling to get free, squealing and squeaking in desperation.

Faced with the reality that I would be encountering this situation on a sporadic but ongoing basis, I knew I had to find a solution quickly and I discovered vegetable or nut oil is a relatively effective release agent for the glue.

Today, I am happy to report I have saved the lives of many dozens of innocent rodents, all of whom have a very strong will and desire to live and be free. A perfect example of this is one of the mice I found early one morning last year who was in really bad shape on the glue trap. She was barely alive and in fact her breathing was so shallow I had assumed she was long dead by the time I found the glue trap in the trash. I stared intently at her body for a couple of minutes and it was then I thought maybe I had seen some very slight movement. It was the middle of winter so I took her into a storage room that was quiet and held her up close to my mouth and began to exhale slowly, the warmest breath I could possibly summon from my lips. After what must have been fifteen or twenty minutes of constantly breathing like this onto her body, and feeling a bit dizzy myself, she kicked her only free leg a little and her breathing became noticeable… she was alive!

I was able to start the release process then using the small jar of almond oil I keep in my storage closet. You have to carefully pour some of the oil in the places where the fur and the glue are in contact, which for most stuck mice is almost everywhere including their tail and even their head. Caution must be taken not to inadvertently drown them with oil because if their head is stuck to the glue trap and the poured oil spills over their nostrils and mouth, they are unable to make the normal reaction they would otherwise make, which is to jerk their head to dislodge the oil. I used my finger to carefully and gently push, pry and lift her tail, legs, body and finally lift her head off the trap. This took longer than usual because she was too weak to assist in her own liberation. I then carefully placed her in a small box with air holes in it that I had made just for this purpose. At the bottom I have a piece of old, clean, soft, cotton T-shirt crumpled up that I use to give added comfort. She was relatively motionless after being released and her body stiff. This was very troubling to see so I continued warming her with my breath. By lunchtime she was able to move herself slowly beneath some of the folds of the T-shirt. I put a water drop on my finger and put it to her mouth and some of it seemed to melt into her mouth but I could not be certain because her mouth was so tiny. I continued with this routine until the end of my workday when I was then able to get her home and take better care of her. I don't have room here for all the details of her recovery, but she did in fact make a full recovery. I released her into an old storage shed on a piece of disused property miles away from any house where traps might be used and hopefully, she and all the others I've freed have lived out the remainder of their lives in freedom.

I wasn't born with special talents or gifts that make me better suited than anyone else to help someone in need, nor was I born with a particular propensity to be kind and compassionate – all of these things I learnt, and some of them I struggled and still struggle with. The only real difference I am aware of between me and someone who hasn't done something personal to spare or save the life of an animal yet, is that I was presented by chance with some additional opportunities to test my heart. In other words, I am convinced that any of you reading this very abridged story of my life is capable of doing at least as much for the animals as I have been able to do.

■ SEEING THE BIG PICTURE
Gary Smith

"Veganism at its core is about justice."   ■

—Gary Smith.

Gary Smith is co-founder of Evolotus, a PR agency working for a better world. Evolotus specialises in nonprofit documentary films, animal advocacy campaigns, health/wellness, natural foods and socially beneficial companies. Gary blogs at *The Thinking Vegan* and has written for *Elephant Journal, Jewish Journal, Mother Nature Network* and other publications. Gary and his wife are ethical vegans and live in Sherman Oaks, California, with their cat Chloe and two beagles, Frederick and Douglass, who were rescued from an animal testing laboratory... ■

My journey into veganism started about twenty years ago. I ran into an old high school acquaintance who lifted weights quite seriously, and I began to work out with him. He avoided red meat because of the high fat, and would not eat any foods with a fat content over twenty five percent. As we worked out more, I became more open to new dietary ideas and began to adopt some of the same eating habits, giving up red meat and eschewing high-fat foods.

One evening I was listening to a late-night radio program and the host mentioned a book called *Diet For a New America* by John Robbins. I bought the book

▶ Gary Smith with Douglass, Kezia and Frederick.

the next day and I remember quite clearly thumbing through the first few pages. The pictures of farmed animals in confinement stunned me. I had no idea the meat I was eating came from factories and heavy confinement and at that moment, I went vegan. I called my best friend and explained the photographs in the book. He went vegan on the spot, without even seeing the pictures. So I became vegan and influenced someone else to do the same, on the same day.

I knew abstaining from eating meat, dairy and eggs would bring changes into my life, but I did not know the extent of what those changes would bring. What I had not anticipated was the emotional and spiritual shifts that would occur from this change. Early on in my vegan journey, my political beliefs began to fall apart. Rapidly. I had been a young, obnoxious Republican and was obsessed with Ronald Reagan. I wanted to be a wealthy, successful businessman and the first time I was eligible to vote in a presidential election, I voted for George Bush Senior.

I also had inner stirrings that would later reveal themselves to be a spiritual/philosophical shift. I wasn't actively searching for anything, nor was I actively questioning myself or my beliefs, but a process was unfolding, whether I liked it or not.

My workout buddy and I signed up for a class on nonviolence. I remember very clearly sitting in class the first day and realising everything made sense. All of the searching and questioning I had been doing was about nonviolence at its core. If Gandhi, Tolstoy and Martin Luther King Jr had followed the philosophy of nonviolence, then I wasn't going crazy after all.

I gradually began to eat dairy, eggs and fish again and continued in this way for the next ten years. It is my single greatest regret. I never felt comfortable internally while I ate those products. Emotionally, I felt disconnected and uneasy. So, I gave up fish and became vegetarian. Six months later, I decided to go vegan for a week, just to see how it felt again. Nearly seven years later, I remain vegan.

This time, the experience has been remarkably different. I was really only vegan in terms of food, as I had no real grasp of the concept of animal rights. I didn't think about animals used in entertainment or vivisection and I continued to wear leather, silk and wool.

When I became vegan again, I immediately felt I was home.

Around that time, my wife and I started a PR agency called Evolotus. Initially, we focused on companies and organisations that we supported, and tried to match them up with sympathetic media. As time went by, we realised Evolotus could function more as a tool for our activism. Even though it is important that supportive media are aware of what our clients do, it is just as important that mainstream media and their audience become aware of veganism, animal rights, climate change and other social justice issues. Learning how to live in the world of social justice activism, and understanding how to tell a story the mainstream media will not reject outright, is a skill we have developed in our activism toolbox.

We began working with Mercy For Animals on their Farm to Fridge tour, when they took their twelve-minute film about animal food production to forty-one cities, and have since worked on publicising three of their undercover investigations into factory farms. We worked with Animal Defenders International on the US Travelling Exotic Animal Protection Act, a Federal Bill to ban the use of exotic animals in travelling circuses. We worked on the Fur Free West Hollywood campaign, which made West Hollywood the first city in the United States to ban the sale of fur apparel. We have worked on numerous documentaries about animal rights and veganism, such as *Earthlings, Got the Facts on Milk, Forks Over Knives, Skin Trade* and many others. These campaigns have resulted in coverage in national mainstream publications and television programs, enabling the issues of animal rights and veganism to reach the wider public via Evolotus. And better yet, these stories are being taken seriously and respected by the media. Over the years we have been doing this work we have seen a great shift in how the mainstream media regard our clients and our issues.

Getting media to cover animal rights issues is vastly different from hands-on rescue. A few years ago my wife and I began helping to rescue beagles released from animal testing laboratories. Watching the first rescued dogs run around the yard, come up to us, and generally find some version of happiness was heartwarming. Being in their presence touched and changed me.

Getting universities and private testing facilities to give beagles to animal rights activists is about the most difficult task you can imagine. They do not want the public to know they are testing on dogs, and having them out in the world creates that possibility of exposure.

We rescued nine beagles on 8 June 2011. When we pulled up to the liaison's contact point, my heart broke. I was frozen for a few moments in deep grief as all nine of them were drooling, had piss, shit and vomit in their cages and looked frightened. I snapped out of it and helped to move them to the van. We took them to a friend's yard where we opened each carrier one at a time. It took about ten minutes before the first beagle had the courage to step outside for the first time. Within another ten minutes, they were sniffing each other, us, exploring and acting like dogs, as much as they could. There was no barking, of course, as their vocal cords had been cut by the breeder so they would not disturb the researchers.

We got back to L.A. around ten that night to a throng of media, and the dogs were assigned to foster homes. The next morning, I received a call from one of the foster families who said their current dog wasn't happy with the situation. They dropped him off at our house; the poor fellow was still scared and disoriented beyond belief. We intended to keep him for a couple of hours, but a few hours turned into five weeks! Watching Malcolm go from a frightened victim of violence into a happy, mostly adjusted puppy (in the body of a two-year-old dog) changed my life. I still get teary when I think about him. I didn't expect to fall so deeply in love with him.

This experience opened my eyes to focusing on individual lives at the same time as focusing on the abstract numbers such as ten billion land animals. Malcolm also opened my eyes to single-issue campaigns because he and his beagle friends would have been overlooked by vegan education outreach.

I was happy with the media attention we were able to get. We chose to tell the happy story about beagles who had been rescued from testing labs and have a chance at a great life, over the story of the horrors of animal torture. The media did a fantastic job of taking our story and filling in the blanks, asking why they are used in labs, why animals are tested on for household products, and generally asking all the right questions. In six years of doing activist PR, I have never seen such overwhelmingly positive and supportive comments on articles and TV stories. Readers and TV viewers really understood the issue, and I could see the impact it had. As a result, many people threw out all their make-up and detergents and found cruelty-free products to substitute what they had used before.

A few months later, Frederick and Douglass entered our lives. Letting Malcolm go to his forever (adopted) home was one of the hardest things I've ever had to do, but a few months later forty beagles were released from a laboratory in Spain that was going out of business. We were ready to adopt (although our cat would no doubt object). We ended up fostering eight of these dogs, and helped to place them in forever homes. Two special guys remained, and to say they have changed our lives would be a massive understatement. We are completely focused on making sure they are happy, healthy and at peace after the five-plus years they were confined in a laboratory. They still have emotional and physical scars, but with each day that goes by and each belly rub, they grow more comfortable and adjusted to freedom.

My path to activism has changed and continues to evolve with experience and knowledge.

Veganism is much more than what one eats and wears. At its core it is about justice; a social justice movement that gives an animal the right to be left to his or her own devices. As such, advocating for veganism is much bigger than convincing individuals to become vegan. It's also about fighting against the industries that profit from the use of animals. It's about fighting against governments that protect the rights of those industries to use and abuse animals. Ultimately, it is about reaching a public that allows and perpetuates the abuse of animals, and educating them about speciesism.

Fighting industries is a difficult game. It involves so many stakeholders, including suppliers, wholesalers, banks, retailers and the like. If enough economic damage can be brought to enough businesses, the US Government will have a harder time continuously bailing them out.

Sea Shepherd's 2010-11 Antarctic campaign is a good example. For six years, Sea Shepherd has caused economic damage to the government of Japan. Japan has been killing fewer whales, which means a loss of revenue, as well as spending more money on additional ships, weapons and manpower. In this particular campaign, Japan cut their whaling season short, not because of public pressure or a marketplace decrease in the demand for whale meat, but to stop even greater economic losses.

The consumption of vegan products alone is not going to create the kinds of changes we need for the planet. Not eating animal products doesn't necessarily save lives. It stops the breeding of some animals, which is wonderful, but we are talking about fifty five billion land animals used globally for food, trillions of fish, millions of animals violated in the name of science, millions killed and skinned for clothing, thousands exploited for human entertainment and millions of dogs and cats bred for the whim and pleasure of humans. A few people going vegan is not going to make any significant change globally, particularly when we factor in increases in animal consumption and population growth around the world. If we truly wish to create real change in terms of the holocaust against animals, we have to do more than hand out leaflets.

Rescue Story

Desert Tortoise Rescue at the Kerulos Center, Oregon.

▶ Desert Tortoise rescue at The Kerulos Center, Oregon, USA.

The Kerulos Center's Tortoise and the Hare Sanctuary provides lifetime care for special-needs desert tortoises and rescued rabbits (www.kerulos,org). The endangered Desert Tortoises, who can live up to one hundred years of age, come from a government facility that is closing. Healthy Tortoises will be reintroduced to their native habitat, but those who have been abused or have developed shell and limb deformities from poor care as 'pets', need sanctuary. Lomahongva (Beautiful Clouds Arising), shown above, was kept in a closet for more than one year and sustained severe injury to her back leg. During warm months, the Tortoises will live in their Oregon geodesic domes and winter in their hibernation barn, Je t'attendrai ('I will wait for you'). To honour their Southwest US origin, the Tortoises have been given Hopi names.

AUSTRALIA

■ INTERVIEW WITH
Pam Ahern
Founder, Edgar's Mission Farm Sanctuary, Melbourne, Australia

"I think it is the power of kindness that really changes people."   ■

—Pam Ahern.

When the porcine stars of *Charlotte's Web* needed a home after the completion of filming at Greendale, Victoria in 2005, they were fortunate enough to become residents of Edgar's Mission Animal Sanctuary in Willowmavin, Victoria. Over the years, the sanctuary has been home to thousands of animals who have been rescued from abuse and neglect from a variety of situations, including at the eleventh hour on their way to the slaughterhouse. Many of them have been rehomed, and Edgar's is currently a forever home to three hundred and fifty animals. Their guardian angel is Pam Ahern, a tireless animal advocate and educator who self-funds this two thousand dollar a week venture…   ■

▶ Pam Ahern and Maid Marian.

Pam, how did you come to run Edgar's Mission?

Edgar's Mission was something I never really set out to do. It all came about because of my love of Edgar. I was working with Animals Australia on the Save Babe campaign, which was raising awareness of the plight of factory-farmed pigs in Australia. Most people are not aware of the situation, and that farm animals have been specifically exempted from The Protection of Cruelty to Animals Act. This means things can be done to farm animals that would never be allowed to be done to domestic pets with regard to cruelty.

The Save Babe campaign was timely because the Code of Practice for pig farming was being reviewed. James Cromwell happened to be in Australia at the time. People automatically identified with James as Farmer Hoggett in the hit movie *Babe*. He is passionate about helping animals and people, and he does a lot of work with the Native Americans who have been displaced from their land. We got in touch with him and he couldn't do enough to help us. We needed a pig for a photo shoot and that's where Edgar came in. We procured a Landrace Large White Cross from a piggery and we called him Edgar Alan Pig. A sanctuary was then needed to provide lifelong loving care for our porcine star so we created Edgar's Mission, naming it in his honour.

Edgar and I would go for walks in the park and people came from everywhere to see my pig and marvel at him. Edgar would grunt his "hello" and so a dialogue began with people I would never have had the opportunity to speak with before. They were interested in learning about Edgar and were horrified to learn about the treatment of animals like him. I realised then that the best ambassadors for changing the way we think about farm animals are the animals themselves. Edgar's Mission really grew from the love of my pig!

I had little to do with pigs before Edgar, but I had been inside piggeries where I learnt an important lesson. I would hear them grunting and I thought this was just because people had come into their shed. I was later to learn, however, that the sound they were making was actually a deep, guttural greeting that they offer as a "hello" to the humans who come in. Given everything our species has done to them, that they could still say hello to us brought tears to my eyes.

They seem very forgiving, don't they?

They are incredibly forgiving. I've had important teachers in my life but the most important have been animals and their capacity for forgiveness. Humans carry grudges about all sorts of things but animals, particularly the abused animals who have come to the sanctuary, just don't know about grudges. They feel the kindness and repay it a million times over. Alice, who played the mother of Wilbur in *Charlotte's Web*, was a special example. For four or five years she had been in a factory farm, producing litter after litter of piglets, each lot being taken from her at only a few weeks of age. After the movie, she went back to the farm where she was bound for the slaughterhouse. Luckily for her, Paramount found out. They were horrified so they bought her and that's how she came to our farm. Alice had never known human kindness and when she arrived, the first thing she did was to bend down and eat grass. The farmer who had brought her was shocked and he said, "My God, that's the first time this pig has seen grass!" That day was a day of many firsts for Alice. It was the first time she saw sunlight, smelled fresh air and took more than a few steps. Sadly for most pigs, they only ever get to do these things on the last day of their life, as they are trucked off to abattoirs.

What was the big step from that initial campaign to having a sanctuary for so many animals?

It's probably something I've been building up to all my life as it marries two of the most important things for me, my love of animals and my sense of justice. I've always loved animals and had an affinity with them and over the years I've learnt so much about them, how to read their behaviour and how to understand what is important to them.

The other thing that motivates me is my sense of justice. Many people who visit Edgar's Mission say, "I never thought about that before," or "I had no idea about this before." The Mission is a place where I would have loved to come when I was a child, to have had my feelings and concerns for animals validated. We all have feelings for animals and want to care for them but so many in our society dampen and squash that in us and when that happens, I think a part of us dies.

It's about our capacity to care, which should have no boundaries. You don't have to be an animal lover to care about these things, you just have to be a decent human being. I think most people are decent but they are simply not aware.

The gentle animals at Edgar's Mission are far better teachers than I am. Just spending time with a pig, hanging out with a sheep, stroking a chicken, seeing a turkey doing what turkeys do, are all wonderful things. On some level Edgar's Mission has something to offer everyone. It may just be realising that animals are sentient, emotional creatures.

During this process you became vegan.

I was vegan before Edgar came into being. I cared deeply about animals and I remember seeing an ad in the paper about products that weren't tested on animals, explaining they were cruelty free and that there is no need to test on animals.

As a result, my mother and I attended an 'anti-fur' rally. I remember saying apologetically to the lady who organised it, "Look, we do eat meat but is it okay if we still come along?" She said, "You know, it's not so much about what's on your plate but how it gets there and we just want you to think about these things." Her single act of kindness and encouragement had a huge impact on me and my style of activism has been influenced strongly by her.

At the rally I heard about Peter Singer, author of the hallmark book *Animal Liberation*. It was from reading this book I learnt about an experience Peter had in England. He'd been invited to the local chapter of the RSPCA. At afternoon tea the ham sandwiches came out and Peter thought, "How odd." I thought "How right." How can these people profess to care about animals and eat them at the same time, and expect to be taken seriously? It was my "*Aha!*" moment. I could not go on advocating for animals, asking people to care about them and trying to awaken compassion in others and yet eat meat and expect to be taken seriously. At that moment my life and my menu changed forever.

Would you say that being on a vegan diet has benefited you health-wise?

Absolutely. And the great thing was, the more I read and learned, the more boxes this lifestyle choice ticked. Not just health, but environmental, spiritual and energetic levels as well. I couldn't cope with eating meat again. If somebody said, "Oh, you've got to eat meat or you're going to die," I think it would be time to say goodbye to Pam!

I've been a blood donor since I was eighteen. Whenever you donate blood, your iron levels and blood pressure are monitored. I had a history of what my iron levels were like and to my surprise, both my mum's and mine increased as a result of being on a vegan diet. I think it was because of being more conscious of what we were eating – no more processed foods, more fruit, vegetables and legumes. Our health improved phenomenally. I can go all day fired by passion and the love of my pig and also wonderful vegan food, and rarely do I get sick. I believe that's a testament to my diet, my lifestyle and my beliefs.

What has become the single most important thing in your life now?

Keeping going, creating change, creating awareness. Everyone thinks about changing the world but only a few think about changing themselves. If we want change to happen, it's up to each individual. I truly believe in the goodness of the human heart, I will not give up on that, it is just getting people to think and make the connection.

If you gave people one message, what would it be?

To think about the really important question, "If we could live happy and healthy lives without harming others why wouldn't we?"

◼ THE WAY TO A KINDER WORLD
Kyle Behrend

> *"I remain happy, positive and upbeat. I find it energises, engages and encourages others to see the world from another creature's point of view. I am mindful not to be judgmental or harsh with anyone. That certainly is not the way to guide people to a kinder world."* ◼

—Kyle Behrend.

▶ Kyle Behrend and Mrs Peaches.

I found my way to Australia via London, where I headed after finishing university in South Africa. I met an Australian girl and decided to travel to her homeland with her. I found Australia to be a wonderful place; picturesque countryside and many opportunities. But I also found much more, I found my calling. I learnt about Edgar's Mission, a not-for-profit sanctuary for rescued farm animals, and it was at this busy and happy place where kindness bubbled to the fore once I stepped inside their farm gate – it touched something deep inside me. I have always cared about animals and social justice but in the past few years there was a growing need for me to do something more.... ◼

Like many, I feel we live in troubled times; we are indeed at a cusp and which way we tilt will determine the future of the planet. My take on this is that kindness is the key to a better world for all, kindness towards each other, towards the planet and towards animals. There is no doubt our environmental footprint is very much in the spotlight, we are encouraged to take shorter showers, use recycled materials, eat organically and travel less. But I feel our greatest test comes from how we treat animals, our fellow inhabitants on this planet, and if we look at our past report card on this we haven't done too well. I truly believe people are good of heart and that many have just lost their way. Through my work with Edgar's Mission I believe we can help people reconnect with their inherent 'goodness'.

I started out volunteering at Edgar's Mission. This gave me the opportunity to do something with my life that I feel made a positive difference to the world and all the creatures we share it with. Sadly today there exists a great disconnect between people and farm animals. Edgar's Mission helps bridge this void.

Not long after I started volunteering I was offered a fulltime role. Prior to this, all the day-to-day activities were carried out by the founder and director of this magical place, Pam Ahern. I now live at the sanctuary and can think of no place I would rather be. The sanctuary is home to more than three hundred and fifty rescued chickens, pigs, cows, sheep, horses, goats, chickens, ducks, geese, rabbits and even peacocks. My daily tasks include animal feeding, animal husbandry, farm maintenance, administration, photography, maintaining the website and *Facebook* page, helping with the monthly e-newsletter *Trottings*, outreach work to markets, schools, community events and aged care facilities, and conducting tours for visitors.

I really enjoy conducting the farm tours. It is amazing how the touch of a gentle cow or the grunt of a friendly pig can really help people put in perspective what their dietary choices are doing to these innocent creatures. Every animal at the sanctuary has a unique story to tell, and they all are united in that their arriving at Edgar's Mission was brought about by an act of kindness by someone not wishing harm to come to another creature. There is no doubt people empathise with farm animals once presented with the individual creatures and many are shocked, even brought to tears when they learn the emotional capacity of these gentle souls is not unlike that of their beloved pets. Over and over I hear, "I have never thought about that before." It really is the light bulb moment for many.

We work very long hours but I love the work we do and would not have my life any other way. Nothing comes easily, and I think it motivates others to see how much time and effort we put into helping animals, with nothing to gain except a kinder world for all.

Every day in Australia about twelve million chickens live in battery cages, with not even enough space to extend their wings. Knowing this can be stressful and unpleasant, with many people preferring to switch off. But in knowing the reality of our choices we are given the opportunity to make informed decisions so that our actions can truly reflect our ethics. If we simply dwelled on the cruelty in the world there would be no change – we would become depressed, despondent and slip into a world of despair. Yet every day I am reminded the greatest tool for change is us. Everything we do, say, and even don't do, tells the world so much about the sorts of people we are.

Last year we were contacted by a battery hen farmer who decided he didn't want his spent hens to go to slaughter and determined it was cruel to confine these intelligent, curious and inquisitive birds in tiny barren prisons. With an undertaking he would not restock the cages we assisted in what has become Australia's biggest rescue of farmed animals. The experience of walking into the shed that contained all the chickens is one that will haunt me forever. Most of us have seen pictures of hens in cages but nothing can prepare you for the sight, sound and smell of those hell-holes. I was sickened to see the hapless hens trying to eke out an existence in such a sad, sad world. I wanted to race out into the streets of Melbourne and take everyone by the hand and make them witness what they were paying someone to do.

Whilst seeing animals in such a terrible state and witnessing the condition many animals arrive in is heart wrenching, I remain happy, positive and upbeat. I find it energises, engages and encourages others to see the world from another creature's point of view. I am mindful not to be judgmental or harsh with anyone. That certainly is not the way to guide people to a kinder world.

And if I were to suggest to you the single most important thing one can do to make the world a kinder place I would have to say adopting a cruelty free lifestyle – for your health, for stopping animal cruelty and suffering, and for helping our ailing planet – it really is that simple.

■ SOUP'S ON! OR HOW I FINALLY OPENED MY EYES
Patty Mark

"Not everyone can or will do Openrescue but everyone can end any part they may have in causing violence to others."   ■

—Patty Mark.

Photo credit: Noah Hannibal/alv.org.au.

▶ Patty Mark and rescued piglet with swollen back leg.

Patty Mark is the president and founder of Animal Liberation Victoria(ALV)… ■

Soup, it took a pot of soup to wake me up. I considered myself some-one who loved animals, I would pat dogs, cuddle cats and 'talk' to hors-es or cows over country fences. I grew up in a small country town in Midwest USA where animals were a daily part of everyone's lives three times a day – on our plates and in our cups. I don't recall all through school and university ever meeting a vegetarian, much less a vegan or hearing the words 'animal rights'. Of course we were always taught not to be 'cruel' to animals but this was never connected to killing them and taking total control of their lives before we did. It never crossed my mind, not once, that animals were our slaves. Then in 1974 my whole life changed. I married an Australian in London and we cycled overland to Australia through Europe and Asia – it took us fourteen months.

Early on in this trip we were in rural Greece cycling through the olive groves, all our belongings packed onto the back of our bikes, often with a bread stick and block of cheese under the elastic strap. I called to my husband to stop when I saw a herd of goats with their kids on the side of the road. I always stopped when animals were near as I felt so drawn to them. These goats even let me pat and play with them, I was happy and full of joy. It wasn't long after this break that we pulled over for lunch. It was just outside a small village at a roadside stall under a tarpaulin. There were a couple huge pots with lids on the fire. We didn't speak Greek so we pointed to the lids to see what was available to eat. As the man lifted the lid, staring straight at me was a goat's head – it was Goat's Head Soup.

It took that shock to make me realise who meat was. And I decided then and there to stop eating animals. It took me another three years to accept that fish were also animals and twenty more years to understand that milk, cheese, dairy and eggs also meant the slavery and death of animals.

It's now forty years since I passed on the goat's head soup and I think how different things are. Most students at University would know a vegan and definitely some vegetarians. And animal rights is much discussed if not fully understood. Knowledge and visual evidence of what is happening to animals is widespread on the internet for all to see. The game plan has changed dramatically as instructions are now at our fingertips and the ball is in our court.

My own learning curve starting back in the 70's was wide. After settling in Melbourne in 1975 we had two children – I didn't feed them animal flesh either, but we all consumed dairy. In 1978 I was so distressed about the plight of battery hens forced to live their entire lives in tiny cages that I put a handwritten notice in my local milkbar – it said in big letters: HELP THE HENS. A journalist saw it as a novelty, mentioned it in the popular *Sun* newspaper and this brought seventeen people to my lounge room for the inaugural meeting of Animal Liberation Victoria (ALV).

Thirty-six years later ALV is still trying to do all we can to help hens, but not just to get them out of battery cages into sheds or even to fields and paddocks, but to stop using them all together. What started as an animal welfare organisation trying to better the conditions for animals evolved to become a vegan abolitionist organisation working to abolish animal slavery and to promote veganism.

Personally I've come from a position where I was too shy to say I was a vegetarian and where I thought vegans were fanatics – so we definitely didn't want to go there! – to now being someone who firmly believes that promoting veganism is the single most important thing an animal activist can do. That it's just as wrong to enslave animals as it is to enslave humans, that it's wrong to unnecessarily cause someone else pain or to kill them to suit my own desires. What helped me dramatically to cement this transition was Openrescue.

Openrescue

In 1993 a woman rang who told me she worked inside a battery hen farm. She told me that many hens were packed seven to eight in cages that were supposed to hold four. She said some hens would fall down into the manure pit where there was no food or water and that at lunch-time workers used these starving hens for 'target practice'. I was dumbfounded. I knew that some producers would overstock the cages – I'd seen this personally myself – but I had no idea what she meant by a 'manure pit' and this talk of target practice was too eerie to contemplate.

Back then I thought I knew almost everything about battery cages, the Department of Agriculture had even taken me on a few 'tours' of egg factories. All I'd ever seen was the single tier system where the cages are raised above the ground with the hen's droppings collecting in piles directly beneath the cages. It's hard to remember now how little we knew about what was really happening, back then everything was out of sight and out of mind. I asked someone I knew who lived near this farm if he could possibly work there to confirm what this woman was telling me. He lasted three days. Then a friend, Diana, who was helping ALV at the time, offered to go in at night and try to get some footage. I was in total awe of her bravery. The footage she brought back reduced me to tears, there were hens buried in their own faeces, many lying dead around cesspools of leaking water from 'above', mixed with the excrement. Sick and dying hens were slumped in despair in what was an enclosed 'manure pit' with multiple tiers of cages on the first floor above.

I asked Diana if she'd go back there with me so we could rescue them – she agreed, so I asked a few others as well. Then I showed Diana's footage to Derryn Hinch who produced *Hinch at 7*, a national TV current affairs program. He agreed to send a film crew with us and what followed was our first Openrescue. We didn't cover our faces, we did 'trespass' but we acted responsibly and we peacefully rescued all the hens we found trapped in that manure pit. None of them would be 'target practice' the next day. Our action was televised nationally and called, *The Dungeons of Alpine Poultry*.

Twenty-one years later we continue getting as many animals out as we can, and the numerous arrests, court cases and short imprisonments haven't dented our resolve and commitment. We do exactly what we would want someone to do for us if we were the ones 'inside' waiting – and hoping.

Openrescue is an act of non-violent civil disobedience that involves breaking laws in order to give aid and rescue to individuals who are neglected and in peril, and to document their conditions. The other imperative is this. Innocent and defenceless lives are at risk – individuals who are enslaved and unable to help themselves. It is also about *Opening* - whether it's a door, a gate, a cage, one's identity or a mindset. To be an Openrescue activist one's passion for justice and non-violence must override fear – the fear of breaking unjust 'laws' and the consequences to oneself that may follow. Openrescue may involve one's own incarceration, however, there is an unparalleled sense of freedom when one steps up to help someone else who is imprisoned, tormented, tortured, sick and/or dying.

Openrescue activists could be called the underground SES (State Emergency Services). In reality we are doing exactly what the dedicated workers at the SES do, working hard to help others in dire need. But it is more than that, we are also working to abolish the property status of animals. This makes Openrescue trailblazing work. Think back to the *Underground Railroad* when some 100,000 slaves – some humans were also considered 'property' at that time – were helped to escape to freedom between 1850 and 1860. Or consider the *Diary of Anne Frank,* which moved millions and was a major influence on me in my formative years. There are humans willing to risk their own lives not only to help strangers but to end an injustice. We share sentience with animals, why should they be excluded from moral consideration and the freedom to live their own lives?

Currently, when Openrescue activists go into action and are caught, it becomes trespass, burglary and theft. We put our own freedom at risk when we dare to 'break and enter' into the sinister and cruel underworld of animal agriculture. We immediately reach out to gather the sick and crippled before us, as there are so few of us and these beings need urgent help – but they *all* need to be free – this is abolition. There are countless animals who are enslaved, denied and dominated by those who have total control over their lives. To engage in these altruistic Openrescues exhibits integrity and empathy, both traits that should be fostered in our humanity, not criminalised.

Not everyone can or will do Openrescue but everyone **can** end any part they may have in causing violence to others. Rape, murder, child abuse, bullying and family violence won't end overnight or even in our lifetimes but as a society we oppose it and punish those who commit any violence against others. Likewise, the human population won't go vegan overnight, but that doesn't mean we continue, rationalise or turn a blind eye to the murder, rape and violence against animals.

Links:

https://www.facebook.com/animalliberationvictoria

veganeasy.org

humanemyth.org

■ INTERVIEW WITH
Lynda Stoner
Animal Liberation New South Wales

"The question is not, 'Can they reason?' or 'Can they talk?' but rather 'Can they suffer?'"   ■

—Jeremy Bentham.

▶ Lynda Stoner and Minty.

Fulfilling a childhood dream, South Australian Lynda Stoner became an actress. She was popular onstage and on television and starred in several series including *The Young Doctors*, the police drama *Cop Shop*, and *Chances*. In 1986 she played the glamorous villain Eve Wilder in the cult soap opera *Prisoner*. Her credits include many guest appearances and two documentaries, one set in Mali in West Africa and the other about whales, produced by Laurie Levy.

In addition to her love of acting, Lynda discovered her profound love of animals of all kinds, and by the early 1980s she had become a prominent spokesperson for animal rights. This has now become the primary focus of Lynda's life…   ■

I remember seeing you on the television screen in popular shows like Cop Shop. *An activist working for animal rights seems a long way from the work you were doing. What took place in your life that prompted you to leave a successful acting career to work on behalf of the animals and when did you first realise you wanted to devote your life to animals?*

Since childhood I wanted to be an actor. I 'knew' as a little person that's what I would end up doing with my life. I was also surrounded by animals while growing up, chickens, dogs and cats. Aside from my sister, my best friend was my dog Toby. I used to discuss all of life's issues with him. It was into his ears that I whispered my hopes and all manner of childhood secrets. When he died I was inconsolable. I turned a backyard shed into a memorial to him and started the *We Love Toby* club. The fact my sister and I were its only members was not a deterrent. I didn't think my heart would ever heal.

I grew up seeing chickens running around our huge backyard during the day and sheltering in comfort and safety in their coops at night. I adored them. We gave them names and enjoyed their individual quirks and their intelligence and inquisitiveness.

School plays led to years of working in theatre and then television and film. I did scores of theatre work, but I guess the shows I am remembered for were *Young*

Doctors, Prisoner and *Cop Shop*. It was during my first few weeks of filming *Cop Shop*, when I stopped in my tracks as TV news showed footage of seal pups in Canada being bludgeoned to death and sometimes skinned alive. The image so distressed and haunted me that it became the pivotal point in me seeking out information about other animals being persecuted for skins and food.

With perfect synchronicity, Peter Singer's legendary book, *Animal Liberation,* had just been released. It took reading just the first three chapters to have me swearing off eating animals. I went home that night and threw out all leather and cosmetics tested on animals. It was an epiphany. My entire life changed that day and pretty much everything from then on has been determined by what I learnt then. I have to say I was strident in those early days and, on reflection, probably an aversive advocate for animals. I was fuelled by passion and simply could not comprehend why, once people knew of the savagery of our treatment of animals used for food and clothing, they didn't become vegetarian immediately (veganism wasn't heard of back then). It led to all manner of heated arguments with work colleagues and friends. Although these arguments were gut wrenching and horrible, they were the catalyst to ensuring I read and learnt everything possible about all animal rights issues so I had informed responses rather than just emotional ones.

It's easier for most people to choose not to listen because there is no getting away from the fact that as long as they consume animal products they are complicit in the suffering of those animals. I continued to be involved in the entertainment industry but any spare time was spent working for the rights of animals. Having a high profile back then meant I was better able to get word of cruelty and suffering out to a wide audience, for which I was tremendously grateful. It didn't hurt either that I thoroughly enjoyed acting. Animal rights began to take up more and more of my life and these days I just do the occasional acting role.

Were you vegan at this stage of your life? Why did you choose to go vegan, and was it an easy transition?

As mentioned I became a vegetarian in the proverbial blink of an eye. Vegetarianism was seen as 'odd' back then, and veganism was a lifestyle no one mentioned. I had to do a paper about the suffering of dairy cattle and happened to be eating a pizza with cheese at the time. I almost regurgitated because the cheese suddenly tasted disgusting. That was it. For someone who had consumed massive amounts of ice cream, cheese, yoghurt and cream from cows, I found it a doddle giving those things up – I just had to recall what I'd learnt about the suffering of cows and calves. These days of course, there is nothing you cannot enjoy along those lines made from soy and other healthy alternatives, without causing suffering.

What made you join Animal Liberation specifically, and how long have you been involved with them?

I joined Animal Liberation because of Professor Singer's book and because this was the only organisation I knew of working for the rights of *all* animals, not just companion animals or exotic animals or native animals. I was also inspired by Christine Townend, who started Animal Liberation in NSW thirty-five years ago.

She is a phenomenal person who forced herself to go into intensive animal factories and confront 'farmers' and industry. Animal Liberation was the only organisation at the time regularly doing undercover work and exposing the cruelty of
animal industries. It is not beholden to any government or other institution and
therefore has the freedom to tell the truth without constraint.

*Many stars take on causes and then we don't hear about them after a while.
You have stayed the distance with Animal Liberation. How long have you
been involved, and what is the driving force that has kept you committed
to this kind of work?*

I have been involved with Animal Liberation for more than three decades. The
driving force for me is the ongoing minute by minute suffering of billions of animals, whether they are used for food, clothing, so-called 'entertainment' such as
rodeos, circuses and zoos, research and all the other ways humans have found to
exploit, profit from and abuse non-human animals.

Do you think your celebrity status has made your campaign more effective?

Definitely. If I hadn't been known to Australians back then, few would have lis-
tened to me. That's unfair but it's reality. These days we have the internet and social
networks, and people have many ways of being heard, but then it was newspapers,
radio and television that provided immediate access to the public. I think, too,
the fact I was completely immersed in learning everything possible about animal
suffering meant I was better able to speak for them because whatever was thrown
at me, I always had informed truth to respond with.

How has your family been influenced by your work?

Profoundly. My biological family lives the most cruelty free lives possible. Many
in my stepfamily also live cruelty free. When I first met my beloved stepdaughters
Kate and Jo – they were just twelve and eleven – I was nervous beyond speech. My
husband-to-be helped relieve some of that fear by sharing that they already loved
me because I worked for animals! It was the girls who took me to my first duck
rescue at Lake Cowal because they'd been the year previously. My ex-husband was
also actively involved with Animal Liberation for twenty years and did much to
further the animal rights cause.

*Did you raise your son Luke as a vegan, and if so, was that challenging in a
predominantly non-vegan world?*

Luke was conceived vegetarian and has continued throughout his life to live
cruelty free. When he was a little three-year-old Botticelli angel, he took on, by
himself, bigger boys at the beach who were stabbing a jellyfish. While in infant
school, he stood up at assembly and spoke about the plight of battery hens.
He was teased and ridiculed at school for being vegetarian, but nothing and
no one could sway him from his powerful love and protection of animals. We

always had dogs, and they slept with him and became his best friends, as Toby had been mine. He's had time during these past twenty-seven years to disavow himself of these beliefs, but they are his own. We obviously influenced him, but there is something intrinsic in Luke's core that would never knowingly harm anyone or anything. He used to be like a magnet, attracting 'stray' animals home and we always had a menagerie when he was little. He simply had to have another species to nurture and love. Heaven forbid if you almost stand on an ant when he is around – he will move quickly to save any living creature, so you'd better move quickly, too! His love of all species and any suffering to them causes him considerable heartache, but there is strength in him coupled with compassion.

Tell us about the campaigns that are closest to your heart. What are you currently focusing on?

All the campaigns we work on are close to my heart. I am currently focused on getting a ban on battery cages – it will be good when Australia catches up with much of the rest of the world – banning pig dogging, dairy and leather.

What would be one of the most heartfelt moments you've experienced?

I was giving a talk at the Garvan Institute against the testing of animals to a packed room of animal experimenters. I thought the woman sitting in front of me was 'one of them'. She turned around after my talk and asked to see me outside. She said that what she'd heard had changed her life. This woman is in a highly influential position in the medical field and now devotes her life to stopping the use of animals for medical experiments. From a sea of fear in my stomach before my talk commenced came a wonderful and totally unexpected outcome. This woman has gone on to do magnificent things for animals.

It is always a powerful mix of emotions when we rescue animals from factory farms: the grief of leaving so many behind and the absolute joy at rehabilitating those we are able to rescue and provide whole-of-life care for. You never become jaded to the exquisite moments when a hen takes her first step, stretches her wings for the first time and lifts her face to the sun.

What are some of the most difficult challenges you've faced?

Being in battery sheds and sow sheds, seeing animals who have been mutilated and existing in the most barbaric conditions and having to walk away. Taking on the rodeo community with its inherent violence. Watching the apathy in people's faces when they hear their choice of eggs and bacon for breakfast has caused unimaginable pain – and to have to remind myself I wasn't born a vegan – it's been a journey of learning, that people can and do change.

What is your definition of success in this work?

Literally and metaphorically – when the last cage is relegated to museums, that's when we will have made real inroads for animals.

What message would like to get out to the public now? How can they help to make the difference to the extreme suffering that animals are experiencing?

There is one simple thing people can do to directly stop the suffering of animals, improve their health and stop contributing to climate change and the damage to our planet – go Vegan!

What do you envisage in a perfect world for all animals (and humans)?

Human beings, particularly those of us in affluent countries, have choice of lifestyle, choice of alternatives to using animals, and that alone would ameliorate the suffering of billions of animals. If we all became vegan, there would be so much more food to provide to developing countries and humans in need. There is no such thing as world perfection but that would take us a long way to Utopia.

Are we making progress?

Yes. You only have to marvel at the number of young vegans and vegan restaurants and vegan options to know a corner has been turned, that a pricking of mass psyche is occurring on behalf of animals, and we cannot go back.

Can you share your favourite quote with us?

"Wars will never cease while men still kill other animals for food, for to turn any living creature into a roast, a steak, a chop, or any other type of 'meat' takes the same kind of violence, the same kind of bloodshed, and the same kind of mental processes required to change a living man into a dead soldier." This was written in 1943 by the feminist vegetarian **Agnes Ryan.**

And the following for many reasons...

"The animals of the world exist for their own reasons. They were not made for humans any more than black people were made for white, or women created for men."   ■

—Alice Walker.

■ THE JOURNEY TO BRIGHTSIDE
Emma Haswell

"It is hard for me to describe or talk about because for me it's like breathing. I just can't stop. I can't stand the thought of letting them down, of turning my back on them. It is like I can feel their suffering all the time. They are in my thoughts day and night." ■

—Emma Haswell, Founder of Brightside Farm Sanctuary, Tasmania .

▶ Emma Haswell and Matilda.

I grew up in a conservative family who farmed in the midlands of Tasmania from 1823. I adored my grandfather who had been a farmer all his life. I followed him like a mini shadow so when I left school I worked on sheep grazing properties, a dairy and even a cattle feedlot. I saw terrible cruelty in most of those jobs. I now know those incidents were prosecutable offences under the Animal Welfare Act and yet at the time I kept quiet. It was the way things were done in the world of farming. I witnessed unspeakable acts of cruelty that were so accepted in the industry yet hidden from the public.

I then went on to run a small two hundred acre corner of my family farm where I had superfine merinos. I decided that if we ate meat we should eat animals from our farm that were born there and died there. Animals I knew had been happy. It was at this time I turned vegetarian and it all became personal for me. I started to see a bigger picture. I developed a real love for animals. I guess reality kicked in for me.

My daughter and I moved to London. I took her to a charity dog show where I picked up a flier about greyhounds being exported live from Australia to Asia. Horrified, I joined the anti-greyhound racing organisation as their North London coordinator. I held a stall at a vegan festival and happened to read a flier on the truth about dairy and became vegan overnight. I learned about factory farming and sow stalls. I was thrown into a world I had always been too scared to look at. I had loved animals but could not face knowing about their suffering. All of a sudden I was strong enough to open my eyes and see. I wanted to use my love of animals to become strong for them and become their voice.

I attended protests in Cambridge against the Cambridge Primate Lab where I was incredibly lucky to be present for Mel Broughton's unforgettably empowering speeches against the lab[1]. Seeing Mel's deep sense of compassion, gentleness, selflessness and determination was life changing for me. Here was a man fighting animal abuse even if it cost him his own freedom.

I believe everyone has a right to be an informed consumer and many people in London told me they turned vegan or vegetarian after someone came to their school and showed them the truth about meat production. So, it was in the UK I decided to aim for three things: founding a farm sanctuary, conducting undercover investigations into factory farms, and educating students. The meat, egg and dairy industries spend millions on marketing their products and hiding the truth about where those products actually come from.

I returned to Tasmania and founded Brightside Farm Sanctuary. Brightside is home to about three hundred rescued animals who are ambassadors for their kind. I tell their stories while they show people how truly wonderful they are. We find new homes for hundreds of neglected, rescued and unwanted animals each year and I speak to about five thousand students every year about factory farming and animal rights.

Together with my remarkable, incredibly brave and dear friend Diana Simpson, I have conducted several undercover investigations into factory farms in Tasmania. We have successfully caused the closure of two horrific factory farms that resulted in one of Tasmania's largest pig farmers being charged by police and convicted of aggravated cruelty.

Through doing this I learnt a very valuable lesson. I saw first-hand how industry and government departments lie to protect themselves and those around them and I saw the terrible things people do to other animals. I discovered that no one was there to help the animals of Tasmania and there was no one I could call in to fix things. I realised that with Diana's help I would have to do it myself. I learnt that one person who stands up to be a voice for the animals has a lot of power to create change.

Together with the wonderful Brightside pigs we have been instrumental in banning sow stalls in Tasmania. Brightside pigs have been walking the footpaths of Tasmania and visiting Parliament House for nine years. They have graced the screen on our evening news and the front pages of newspapers many times and appeared on programs such as *60 Minutes, Stateline, 7.30 Report* and *Australian Story* and they have walked the hallways of many Tasmanian schools. To our wonderful pigs, especially Lynnie, who I rescued as a tiny dying piglet in a factory farm, I am indebted.

Every day I am driven by the fact that codes of practice provide animal industries with a defence from cruelty prosecutions by making gestation crates for pigs and battery cages for hens the recommended way to keep animals. How can this be when animal welfare laws state that it's an offence to be cruel to an animal, to overcrowd an animal, to torment an animal or to fail to provide an animal with exercise?

The things I have seen in factory farms and the shame I have felt at being a human will stay with me for life. Like the hens dead in their hundreds in battery cages where their live cage mates were forced to live on top of their rotting bodies, or the live hen I found discarded and buried in a pile of rotting corpses and manure. Or the skeletal mother pigs incarcerated in six foot long and two foot wide crates, too weak to stand with swollen legs and only their eyes indicating they were alive. I've found a mother pig alive and unable to move but seething with maggots and left to die on wet concrete in a pool of faeces, mud and maggots. Or the times we have seen tiny four-day old broiler (meat) chickens unable to stand because of their grossly oversized bodies, just lying there unable to reach food and water, dying a slow death of starvation and dehydration.

I wish everyone could see inside a factory farm or a slaughterhouse and witness the level of suffering inflicted on every animal, every day. I have promised those abused and suffering animals I have met that I will do everything I can to help them. I have promised them I will never give up.

In order to be the best leaders I believe we must lead by principle, we must live by our convictions – and we must be strategic in our thinking. The animals need all of us to be helping them and speaking up for them. Please don't forget them. We are all they have.

Endnote:

[1.] Mel Broughton is one of the UK's most prominent animal rights activists. He co-founded SPEAK, The Voice of the Animals, in 2004 with Robert Cogswell. The campaign was designed to stop animal testing in Britain.

■ LIFE WITH PÅSKE
Anna Hall
Companion Rabbit Advocates

"If we could learn to tread as lightly upon the earth as rabbits do, there would be no global warming or much in the way of world hunger. They enjoy their vegan diet, produced with minimal carbon production and water usage. They value a short excursion into the garden or some human affection much more than material gifts and are able to reward their human companions with genuine and treasured affection." ■

—Anna Hall.

After receiving her Master's Degree in Applied Management, Anna Hall worked in health care in both clinical and management roles in the UK, Norway and now in Australia.

Anna recently founded Companion Rabbit Advocates in an effort to improve the lives of these marginalised creatures in Australia. She also campaigns for other sentient beings, including running a monthly animal activism stall and assisting other animal rights and welfare organisations. Anna is currently treasurer of the Animal Justice Party and secretary of Animal Liberation NSW. She lives with two rescued rabbits, who are now rescuing her after the recent loss of her much-loved husband, John Sargent, a valiant supporter of all things rabbit... ■

Påske, which means Easter in my mother's native tongue Norwegian, arrived at Easter in a large cardboard box. She was delivered to us after being rescued for fos-

▶ Anna Hall.

tering. We were responsible for helping this frightened little grey bundle of rabbit with enormous beautiful ears to transition from a life of terror to one that promised peace and care. One of those ears had a sizeable hole in it made by an agricultural identification tag, which had been removed by the vet. Påske was rescued from a factory farm, where like hundreds of other rabbits, she waited to be decapitated with a circular saw, in front of other rabbits.

The rescuers found the farm was filthy with numerous dead rabbits lying around in various states of decay. Påske was huddled in one corner of a cage, a place where she was as far away as she could get from one of those dead rabbits. She was one of the lucky five to be rescued and re-homed. Some farmers dispute that rabbits are animals, as they do with chickens here and in the US and so believe they are not covered by limited legal protection offered to other 'livestock' guided by current animal welfare Model Codes of Practice[1]. Rabbits therefore are not afforded the most basic decency to minimise their suffering before slaughter.

Påske had previously lived her life in a large fetid shed strewn with faeces and urine. She had been forcibly taken from her mother when she just one month old. She was kept in a wire cage that cut into her soft paws and offered no stable support to develop healthily, so of course she had problems with walking and coordination when first rescued. Rabbits in rabbit farms are crammed into cages in much the same manner as battery chickens, a practice now banned in Europe. Påske's monotonous diet of minimally nutritious pellets served only to cause unnatural weight gain. All of this suffering is the result of one goal: to make the farmer more money and permit a cheap source of rabbit fur to wear and flesh to eat.

Påske quickly recovered her appetite and devoured everything we provided her. She did this with noisy enjoyment, grunting away with excitement. Over the next few days she learnt that she could relax while being cuddled. She even began to enjoy it. Even more enjoyable for her was exploring our bathroom. This improved her coordination so much that she soon loved to complete small running circuits and undertake a few binky jumps. For people unfamiliar with rabbit culture, a binky is a slightly twisting jump undertaken as a sign of joy and an indulgence of pure rabbitness. Her coat, which had been coarse on arrival, gradually became soft and silky. She became less terrified of humans and allowed us to pet her and even initiated affection towards us. After all she had been through in life this was a truly touching and triumphant moment.

Påske has transformed from a fearful 'agricultural commodity' to someone who realises her expressive, gentle, sentient and vital self and she touched us greatly.

Animal rescue can be complex. Often, rescue happens under conditions of crisis and building human community is critical. This was the case for Påske. If we had been unable to take her in and care for her immediately, she would have been left in that wire cage to die. Because there was a network of care, Påske was able to live. This experience made me reflect on how tenuous life can be and how much is based on chance and the nature and quality of relationships.

I always learn from animals and find them an endless source of inspiration and mentorship as to how to move forward and become a better citizen of this earth. Påske reinforced my belief that the only differences between 'livestock' and 'pets' are the labels we put on them and the animals' experiences. New Zealand or Florida White rabbits are common as pets; but they are also used on farms and in laboratories.

Over the years of observing and interacting with these wonderful creatures on a daily basis, I decided I could not eat other sentient beings. As I became more involved with animal advocacy work and ideas, and as I became more fully aware of the real cost of egg and dairy products, my diet became increasingly vegan.

My rabbits have taught me about living mindfully. They are overjoyed by a nice morsel to eat, or to see I have risen for another day. I am not as smart as that and take many of these things for granted, rather than as worth celebrating. Rabbits have excellent memories but they put unpleasant occasions such as a stressful visit to the veterinarian behind them and do not let fear or anger spoil the rest of their day. Their ability and speed to forgive puts me to shame at times and that alone makes them great mentors.

From farm property worth a pitiful few dollars, Påske became a fun-loving individual in a luxurious home. She became an inspiration to many, even featuring around the world in a Quaker Animal Concern newsletter. Thank you, Påske, for teaching us how to become rescuers. Thank you too to those young people who selflessly went to great lengths to rescue her in rural New South Wales. Påske's story underscores the urgent need for effective and far-reaching animal rights legislation, worldwide commitment to plant-based diets and compassion.

Endnote:

[1.] Exclusionary policies: The Humane Slaughter Act (HMSLA) is criticised by animal rights advocates and the Humane Society of the United States for only including cattle, pigs, and sheep but not poultry, fish, rabbits or other animals routinely slaughtered for food. After a 2004 PETA undercover investigation which publicised abuse of chickens by employees of a West Virginia Pilgrim's Pride slaughterhouse that supplied chickens to KFC, PETA was joined by the Humane Society in calling for the Humane Slaughter Act to be expanded to include birds.

■ COMPASSIONATE ACTION AND DEEP PEACE FOR ANIMALS
Billie Dean

"It is not about being angry and hurling destructive words and thoughts at others. It is about standing up and saying 'No' to the old ways of thinking and being that don't respect the other species who share our world. And it is about saying 'Yes' to social change. It is about embodying the return of the Divine Feminine, that inherent connection to all life we all have, the free, wild, intuitive, instinctive self that has been suppressed for so long. And walking the loving, compassionate, respectful path that honours our Mother Earth and all her children." ■

—Billie Dean.

▶ Billie Dean with foal Arthur and his mother River.

Billie is the founder and CEO of the Billie Dean International Deep Peace Organisation, dedicated to creating peace and protection for all animals through the arts, education and compassionate action. She is an author and a filmmaker and runs *Rainbow Fianna: Wisdom School for Earthkeepers*, teaching others how to listen to the old silent language, with ethics and ancient wisdom. With her husband Andrew Einspruch, Billie runs a forever home for horses and other animals.

Billie Dean has always been compassionate towards animals – she is an innate interspecies telepath, and since childhood felt the pain of other species, including animals and trees. A vegan and animal rights activist, Billie has been meat free since the early 1970s. Her family is too, including the six dogs... ■

"I don't want to be dog meat."

The silent plea came hurtling through the airwaves from a small round brumby stallion with frightened eyes. I was out in the bush as a filmmaker – hired to film the humane capture and training of wild horses. But as an innate telepath, empath and animal sensitive, the animals in trouble always know I can hear them.

My heart thudding with his pain and fear, I made him a promise he would never become dog meat. And I always keep my promises.

Finn, as he became known, was so frightened of his fate he attacked the natural trainers who tried to train him. I stepped in at that point, revealed my true nature as an animal sensitive and offered to take Finn home to join the other horses who ran free in peace on my property. Finn knew he could trust me. He never showed any aggression to me at any time, and never to anyone else ever again.

The thought of any of the sweet horses trapped that summer ending up in anyone's rough hands or winding up as dog meat had us all shuddering, and my husband Andrew and I ended up with all eleven of them. We'd been active animal advocates for a couple of decades by then, and used our country property as a refuge for the animals who called us for help.

Wild horses are different from domesticated horses only in that they have been free and have not been hurt by humans. They are gentle, shy and sensitive. While I have studied natural horsemanship techniques, we threw them all out the window with these horses. We built a relationship through telepathy and trust.

And they taught my students a lot – especially about the nature of the human as a predator. And how not to be one.

A few years later, my wonderful Appaloosa mare friend Montana left this plane and she told me that because of the times we live in, we needed more horses.

"More horses!" I said, surprised. We cared for thirty-odd rescued horses at any one time, and it stretches the pocket.

"The world is changing," Montana told me. "And more horses will help you hold a high vibration."

As is the shamanic nature of animal teachers, she left me with that thought to puzzle out for myself.

The road to peace is found by taking the path of the heart and acting with compassion when you are called. So I wasn't surprised to hear the voice of a wild stallion from Kosciusko National Park one day during my daily meditations.

It was another cry for help – tinged with the fear of death.

Today we all have to take a stand against the old and dying patriarchy – that so-called voice of authority that says animals don't have souls and killing them is our right. That it is okay for humans to cull because the animals are taking up too much space. That it is okay for humans to slaughter and maim and kill for our own benefit.

It is not. And that thinking is completely unacceptable if we are to have true peace on the planet. I don't think it is any coincidence that Pythagoras and Buddha lived at the same time in history and both believed in the transmigration of souls. There is a lovely story of Pythagoras, who never ate meat, helping a dog who was being beaten. He stopped the man, saying, "The soul of this dog belongs to a friend of mine – I recognised his voice when he cried."

Native wisdom also tells us the world is alive, and every animal and plant and stone has a voice for those who listen. This has been my experience all my life.

So we offered to take the stallion and his family, trusting in the way of Spirit and telepathy that all would be in Divine Order. But it seemed a few more horses heard the call and we ended up with fourteen brumbies straight out of the bush, including several pregnant mares and some orphaned colts and fillies.

This brought our horse count to more than forty – far more than we could easily afford. But we said "yes" anyway, because that is the nature of compassionate action and we weren't going to turn away those who had called us. There is always a higher reason.

Montana's words came back to me when the horses came off the truck one by one on that sunny winter's day. To think these young and innocent wild beings would have been hauled off to the slaughterhouse was unthinkable. It filled our hearts to brimming knowing they were now safe. We settled them in to a paddock by the house and they learned about human life as we built relationships, hanging out with them as we shovelled manure (lots of it!) and feeding out hay.

A few weeks later, our beloved dog Raffi passed, leaving a huge hole in our family. We have seven or eight rescued dogs at any one time (they have to all fit in the van for outings), but Raffi was a very special blue heeler with a huge personality. He and our daughter had a very close bond, and Raffi was the star of our feature film *Finding Joy*, and also starred in our 'dogumentary' *7 Days with 7 Dogs*. He taught my students telepathic communion with all of life, and was an irrepressible, joy-filled character.

His passing numbed us with grief.

I couldn't sleep in the bedroom where his empty body lay on the dog bed he had chosen to die on. I cuddled the other dogs and sat by the fire, drawing in the warmth from an old-fashioned hearth. As in life, Raffi had been very matter of fact in his dying process, knowing exactly what to do and asking us to quietly hold space and listen as he sweetly slipped into the spirit world, shouting his freedom and the return of his eyesight with his ebullient charm.

But even being able to see and hear the world of spirit doesn't always ease the pain of physical loss. Our family missed him in the car and around the house. We couldn't believe we wouldn't be able to cuddle him again.

The brumbies, however, had a special gift for us to lift our spirits, and as Montana had foretold, also lift our vibration – so very important for this time of change on Earth. We all have to embody the high vibration of joy and peace, to lift up the energetic matrix of the planet, which has been sunk low in a dense, murky mire of doom, gloom, depression and fear.

I was feeding out hay in the early morning after Raffi's passing when I noticed a tiny new foal in the herd. He was perfect and beautiful and both he and his wild mother gave me the honour of allowing me to touch him. What complete joy! It is the second time this kind of miracle has happened to us, showing us the perfection of life when we allow the natural processes to happen and listen with all of our senses.

The foal indeed helped us all tremendously with our grief, and a great peace settled over the animals on our property once again. I thanked the horses for their great gift, and Raffi for his usual impeccable timing.

I've noticed every death has its own perfect timing, and lessons from the animals are everywhere if we choose to listen.

Now more than ever, it is time to honour the other species who share our planet. The animals have been holding so much grief and they tell me over and over that they are finished suffering. They deserve peace and freedom as much as we do.

There are many in spiritual circles who say everything is perfect and the world is simply an illusion. I would say yes, however all the great spiritual leaders and thinkers of our time call for compassionate action. To not respond to a call to the heart and help others in need misses the point of what it is to be human on this planet at this time. And if you can't help physically, you can support a bigger effort. You can work on yourself, and you can make your voice heard.

As Gandhi said, "You can be the change you want to see in the world."

So consider the personal choices you make every day, and ask yourself, are you helping or hurting another species by that choice? As each one of us awakens and makes enlightened choices, we pave the path of peace – not just for humans, but for all species.

Links:

www.billiedean.com

www.deeppeacetrust.com

www.wildpureheart.com

Rescue Story

Albert and Einstein arrive at Brightside Farm Sanctuary, Tasmania.

Two baby camels, Albert and Einstein, were rescued by Brightside Farm Sanctuary at a meat sale in Victoria. They have landed on their feet and now lead happy and safe lives at the sanctuary in Tasmania.

▶ A happy Albert with Emma Haswell.

"In November 2013 we went to a sale in Victoria to rescue wild donkey jacks who had been captured by dealers in the Northern Territory and sent to a Victorian sale notorious for its 'meat buyers'. The same dealer also had a number of camels they had captured from the wild in South Australia and transported to the sale.

It made me so sad seeing the camels the night before the sale. They were huddled together in groups – the baby camels were protected by the adults. I knew the next day they would all be separated although the babies were much too young to be weaned.

And that is exactly what happened. As the auction progressed the wild camels were sold one by one. There was no way of knowing which baby belonged to which mother. Some people bought one baby and laughed about how they would get him or her into their trailer. I found the whole thing terribly distressing. The way the camels were handled reminded me of how Australian sheep are handled in the countries we live export them to.

The baby camels let out the saddest wailing sounds as they called for their mothers. The last two young camels of the sale were standing side by side, and the bigger one (Albert) seemed to be taking care of the tiny one (Einstein). I could not have them separated so they joined the donkey jacks we rescued on a large truck for the journey back to Brightside. We filled every bay on the truck and changed the destiny of as many animals as we could that day."

IRELAND

■ CHOICE
Sandra Higgins

"One has to question the extent to which we are truly free to choose when the parts of the world that consume the most animal foods have fashioned this way of eating into a tightly knit socio-cultural tradition, in which vested interests continually suppress our natural compassion and rationality." ■

—Sandra Higgins.

Sandra Higgins, BSc (Hons) Psych, MSc Couns Psych, is a counselling psychologist. She uses the non-violent philosophy of veganism as a major component in Compassionate Mind Training, as a clinical approach to individual and collective psychological distress at her psychology practice, The Compassion Foundation of Ireland. She founded Eden Farm Animal Sanctuary, which is home to more than a hundred residents rescued from animal agriculture and Matilda's Promise Animal Rights & Vegan Education Centre in Ireland... ■

▶ Sandra Higgins with Marian and Maeve.

Many people refer to veganism as a personal choice. The issue of choice is interesting and worthy of examination.

At the outset, one needs to examine the choice of the animals we exploit. They do not have a choice. If they could choose they would choose the liberty of a life not imprisoned by the body of a farmed animal. They would choose to live free of unnecessary pain, they would choose daylight, pleasure and appropriate food, they would choose not to be separated from their loved ones, they would choose not to be artificially inseminated and they would choose to live out their natural lifespans. They do not have a choice. But we can choose to become aware of how our lifestyle choices affect them. We can choose a vegan lifestyle that does not include using goods that entail their exploitation. In that sense, our choice is very closely aligned to our conscious awareness.

One has to question the extent to which we are truly free to choose when the parts of the world that consume the most animal foods have fashioned this way of eating into a tightly knit socio-cultural tradition, in which vested interests continually suppress our natural compassion and rationality. Think of the ways in which the animals we use for food are represented by food companies as 'laughing cows', 'happy hens', or 'smiling pigs' and fish, who willingly and happily swap life and liberty for the pain and death entailed in being transformed into a human foodstuff.

This is how this tradition socially conditions us to accept animal exploitation and suppresses our more benign instincts. It is not a very long tradition in the history of life: 10,000 years of domestication of other animals and the emergence of factory farming in the last century. However, it is long enough and deeply entrenched enough to justify our questioning of choice.

What choice does someone have if they are literally fed animal foods and metaphorically fed the social norm that eating animals is acceptable and necessary, prior to the development of language and critical thinking skills? Choice involves being aware of alternative possibilities: we live in a culture where vegan possibilities are continually suppressed, if entertained at all.

What choice does someone have when, until very recently, veganism and animal rights were socially disparaged?

What choice does someone have when information on the health benefits of a vegan diet is not, until recently, included in professional dietary guidelines, and where it remains sidelined by professionals who continue to recommend animal sources of the same nutrients that are available from plant based sources?

What choice does someone have when the damage our consumption of animal foods inflicts on the environment, and on the human farm and slaughterhouse employees, and the degree to which it contributes to world hunger, is continually suppressed by louder, more powerful research voices, funded by the very industries that profit from animal exploitation?

What choice does someone have when the animal food industry harnesses the public need for a clear conscience and sells it to them by working alongside animal welfare measures to foster the myth that the lives of the animals we exploit are comfortable, all the while ensuring continued, if not increased animal food consumption? Which of us, prior to researching the issue, did not believe the lie on the package of 'outdoor reared' pig flesh, eggs from 'free ranging' hens, the milk from the cows living at an idyllic 'organic' farm, or the flesh from the 'grassfed' cow? Do we have a choice when the information we are being sold is inaccurate and calculated to enhance us to purchase? Few of us living in societies that accept the unnecessary killing of sentient beings think to question the ethics of the fact that these animals lose their liberty and their one, precious life in order for humans to have the contents of the attractively packaged meat, fish, egg or dairy carton.

What choice does someone have when they are immersed in a society where few are brave enough to face the horrendous acts that are necessarily perpetrated on other animals in order to eat their flesh, eggs and milk? It is little wonder that when adults are asked to draw their representation of a 'farm', they reconstruct the idyllic myth of interspecies families, frolicking in the tidy, freshly painted farmyards that they have been taught in childhood rather than the facts.

Fact is the mother who bellows for her calf as she is taken from her so that we can have her milk.

Fact is the hen who prolapsed whilst laying the egg that humans so thoughtlessly consume for breakfast.

Fact is the searing, prolonged pain that follows dehorning, debeaking, branding, the extraction of teeth, testicles and tails without pain relief or anaesthesia.

Fact is the premature loss of life of the very young animals who are slaughtered at the rate of billions every year for reasons of human taste, convenience and culture.

Given conscious awareness what do you choose?

■ A PROMISE TO MATILDA
Sandra Higgins

Everyone needs a home. Eden Farm Animal Sanctuary is a lifelong home to non-human animals rescued from the animal agricultural industry. Eden opened in response to my realisation that it is impossible for them to give us their bodies in death, or their eggs or milk or feathers or any other part of themselves in life, without costing them the highest possible price – physical pain, loss of liberty, loss of their children and families, and finally, loss of their lives. I knew I could only offer sanctuary to an insignificant percentage of the millions of non-human animals who we exploit annually in Ireland. Yet I also knew that, to each of those individuals, the sanctuary I could offer was significant and would mean everything to them.

They may be rescued but their suffering is not over. The 'farmed' animals we know today merely resemble their liberated ancestors, and the greater the distance our domestication of them puts between them and the natural heritage to which they are entitled, the more they suffer.

The residents of Eden are ambassadors for a group of beings whose rights' violations constitute what is probably today's most serious social justice issue. But sanctuaries cannot rescue everyone. They run the risk of becoming overcrowded, difficult to manage, and financially stretched. It is also impossible for sanctuaries to mop up the results of the cruelty that is standard farming practice everywhere. For this reason I set up Matilda's Promise, an animal rights and vegan education centre, which is an attempt to stem the problem at its source; the source being breeding other animals for human use in the first place.

The centre is the fulfilment of the promise I made to Matilda, one of Eden's first residents, on the night she died; that I would tell people about why a just world must include equality for other animals, and about the magnificence of the individuals they participate in smothering for something so unimportant as taste and convenience.

One of the first activities at the centre was the production of the documentary *You Haven't Lived Until You've Hugged a Turkey* featuring Maeve, Morgana and Marian, who were rescued by Eden. The film shows who these turkeys are that we breed and harm and kill so unnecessarily. In this film, the turkeys speak to us in language that we share – body language and the language of emotion. They speak to us of justice and of love.

The film is supported by contributions from experts on the most recent scientific data on avian and other non-human animal sentience and cognition. It calls attention to the fact our breeding and exploitation of all non-humans causes unnecessary and severe suffering to beings whose capacity to suffer is of equal significance to our human capacity to suffer; whose liberty is as important to them as our human liberty is to us; whose right to life is as important to them as our human right to life is to us.

Many people thank me for what I do for the animals but my response is that a sanctuary can only support a few animals. Every person can save the lives of many animals by going vegan.

Link:

www.edenfarmanimalsanctuary.com

Rescue Story

Casper comes to Hillside Animal Sanctuary, England.

Casper came to Hillside in an emaciated condition. He has such a kind nature and it is hard to imagine how anybody could have treated him so badly.

Casper is enjoying life at Hillside after just a few weeks of basic feed and care after being rescued from a life of neglect.

▶ Casper arrives at Hillside Animal Sanctuary.

▶ Casper, just a few weeks later.

Photo Credit: Connie Pugh and Farm Sanctuary.

Photo Credit: Connie Pugh and Farm Sanctuary.

Photo Credit: Connie Pugh and Farm Sanctuary.

Photo Credit: Connie Pugh and Farm Sanctuary.

The Food Revolution

■ A COMPASSIONATE COOK SERVES UP A NEW WAY OF THINKING.

Interview with
Colleen Patrick-Goudreau

A Prayer for Humans on Behalf of Animals

"My hope is that we can navigate through this world with the grace and integrity of those who need our protection. May we have the sense of humour and liveliness of the goats; may we have the maternal instincts and protective nature of the hens and the sassiness of the roosters. May we have the gentleness and strength of the cattle, and the wisdom, humility and serenity of the donkeys. May we appreciate the need for community as do the sheep and choose our companions as carefully as do the rabbits. May we have the faithfulness and commitment of the family of the geese, the adaptability and affability of the ducks. May we have the intelligence, loyalty and affection of the pigs and the inquisitiveness, sensitivity and playfulness of the turkeys. My hope is that we learn from the animals what we need to become better people." ■

—Colleen Patrick-Goudreau.

▶ Colleen Patrick-Goudreau.

Colleen Patrick-Goudreau is a well-known, inspiring and sought-after speaker on living a compassionate life and has motivated countless people to think differently about our relationship to animals, giving them the tools and resources they need to live according to their own values of compassion. Colleen is the author of three cookbooks. She is an expert on food/cooking/nutrition and, with the publication in 2011 of the *Vegan's Daily Companion: 365 Days of Inspiration for Cooking, Eating, and Living Compassionately* and *The 30-Day Vegan Challenge*, she has produced the ultimate guides for leading people to a compassionate, joyful vegan lifestyle... ■

Two books influenced your decision to become vegan, A Diet for a New America *by John Robbins, and* Slaughterhouse *by Gail Eisnitz. Please describe the journey from those early days to the creation your work as an author, educator and speaker, and what you hope to achieve in your outreach.*

Especially after reading *Slaughterhouse*, it was just a visceral reaction to do *something* to help. I became vegan immediately after reading it; I knew the *least* I could do was not contribute to what was so difficult to read about. Every fibre in my body was repulsed by the violence against animals committed by desensitised, damaged people. I'm not someone who lives in despair, so I very naturally started figuring out how I could be part of the solution. I think I was like everyone else who goes through this: I talked to whoever would listen, including my husband, who became vegan not long after me, and I got to know various organisations and seeing how I could get involved. I started leafleting, tabling and showing slaughterhouse footage on a TV screen in the middle of Berkeley on Friday nights. I wanted people to know and to see what was happening. However, it was people's responses to this truth that led me to create the work I do now. Most people were appalled and they asked the same questions about food, nutrition, ethics and how to handle social and family situations. I knew that as important as it was to give people information about what was going on, it was equally important to give them the resources they needed to make the changes they wanted to make. So that's how I started teaching cooking classes and workshops, which led to my cooking DVD, which led to my podcast, which led to my books, which led to where I am now.

In a transcript from *Compassion on a Plate* (Radio KQED 'Perspectives') you made the following statement, *"I have yet to meet a non-vegetarian who doesn't care about the treatment of animals raised for human consumption. Even people who eat meat, aware on some level that the experience is unpleasant for the animals, will tell you that they object to 'unnecessary' abuse and cruelty. They declare that they buy only 'humane' meat, 'free-range' eggs and 'organic' milk, perceiving themselves as ethical consumers."* Can you elaborate more on this issue, particularly the traps consumers can fall prey to in their efforts to support a supposedly cruelty-free industry?

I believe people want to make choices that reflect who they really are, that is, kind, compassionate people. I don't believe people wake up in the morning trying to figure out how they're going to contribute to violence or cruelty that day. But I also believe we underestimate people. They are encouraged to do just enough to make it appear as if they're making changes without having to really do anything. Labels on animal products, whether it's animal-based meat, milk or eggs, feed into this, but exploiting an animal for her reproductive outputs, valuing an animal only for what she can 'produce' for humans, breeding animals only to destroy them, and killing animals – anyone who is part of this – is inherently violent. There is simply no way around that. We try to find a way to feel better about our participation in this violence by throwing around words that make us feel better: humane, free-range, compassionate meat (?), organic. To the victims themselves, those labels mean absolutely nothing.

There are now many large-scale projects that assist the poor and disadvantaged through the donation of live animals. However, when we start to examine the suffering of the animals involved, our desire to give assistance to these people conflicts with our desire to protect animals (for example, The Heifer Project International). What are your thoughts about this? Are there projects that can protect the interests of both sides?

Projects like Heifer operate on the basis that since we've always done something one way, we have to keep doing it. The theory or practice becomes romanticised and subsequently entrenched in our cultural memory. Animal agriculture is so ridiculously romanticised in our society that we forget there is another way. If we raised the bar and started looking forward instead of looking backwards, we would find all the solutions we need. We would be able to feed people healthy, life-promoting foods rather than life-taking foods; we would stop perceiving and treating animals as mere commodities for us to trade, sell, strip and kill. We can do so much better, but we need to change our measuring stick.

Turkeys have a special place in your heart and yet three hundred million birds are killed each year in the US. What is missing in people's perceptions that would allow them to see them differently and reduce such widespread slaughter?

When people meet turkeys, they're more surprised by them than by other farmed animals because we've been taught that birds are stupid ('bird brain') and that they don't have individual personalities. So when people meet these curious, playful, affectionate animals – each of whom has a unique personality – they're very moved. Most people comment on how turkeys act just like their dogs and cats do. The more we change our perception of animals, the more we will change our treatment of them and be repulsed by the consumption of them. So, I encourage everyone to find their nearest farmed animal sanctuary and visit these amazing individuals.

In another article from Perspectives (December 2007) you state:

"We, the victors, the authors of history, depict animals as savage, vicious and violent, and humans as civilised, intelligent and compassionate. If animals were tellers of this tale they would be an entirely different story..." How so?

Well, the victors are the ones who get to shape the story, right? So, the humans are the ones who create the perception of animals in order to justify our control of them. If they're 'savage' then we need to tame them. If they don't feel the way we do, then we can hurt them. If they don't have relationships as we do, then we can destroy families. When humans can demonstrate humility and learn to share this Earth rather than dominate it, there will be hope for all of us – humans and animals.

In one of your articles you refer to 'Excuse-itarians' (Satya Magazine, October 2006). Can you elaborate on this breed?

These are the folks who romanticise the killing of animals to such a degree you'd think the animals were lining up to be used and killed. Excuse-itarians use different terms, though. They prefer to call themselves 'locavores' or 'homesteaders'. I prefer the term 'slaughter hobbyists'.

How would a 'Rhetoric Revolution' assist the move towards a plant-based diet?

We use language that holds up animal products as if they're the barometer for everything else, and then when it's NOT an animal product, we call it *fake, faux,* an *alternative*, a *substitute*, a *replacement*, or an *analog*. We need to stop using words that make plant-based foods seem inferior and unappetising. Who the heck wants to eat an analog? I encourage us all to use words that speak truth, including taking back the word meat. The word meat is based on the word *mete*, which originally referred to something that was eaten rather than drunk. It was solid food versus a beverage, and we still use the word today when we say coconut meat or nutmeat.

Call it cow's milk if that's what it is. Say almond milk if that's what it is (not dairy substitute). Even say animal-based meat versus grain-based or plant-based meat.

How possible is it in your view to foster solutions that do not harm others?

I think it's not only possible – it's essential. Everyone says they want to make a difference, effect change, live a meaningful life. Everyone wants to make a difference, and yet I think we forget that in order to make a difference we may have to do something different. Being vegan is an opportunity to have a huge impact and make a huge difference. The biggest misconception about being vegan is that it's an end in itself, but for me being vegan is not an end; it's a means to an end, and that end is unconditional compassion and nonviolence. It's not about being perfect and pure; it's about doing everything we cannot to harm someone else. There is so much we can do, and being vegan is an easy and effective opportunity to foster compassion and not harm.

You are renown for your wonderful vegan recipes. Which of your resources would you suggest for a person beginning their vegan journey and how would you encourage them to go about it?

I'm proud of all my books: *The Joy of Vegan Baking* which is now part of thousands of people's repertoires who use it to demonstrate you don't have to deprive yourself of traditional, homemade treats. *The Vegan Table*, organised as an entertaining book to guide people in creating delicious recipes for themselves and loved ones and to learn how to create menus and plate different recipes together. *Color Me Vegan* encourages people to eat by colour which makes it easy for them by organising all the recipes by the highest concentration of colour (such as blue/

purple, green, orange, red and yellow). *Vegan's Daily Companion* is three hundred and sixty five days of inspiration, with each day of the week providing a different theme. Mondays are food, Tuesdays are effective communication, Wednesdays are health, Thursdays are animals in the arts, Fridays are stories of hope and rescue, and Saturdays/Sundays are recipes.

I'm not someone who lives in despair, so I very naturally started figuring out how I could be part of the solution. I think I was like everyone else who goes through this: I talked to whoever would listen, including my husband, who became vegan not long after me, and I got to know various organisations and seeing how I could get involved. I started leafleting, tabling and showing slaughterhouse footage on a TV screen in the middle of Berkeley on Friday nights. I wanted people to know and to see what was happening. However, it was people's responses to this truth that led me to create the work I do now. Most people were appalled and they asked the same questions about food, nutrition, ethics and how to handle social and family situations. I knew that as important as it was to give people information about what was going on, it was equally important to give them the resources they needed to make the changes they wanted to make.

The 30-Day Vegan Challenge is the one that guides people to making the transition to veganism. It basically says, "Oh, you want to do it? Great. Let me hold your hand the entire way and answer every question you've ever had, whether it's about travelling, protein, eating out, holidays, cooking, iron intake, talking to family – whatever." It's the culmination of eleven years of my work and really is the ultimate guide for helping people transition confidently, healthfully, and joyfully.

Link:
www.colleenpatrickgoudreau.com

◼ WHEN CHILDREN SHOW THE WAY
Janice Stanger

Janice Stanger, PhD, is a nutrition expert, author, educator and speaker. Her mission in writing the book *The Perfect Formula Diet* is to help people, animals and the planet through providing solid, yet little-known information on whole foods, plant-based diets. She is in her sixteenth year of critically analysing scientific studies on nutrition, weight loss, environmental toxins, and health. Janice has a PhD in Human Development and Aging from the University of California, San Francisco – one of the country's leading health sciences campuses. She is certified in plant-based nutrition through the T Colin Campbell Foundation and eCornell. She also has an MBA from the University of California, Berkeley... ◼

▶ Janice Stanger.

"I'm just not eating it any more, Mom!"

I could tell by the look of resolve on my thirteen-year-old daughter's face that she was determined. Rebecca had decided to lead life by her own rules now and this was the latest one. To make matters worse, within a few weeks her eleven-year-old sister Angela decided to take on a meat-free diet as well.

It was 1995, and here I was, a single parent trying to cope with the numerous challenges that having two daughters can bring. To say I was dismayed by their latest declaration of independence would be an understatement. I had been brought up to believe meat was the premier nutrient. Like most of us, my nutrition knowledge at that point was limited to the four food groups taught when I was in school. Every day I consumed, and fed my children, meat, dairy, fruits, vegetables and grains.

I totally believed my newly vegetarian children were at risk of severe malnutrition so I did everything I could to get them to eat meat, but my urgings only strengthened their resolve. So I began a journey of intensive research into plant-based nutrition that continues to this day. My initial goal was simply to figure out how to get them to eat enough protein to stay alive.

I was in for a surprise. Not only did I learn that a vegetarian diet was actually healthier than meat-based eating but at age forty-four, swayed by the compelling evidence, I became a vegetarian. The pressure was off the kids and we now shared the same conviction that what we were doing was not only benefiting ourselves but all the farm animals whose lives were being spared. The transition was unexpectedly easy and I never missed meat after I stopped consuming it.

We never know where the first step in any journey is going to take us and this was no exception. The more I continued to learn about nutrition and the dairy and egg industries, the more I discovered facts that were very troubling to me. Those facts were pushing me to the precipice. I wanted to go vegan.

At that point we were still consuming loads of dairy foods and eggs. The inconvenience I perceived of being vegan and the inability to get food at client lunches and other work-related gatherings seemed too big a barrier.

So I decided to do the one thing I thought would alleviate the growing guilt that gnawed at me from continuing to eat dairy. I joined a tour to a small family dairy farm near my home in Northern California. I wanted to prove to myself that dairy cows are happy and well cared for.

The visit had the opposite effect. Fortunately, we were spared seeing newborn calves being torn from their mothers and we did see some contented-looking young female cows grazing in a pasture. What was to become my turning point however, unfolded in the next part of the tour.

The owner was quite proud of how cheaply he was able to feed the cows. One of their main feeds was outdated junk foods, such as little cakes sold as human snacks that could no longer be sold as they had expired past their use by date. They were removed from the packages and repurposed for dairy cows. I thought, "These cows are being fed garbage, literally." Dairy products were becoming less appealing.

Then the real blow came. The cows walked into the milking area with filthy, swollen udders caked with mud. Only one employee ran the process. He stood there with a dirty rag and half-heartedly wiped each cow's udder before hooking her up to a machine to be milked. The rag was as dirty as the cows were. No one else seemed to mind or find this disgusting. I could see there was no way to keep the dirt out of the milk. I made my decision in that moment. I was going vegan.

The hard part was knowing what to eat, but after numerous vegan potlucks and the discovery of *The McDougall Quick and Easy Cookbook*, I was set. In 2000, at age forty-eight, I became vegan. In a nice change of dynamics, my daughters followed my lead soon after.

By the time I had adopted a vegan diet, I had been researching plant-based nutrition for five years. On an academic level, I understood all the health benefits. Still, I was pleasantly surprised to see how profoundly my own health was transformed. I shed the twenty-five pounds I had fantasised losing for years. My energy soared and I felt I was ageing in reverse. The headaches, sinus infections, respiratory problems, depression and other troublesome health issues that haunted my adult years just vanished. I had made the step to a vegan diet primarily to end my personal contribution to farmed animal suffering. The leap in my own health was a very welcome bonus.

I decided to share the information I had gathered with others in my book, *The Perfect Formula Diet*. At first the book was going to focus just on the health issues of animal protein. So many people consider only the problems with saturated fat, yet the inflammatory protein in animal foods is at least as dangerous if not more so. As I alternately wrote and delved into the scientific literature, I realised the scope of the book needed to expand to the many other health issues that stem from animal foods, not to mention the environmental devastation.

The Perfect Formula Diet was published in 2009. The book explains how to lose weight and get healthy with six kinds of whole plant foods. While processed vegan junk foods may seem tempting, whole foods support health and the vibrant role models that vegans should be. Whole foods include vegetables, fruit, beans, potatoes, whole grains, nuts, seeds, herbs and spices. Eating each of these in optimal ratios to the others makes healthy food choices and weight loss a snap.

■ INTERVIEW WITH JANICE STANGER ON HER RESEARCH.

You have researched well over two thousand nutrition studies and have concluded that a plant-based diet is optimal for human health. How have you arrived at this conclusion?

To figure out what all these studies are telling us, you need to look at patterns in the data. Each isolated study, on its own, should be treated with scepticism. Was the study well designed and executed? What factors (especially funding sources or other biases) were influencing the researchers? Were the findings a fluke?

Forces that could make any one study questionable will tend to balance out when you look at thousands of studies. The key is to look for consistency.

And not all research is created equal. The most meaningful studies are those that look at the whole picture of what happens when everyday people in the real world eat differently. Do they develop different diseases? Do they live longer? How about their children? This approach is called 'epidemiology', and contrasts with simplistic studies that try to look at just one thing at a time. The world is so complex that no one nutrient or food operates on its own, and pretending it does leads to dangerous conclusions.

The two most important studies of real world nutrition are *The China Study* and observations of Seventh Day Adventists. I urge everyone to read the book *The China Study* by Dr T Colin Campbell. It is truly a masterpiece summarising the author's observations from decades of unbiased nutrition research.

There is no comparable easy-to-understand, compelling book about Seventh Day Adventist studies. However, this research also concludes that the closer a person sticks to a plant-based diet, generally the healthier and longer lived he or she is likely to be.

Amazingly, as much as we are told by government, the media and even doctors that meat is part of a 'balanced diet', there are no studies showing meat is healthy or necessary. While there are some studies that claim to show fish can enhance health, you never hear about the greater number of studies with contrasting findings – that eating fish has no effect on health or is dangerous, upping the risk of aggressive prostate cancer and other illnesses.

Marvel at the thousands of studies that consistently show benefits from whole plant foods, including vegetables, fruits, beans, whole grains, nuts, seeds, herbs, and spices. Any drug that could accomplish what broccoli or apples do would immediately become a multi-billion dollar best seller.

There is much confusion in people's minds about how much protein we need and the best sources. Can you clarify and what do you see as the biggest dangers in the animal protein diet?

Protein is the most misunderstood and overvalued nutrient. Here are some basic facts scientists have known for decades but have not filtered through the media, government, and medical practitioners to most people.

Proteins are linked chains of smaller building blocks called 'amino acids'. The same twenty amino acids form the proteins of all animals and plants. Adult humans can make twelve of the twenty amino acids and don't need to consume. The other eight are called 'essential' amino acids as they must come from food.

Only plants can make the essential amino acids because animals don't have sufficient metabolic energy for this intensive process. Plants, powered by the sun, do have the resources to make all amino acids. Thus all animal protein is nothing but recycled plant protein.

If you eat a whole foods, plant-based diet and get enough calories, there is no way to be protein deficient. Consider that a rapidly growing infant, thriving on breast milk, is getting only five to eight percent of her calories from protein. In fact, human breast milk is mostly carbohydrate, with the energy to fuel the youngster's growth.

Since protein encourages growth, and infancy is the time that people grow fastest, getting five percent of calories from protein is sufficient for adults in almost all cases, unless they have been instructed by their health care provider that they need more for a specific diagnosis. Yet all whole plant foods have at least five percent of their calories from protein, and vegans will average about ten percent of their calories from protein, leaving a wide safety margin for sufficiency.

Animal foods concentrate protein, and this can be dangerous. Animal protein encourages the production of a hormone called IGF-1. Your liver makes IGF-1, which is a key controller of cell division and death, energy metabolism, body size, lifespan, and overall body functioning.

Proteins you eat significantly raise your level of IGF-1 – sometimes to potentially dangerous levels. This is most strongly demonstrated for cow's milk proteins, but all animal proteins have this effect. IGF-1 encourages cancer growth and can speed the ageing process. Proteins from whole, unprocessed plants do not have this effect.

Dealing with high levels of protein also strains your liver and kidneys, which do most of the work of getting rid of the excess. Your body cannot store amino acids you don't immediately need, so it has to break them down. The end result of this process is carbohydrates and fats – not muscle. You don't build muscle by eating protein – that is a dangerous myth. You build muscle by exercising.

Studies show the amount of extra protein athletes need is trivial and easily supplied by the extra calories they eat to fuel their performance. As more and more athletes adopt a plant-based diet, the awesome results make headlines.

How can people be sure they are getting sufficient iron and vitamin B12 if they eat a plant-based diet?

Plants are the base of the food chain on our planet. This means plants are nutrient producers while animals are nutrient consumers. People think they need 'red meat' for iron because of the meat's colour – everyone knows red blood cells are rich in iron. The question then becomes: where did that cow being eaten get her iron? The answer clearly is her food – and the natural diet of cows is grass. Like all plants, grass needs iron for its own survival and absorbs it (and other) minerals dissolved in the soil. Cows cannot make iron and calcium any more than they can make gold or silver.

The key to getting the optimal amount of nutrients is to eat a varied whole-foods, plant-based diet, such as I describe in my book *The Perfect Formula Diet*, or a similar eating plan. When you eat this way, you focus on the overall pattern of your food choices, not individual nutrients. Specific vitamins, minerals, phytochemicals and other necessities will balance out and you will get them in the correct ratios. Unless you have a specific diagnosed medical condition for which supplements have been shown to help, you are safest to avoid supplements and get what you need from whole foods.

Vitamin B12 is the exception and here's the reason. Unlike other vitamins, B12 is produced by bacteria, not plants. So of course bacterially contaminated animal foods are high in B12, but do you want to eat items that could cause food poisoning along with your B12 dose? As a much better alternative, B12 supplements are safe and inexpensive, so take them regularly and also get a lab test at some point to make sure your B12 status is healthy.

Vitamin D is the other nutrient that does not come from plants. Vitamin D is actually a hormone because your skin produces it in the presence of sunlight. The optimal source of vitamin D is the sun. If you cannot or choose not to get adequate sunlight, you might need to add vitamin D to your short supplement list.

What do you say to people who consider a plant-based diet to be boring and tasteless? Where can busy people access some helpful resources?

Tastes change in about three weeks. Any modification in diet, whether to a vegan eating plan or another major revision, can result in the new food choices seeming strange and unsatisfying at first. The key is to give yourself a few weeks to adapt. Try new foods, recipes, vegan cooking classes or videos, and restaurants. Talk with people who have been on a plant-based diet for years. Ask for advice at natural food stores. Search the internet for plant-based ideas.

One site I especially like is fatfreevegan.com, which is brimming with more delicious ideas than you could possibly cook. Don't forget that added oil is pro-inflammatory. If you are eating vegan junk food, don't expect to lose a lot of weight or get to optimal health. So if you are changing your tastes, you might as well go for the summit, which is a whole foods, plant-based diet. Fatfreevegan.com has thousands of healthy recipes. The site of the movie *Forks Over Knives* also has many excellent eating ideas. You can subscribe to their e-newsletter to get wonderful ideas every week.

*One area that creates a great deal of concern is when we put children onto
a plant-based diet. Can you comment on this?*

We have an epidemic of childhood obesity and kids on medication for conditions
that never used to afflict our youngsters. This is frightening. If you are concerned
and have young children, I would advise seeking input from other vegan families
or consult a dietician who specialises in plant-based diets for children.

Even more than health, parents may be concerned their youngster will lack
friends if he or she does not eat hot dogs and pizza. I have seen all the kids I know
who are vegan grow up healthy and enjoy their diet. These young people are plant-
based advocates and do not feel deprived. They can certainly have close friends
who eat an animal-based diet, just as vegan adults do. As for birthday parties, there
are many strategies, such as the plant-based child brings her own vegan cupcake
instead of eating a piece of the big cake. Don't let fear hold you back from giving
your children the benefit of a healthy plant-based diet. You will be setting them on
a course of health with lifelong benefits.

■ HEALTHY PLANT-BASED EATING FOR CHILDREN
Robyn Chuter

▶ Robyn Chuter and family.

Robyn Chuter, BHSc, ND, GradDipCouns,
is a naturopath, counsellor and Emotional
Freedom Technique (EFT) therapist practising
in southern Sydney ...   ■

Throughout my nineteen years in natu-
ropathic practice, I have frequently encountered people who eat a vegetarian
or vegan diet themselves, and are convinced of its health benefits – until they
are expecting a baby. Then they start
worrying that a meat-free diet may not supply the nutritional needs of a pregnant
woman and may not support the growth of babies and children. Their concerns
are often magnified by the concerns expressed by doctors and health professionals,
who admonish vegetarian parents to give their children iron and calcium supplements, and implant fears of protein deficiency.

Let's stop for a moment and consider the logic of this position. On the one
hand, even organisations as conservative as the American Dietetic Association
(ADA) admit to the benefits of plant-based diets for adults; the ADA's Position
Statement on vegetarian diets states that plant-based diets reduce the risk of obesity, heart disease, high blood pressure, type II diabetes and cancer [1]. So how could

this way of eating be unhealthy for *children*? Children are not a different species, after all. They have different nutritional needs to adults because of their rapid growth rate and high need for energy (calories/kilojoules) in relation to their body weight, but these are differences in degree, not in kind. Children don't need to eat different foods to adults – they just need different *proportions* of those foods in their diet in order to support their growth rate.

However, in a society that equates 'healthy and strong' with 'tall and big', many people harbour a deep-seated fear plant-based diets will compromise children's growth and leave them at a disadvantage compared to their meat-fed peers. Nothing could be further from the truth. In this article, I will spell out the health benefits of plant-based diets for children; dispel the myths about protein, iron and calcium; and outline a healthy eating plan that meets kids' nutritional needs and establishes a foundation for lifelong health and protection against the chronic diseases that plague so many adults in our society.

Benefits of plant-based diets for children

When people ask me why I'm raising my children on a vegan diet, my answer is simple: *I want the best for them.* I have a terrible family history of heart disease, type II diabetes and cancer, so I aim to give my children the maximum degree of protection against their possible genetic predispositions to these diseases, by feeding them a diet composed of foods that have been shown, in published medical research, to prevent them[2,3,4,5,6,7,8].

I must stress here that I'm talking about a diet based on fresh vegetables, fruits, legumes, nuts, seeds and whole grains – *not* vegan marshmallows, cupcakes and fake chicken nuggets made from soy protein isolate. This eating pattern supplies ample, but not excessive, unrefined carbohydrate, including highly beneficial resistant starch; protein, including all essential amino acids; and fats, including the essential omega 6 and omega 3 fats. Even more importantly, it supplies a superabundance of micronutrients – vitamins, minerals, antioxidants and phytochemicals – which are not only crucial to our immediate survival, but also shape the expression of our genes in the long run. The exciting field of nutrigenomics is opening up more and more insights into how the foods we eat 'talk' to our genes, creating *epigenetic effects* that may last our entire lifetime – and even influence the health of our unborn children.

For example, studies of what researchers call 'cholesterol tracking' show that if a child eats a diet high in saturated fat and develops high cholesterol when he or she is young, that elevated cholesterol tends to persist through adolescence and into adulthood[9,10,11]. Effectively, the genes that cause cholesterol to be made in response to fat intake may become 'jammed in the *on* position'. So even if that child grows up to be a health-conscious adult who limits his saturated fat intake, he may still struggle to bring his cholesterol down into a healthy range – all because of the foods his parents fed him when he was a child. As the authors of the Cardiovascular Risk in Young Finns study put it, 'exposure to risk factors in childhood induces changes in arteries that contribute to the development of atherosclerosis in adulthood'[12].

Research conducted in Finland has also put to rest concerns that a diet low in saturated fat and cholesterol may adversely affect children's growth and development. The Special Turku Coronary Risk Factor Intervention Project (STRIP) study clearly demonstrated that the neurological development of children on the low saturated fat, low cholesterol diet was *at least as good* as that of children on the control (regular) diet[13].

Girls who eat a diet high in animal protein in early childhood, are likely to reach puberty earlier[14, 15]. Women who began to menstruate before the age of twelve are three times more likely to develop breast cancer than those who started their periods later[16]. Since a girl's age at first menstrual period is strongly influenced by how old her mother was when she passed this milestone, women who enter puberty early may 'transmit' a higher risk of early puberty and subsequent breast cancer, to their daughters[17,18].

It's crucial to understand that it isn't genes as such that are responsible for these adverse outcomes; it's the influences exerted on those genes by *epigenetic factors*. Epigenetic literally means 'above genes': epigenetic factors are the control switches that determine whether, and how, genes *express*, or initiate the production of particular proteins that influence body functions. Dietary intake is an incredibly important epigenetic factor.

A diet based on unrefined plant foods protects children against excess weight and obesity, asthma, allergies, juvenile autoimmune disease and even ADD/ADHD. And just as importantly, it offers profound protection against the development of heart disease and cancer in later life[19].

The protein issue

There's no doubt protein is an important nutrient. But the amount of attention paid to it is totally disproportionate to its role in human health. The daily intake of protein required by children is presented in Table 1. Table 2 shows the amount of protein in average serving sizes of some unrefined plant foods.

TABLE 1

Daily protein requirement for children*

Age of child	Protein requirement (grams/day)
0-6 months	10
7-12 months	14
1-3 years	14
4-8 years	20
9-13 years	40 (boys); 35 (girls)
14-18 years	65 (boys); 45 (girls)

*Reference: http://www.nrv.gov.au/nutrients/protein.htm

TABLE 2

Grams of protein per serving of selected plant foods

Food	Serving size	Grams of protein
Wholemeal bread	1 slice	3.9
Quinoa, cooked	½ cup	6.0
Brown rice, long grain, cooked	½ cup	2.5
Porridge, cooked with water	½ cup	3.0
Banana, peeled	1 (~90 g)	1.3
Chickpeas, cooked	½ cup	7.3
Kidney beans, cooked	½ cup	6.7
Broccoli, steamed	½ cup	1.9
Corn on cob	1 cob	3.3
Kale, steamed	½ cup	1.8
Green peas, steamed	½ cup	3.8
Potato, baked	1 (~200 g)	6.2
Spinach, frozen, steamed	½ cup	3.8
Almonds, blanched	¼ cup	8.0
Cashew butter	1 tbsp	2.8
Sunflower seeds	1 tbsp	1.9

As you can see, meeting the protein needs of children on a plant-based diet is easy. Young children need very little protein, and as they grow, so do their appetites – and their portion sizes! Eating more food inevitably results in obtaining more protein, as long as kids fill up on unrefined plant foods rather than highly processed junk food such as sugary beverages, chips, lollies and biscuits.

What about protein combining?

Many people – including a disappointingly high number of dietitians – still cling to the outdated notion that plant proteins are 'incomplete' (that is, lacking in one or more essential amino acids), and therefore vegetarians must carefully combine different types of plant foods at the same meal in order to obtain complete protein. This is simply a myth, disproven decades ago[20]. All plants produce all twenty amino acids that humans need, in varying proportions. Consciously combining different sources of plant protein in the same meal is emphatically not necessary[21]. Even if you were to only eat one plant food for an entire day (which is not something I'd suggest), provided you ate enough of it to meet your energy (calorie/kilojoule) needs, you *simply could not fail* to meet your protein needs as well.

Furthermore, you would also exceed the required amounts of each of the eight essential amino acids and the twelve non-essential amino acids. In fact, your body employs a fascinating strategy to ensure its protein needs are met: it *recycles* your body protein. The presence of food – even food containing little or no protein – in the small intestine triggers the release of endogenous (self-derived) protein, which comes from sloughed-off intestinal cells and used-up digestive enzymes. In fact, adults recycle over two hundred grams of their own body protein per day in this manner[22], while most take in only one hundred grams or less of dietary protein. This mixing of food derived and recycled proteins results in the ratio of essential amino acids in the gut remaining remarkably constant, no matter what types of food are eaten[23,24].

The National Health and Medical Research Council's website could not be clearer about this issue. "All of the necessary amino acids can be provided in the amounts needed from plant sources"[25]. As if this wasn't enough, the bacteria that live in our intestines also synthesise amino acids, which we can absorb and utilise[26].

The take-home message is: quit worrying about protein, and focus on choosing healthy, unrefined plant foods.

The iron issue

Iron is an essential trace element. The major biological use of iron is in the formation of the protein haemoglobin, which transports oxygen in the bloodstream. Children with low iron levels in their bodies have a higher risk of infection and lower IQ. One of the most prevalent myths about plant-based diets is that they are deficient in iron, and hence vegetarians and vegans are at higher risk of becoming anaemic. In fact, Australian research has clearly shown that vegetarian women's iron intakes and haemoglobin levels are much the same as omnivorous women's; and while the average ferritin (storage iron) level in vegetarian women was lower, similar percentages of vegetarians and omnivores had serum ferritin levels below twelve mcg/L, indicating iron depletion[27]. Only vegetarians who centre their diet on processed foods and low-iron starches such as pasta and white bread, are at risk of iron deficiency. Green vegetables, legumes, nuts and seeds are all rich sources of iron.

Eating dairy products contributes to iron deficiency in children in two major ways. Firstly, milk and milk products are low in iron. When children fill up on milk, yogurt and cheese, they have little room left for healthy iron-rich foods. I have seen quite a few children in my practice who drink a litre or more of milk per day. Their parents complain they can't get these kids to eat any vegetables – no wonder, when their stomachs are full of milk! Secondly, dairy product intake causes 'occult bleeding' from the digestive tract in children with milk allergy, which leads to excessive loss of iron[28,29].

Table 3 shows the daily iron requirements of children, and Table 4 illustrates how rich plant foods are in iron, on a nutrient per-calorie basis. While a lower proportion of non-haem iron (the type found in plant foods) is absorbed than the haem iron found in red meat, fruits and vegetables are abundant in the food factors that increase absorption of non-haem iron, such as vitamin C and citric acid.

TABLE 3
Daily iron requirements for children*

Age of child	Iron requirement (milligrams/day)
0-6 months	0.2
7-12 months	11
1-3 years	9
4-8 years	10
9-13 years	8
14-18 years	11 (boys); 15 (girls)

*Reference: http://www.nrv.gov.au/nutrients/iron.htm

TABLE 4
Iron content in plant foods on a nutrient per-calorie basis

Food	Iron (mg/100 calories)
Spinach, cooked	5.4
Lentils, cooked	2.7
Broccoli, cooked	2.1
Chickpeas, cooked	1.7
Cashews, raw	1.7
Sirloin steak, grilled	1.6
White potato, baked	1.3
Figs, dried	0.8
Chicken, roasted, no skin	0.6
Turkey, breast	0.4
Pork chop, pan-fried	0.2
Milk, skim	0.1

The calcium issue

When I advise parents to get milk out of their children's diets and leave it to the baby cows for whom it was designed, the first question they ask is, "How will my child get enough calcium?" The megabucks spent by the dairy industry on advertising campaigns dressed up as information have been incredibly successful in putting the average Australian in mortal fear of not getting enough calcium. Parents worry that without dairy products, their children won't build strong, healthy bones, and will be at higher risk of fracture – especially as they get older.

Yet the indisputable facts are that populations which consume few dairy products, and have a low calcium intake by our standards, have *lower* fracture rates than high dairy consuming populations such as the US, Scandinavia, Australia and New Zealand[30,31]. The Nurses' Health Study found women who drank two or more glasses of milk per day had a forty-five percent higher risk of suffering a hip fracture than women who drank one glass or less per week[32].

One of the reasons why high calcium intake fails to prevent bone fractures (and may even contribute to them) is that it depresses the formation of calcitriol, the active hormonal form of vitamin D. Without adequate calcitriol, we can't absorb and utilise our dietary calcium efficiently[33].

The vitamin B12 issue

Vitamin B12 is made by bacteria, and if we all ate home-grown vegetables without washing off the B12-rich dirt clinging to them; and drank water from streams that harbour bacteria, rather than chlorinated town water, no doubt we could get enough vitamin B12 to meet our needs. But very few of us live this way anymore, so given the grave neurological consequences of vitamin B12 deficiency, B12 supplementation is an absolute necessity for adults and children on plant-based diets. I recommend oral vitamin B12 sprays and lozenges that dissolve under the tongue because they are readily absorbed. In general, B12-fortified foods such as soy 'meats' are too highly processed, and their added salt and sugar content is too high for me to recommend. Nutritional yeast (available from health food stores) contains vitamin B12 and can be used as a substitute for grated cheese.

The vitamin D issue

Vitamin D is not just a vegetarian issue! Low vitamin D levels are virtually epidemic in Australia, among both adults and children. Vitamin D deficiency increases the risk of colds and flu, allergies, asthma, Type I and II diabetes, autoimmune disease, several types of cancer, rickets and bone fractures[34]. I recommend supplementation throughout winter to all my clients, and year-round supplementation for those with dark skin, Muslim women who wear the veil, orthodox Jewish women who adhere to modest dress, and people who are unable to get sufficient time outdoors are most at risk. Most supplements contain vitamin D3 (cholecalciferol), which is usually derived from lanolin, so is not acceptable to vegans. The D2 form (ergocalciferol) is vegan-friendly but breaks down faster in the bloodstream. A vegan vitamin D3 supplement called Vitashine is now available; it's derived from lichen, and is approved by the UK Vegan Society. I encourage parents to allow their children to play outdoors without sunscreen for half an hour a day during the warmer months. Breastfeeding mothers should supplement their own diets with vitamin D to ensure their breast milk contains adequate quantities.

Putting it all together

Children need diets rich in nutrients provided by minimally-processed plant foods to develop to their full physical, intellectual and health potential. To help

TABLE 5

Nutritional value per calorie of sample foods.

Kale	1000	Kidney beans	81	Chicken breast	31
Spinach	853	Sweet potato	77	Wholemeal bread	31
Bok choy	803	Pineapple	74	Low fat yoghurt	30
Cos lettuce	452	Tofu	71	Eggs	27
Broccoli	376	Walnuts	63	White bread	21
Asparagus	269	Cucumber	57	Ground beef	21
Strawberry	245	Rolled oats	53	Cheese	17
Blueberry	150	Brown rice	46	Potato chips	12
Flaxseed	131	Grape	38	Ice cream	8
Orange	124	Avocado	37	Olive oil	2

Source: Fuhrman J. Aggregate Nutritional Density Index

people grasp the concept of nutrient-per-calorie-density, Dr Joel Fuhrman has developed an Aggregate Nutritional Density Index (ANDI)[35] – a system that rates foods in terms of how much nutritional 'bang' for the calorie 'buck' they deliver. I've included some sample foods and their scores to give you an idea of the relative nutritional value offered by commonly-eaten foods.

And here are some ideas for incorporating these nutrient-dense foods into your child's diet.

Breakfast

- fresh fruit topped with ground linseed/flaxseed;
- green smoothie made by blending a banana with some fresh or frozen berries, mango, kiwifruit or orange, a little fruit juice or hemp/almond/oat milk, ground flax, chia or hemp seed, and green leafy vegies such as baby spinach and/or kale;
- porridge cooked with dried fruit (no need to add sugar!) and served with oat or almond milk, or Birchermuesli – made by soaking rolled oats, sunflower seeds or chopped raw nuts and dried fruit overnight in oat or almond milk.

Lunch

- raw vegetable sticks served with hummus, or bean dip (made by blending cooked kidney, white or black beans with garlic, tahini, lemon juice, tomato paste and fresh or dried herbs);
- salad plus baked potato or sweet potato and hummus or bean dip;
- salad wrap in wholemeal Sorj or lavash bread, spread with hummus.

Dinner

- salad or raw vegie sticks with dip for entrée;
- vegetable and legume soup or stew;
- stir-fried vegetables with tofu, served with brown rice;
- vegetable and legume curry;
- Mexican-style meals such as corn tortillas filled with kidney beans, shredded raw vegies and guacamole.

Snacks

- fresh fruit;
- dried fruit and nut balls – just put roughly equal quantities of dried fruit and nuts or seeds in the food processor and blend until they form a sticky wodge, then shape into balls and roll in coconut;
- frozen banana on a stick – cut a ripe banana in half crosswise and poke a paddlepop stick into the flat end, then freeze until hard; you can roll in chopped nuts or coconut first;
- vegie sticks with hummus, bean dip or guacamole;
- Birchermuesli (I make a big container of it and leave it in the fridge for my kids to help themselves).

My website and my blog have many healthy and delicious recipes that are based on fruits, vegetables, legumes, whole grains, nuts and seeds.

Links:

www.empowertotalhealth.com.au

robyn@empowertotalhealth.com.au

Endnotes:

1. http://www.eatright.org/about/content.aspx?id=8357

2. http://www.ncbi.nlm.nih.gov/pmc/articles/PMC1732406/

3. http://www.ncbi.nlm.nih.gov/pubmed/8134024

4. http://circ.ahajournals.org/cgi/content/extract/circulationaha;106/1/143

5. http://circ.ahajournals.org/cgi/content/full/116/9/973

6. http://www.bmj.com/content/341/bmj.c4229.full

7. http://care.diabetesjournals.org/content/27/12/2993.full

8. http://www.ajcn.org/cgi/content/abstract/87/1/162

9. http://www.ncbi.nlm.nih.gov/pubmed/12801106

10. http://www.ncbi.nlm.nih.gov/pubmed/8134024

11. http://www.ncbi.nlm.nih.gov/pubmed/16028644

12. http://www.ncbi.nlm.nih.gov/pubmed/15702668

13. http://jama.ama- assn.org/cgi/content/abstract/284/8/993?ijkey=0b-
   4f82796a19b3f284997a98ec8f07140e497ffa&keytype2=tf_ipse csha

14. UK Department of Health, Working Group on Diet and Cancer of the Committee on Medical Aspects of Food and Nutrition Policy. *Nutritional aspects of the development of cancer.* London, Her Majesty's Stationery Office, 1998. Downloadable from http://www.nice.org.uk/aboutnice/whoweare/aboutthe-hda/hdapublications/nutritional_aspects_of_the_development_of_cancer_briefing_paper.jsp

15. http://aje.oxfordjournals.org/content/152/5/446.short

16. Pike MC, Henderson BE, Casagrande JT, in Pike et al (eds) *Hormones and Cancer,* New York, Banbury Reports, Cold Springs Harbor Laboratory 3, 1981, cited in Fuhrman J, *Disease-Proof Your Child,* New York, St Martin's Press, 2005.

17. http://www.ncbi.nlm.nih.gov/pubmed/11308097

18. http://www.plosmedicine.org/article/info:doi/10.1371/journal.pmed.0040132

19. Fuhrman J, *Disease-Proof Your Child,* New York, St Martin's Press, 2005.

20. http://www.ncbi.nlm.nih.gov/pubmed/10466163

21. Institute of Medicine. Dietary Reference Intakes for Energy, Carbohydrate, Fiber, Fat, Fatty Acids, Cholesterol, Protein and Amino Acids. Washington, DC, National Academies Press, 2002.

22. http://www.jn.nutrition.org/cgi/reprint/74/4/461.pdf

23. http://www.jn.nutrition.org/cgi/reprint/74/4/461.pdf

24. http://www.ncbi.nlm.nih.gov/pubmed/571014

25. http://www.nrv.gov.au/nutrients/protein.htm

26. http://www.ncbi.nlm.nih.gov/pubmed/10867063

27. http://www.ajcn.org/cgi/content/abstract/70/3/353

28. http://www.ncbi.nlm.nih.gov/pubmed/309064

29. http://www.ncbi.nlm.nih.gov/pubmed/3880888

30. http://www.ajcn.org/cgi/content/full/74/5/571#R27

31. http://www.jn.nutrition.org/cgi/reprint/116/11/2316.pdf

32. http://www.ncbi.nlm.nih.gov/pubmed/9224182

33. http://www.jn.nutrition.org/cgi/reprint/116/11/2316.pdf

34. http://ods.od.nih.gov/factsheets/vitamind.asp

35. http://drfuhrman.com/library/article17.aspx

■ EAT YOUR ETHICS

Lauren Ornelas

"Sometimes it seems we can do things we never imagined possible, when we know it is for someone else." ■

—Lauren Ornelas.

▶ Lauren Ornelas.

Lauren Ornelas is the founder and executive director of the Food Empowerment Project.... ■

I remember being in the line at the cafeteria in elementary school and asking the server not to put 'meat' on my cheese enchiladas. She asked if I was a vegetarian. In my young mind, I wondered why she thought I was old enough to treat sick dogs and cats! I told her no. According to my mom, when she told me what chicken was, I stopped eating them.

Too many factors interfered with my ability to stick with my resolve consistently, but when I was about sixteen, I made the decision to remain a vegetarian. I didn't know anything about factory farming, but growing up in Texas, I was familiar with cows. Seeing them along the side of roads would help me stay committed to my decision, as I would imagine what it would be like if it were my fault one of those cows didn't come home.

One day in my high school ecology class, the teacher presented a slideshow on wildlife management, explaining how hunting was necessary to 'manage' their populations. I raised my hand and said there had to be another way to do this without killing the animals. I continued to raise my hand and ask questions, as none of it seemed to make sense to me. The teacher eventually told me to "talk to someone who cares." I told him I didn't know of anyone. Later he brought me a newspaper clipping about an anti-fur protest by a group called *Voice for Animals*.

I contacted them immediately, and I have been an animal rights activist ever since; that was 1987. I started an animal rights group at my high school with the help of the local animal rights organisation. When I tried to convince that same teacher – who also taught biology – to stop doing dissections, he basically told me I was going to hell.

I was never pleased with the narrow way of teaching most subjects in high school, so instead of getting a college degree, I looked for different activist groups to work with.

I was already trying to do my part to help farm workers by participating in the grape boycott – started by the United Farm Workers to draw attention to the plight of farm workers – and using my food choices to not support the apartheid regime in South Africa. However, after talking to my two mentors in the animal rights movement (I like to refer to John and Kay as my "animal rights parents"), they, like my mom and sisters, encouraged me to go to college and take classes that would make me the most effective animal rights activist possible: speech, to hone my public-speaking skills; political science, so I'd understand the legislative process; ethics, so I could better argue from the moral perspective, and so on. It was excellent advice. Although financially it was a struggle, I was very glad I went.

I started and ran animal rights groups at my university, and I worked for a national animal rights group.

Eventually, my years of activism helped me earn a position running the US chapter of Viva! a campaigning organisation based in England. More than a decade before, I had seen *The Animals Film*, which goes through the various forms of animal abuse. It's where I saw chicks having the tip of the beaks cut off as part of the egg industry's abuse. I remember thinking, "I could never film that."

But as the head of Viva! USA, I would have to do my own investigations of factory farms, from which I created campaigns (mostly targeting corporations). With every investigation I did – from ducks shackled upside down in a slaughterhouse to a beautiful Angus cow being prodded because he slipped on an auction house floor – there was an urgency to intervene and stop the cruelty.

Sometimes it seems we can do things we never imagined possible, when we know it is for someone else.

Fortunately, our corporate campaigns achieved many changes, one of the biggest of which was providing the spark for the founder of Whole Foods Market to go vegan and a grocery store chain to stop selling duck meat. In 2006, I spoke at the World Social Forum in Caracas, Venezuela, where my passions called for me to combine my interests in the liberation of human and non-human animals, as well as the need to protect them and the environment from corporate abuses. The result was Food Empowerment Project, which I founded to help create a more just food system that included veganism and the rights of produce workers. Food Empowerment Project exposes various abuses in the food industry, such as those that exist in the production of chocolate, and working on access to healthy foods in coloured and low-income communities.

Given the horrific abuses faced by animals who are raised for food, promoting veganism is a key part of our work. As we advocate for people to eat fruits and vegetables, we recognise we must work toward supporting the rights of those who pick our food. Farm workers in the US are forced to work in some of the worst conditions, where they are exposed to agricultural chemicals, extreme heat, and where children as young as five years old have been found working. Many do not earn enough to put a roof over their head or put the healthy foods they are picking on their own tables.

By using our name, Food Empowerment Project has augmented the voices of farm workers and encouraged others to get involved in supporting corporate campaigns and legislation. We also campaign for educational basics, and a school-supply drive we organised provided the children of farm workers with backpacks, notebooks, pens, paper and other classroom necessities.

We encourage people not to buy chocolate that comes from the worst forms of child labour, including slavery. In Ghana and the Ivory Coast, it is estimated that approximately 1.8 million children are victims. They work under the threat of punishment if they do not move quickly enough. They carry heavy cacao pods and use dangerous equipment such as machetes. Some are locked in at night and are beaten or killed if they try to escape.

We have a web list of companies, which includes a free app, that make vegan chocolates that we recommend based on where they source their cacao.

To me, veganism is not just a way of eating; it's a way of life. It's about trying to do the least harm and acting for justice. And for me, that goes beyond helping non-human animals. Using our individual choices and collective voices to create change is a great start.

Links:

www.foodispower.org

www.veganmexicanfood.com

www.foodispower.org/chocolate-list/.

■ A PATH TOWARDS MEANING
Julia Schmidt

"It was as if the elimination of animal products from my diet had allowed me to open my eyes and see the animal kingdom properly for the first time." ■

—Julia Schmidt.

▶ Julia Schmidt and Pete.

Julia Schmidt is a teacher in Germany ... ■

After years of worsening allergic reactions to pollen and the subsequent extensive use of antibiotics to fight infected sinuses, my body's immune system was at an all time low. My body finally gave me a very clear signal as my sciatic nerve became terribly agitated and brought with it tremendous pain that after two months finally led to my collapse from exhaustion.

Having spent a terrible time in hospital I spent most of that year lying in bed with a viral infection or some kind of flu. Lying in bed ill at the age of thirty-eight was probably just as frustrating and horrible as to be lying in bed ill at the age of eighty-eight; it just seems a lot more normal to be ill at eighty-eight, but is it?

By chance and much good fortune I came across Dr T Colin Campbell's book, *The China Study*. The veil lifted; the answer was clear. I needed to follow a whole foods plant-based diet.

I say *plant-based* and not *vegan* as the goal was purely health-based at the time. The journey began and as I energetically moved along this path, I experienced numerous health benefits, including reducing my allergies to almost nothing. An interesting development was starting to take place in my mind, the more I delved into this way of eating and living, the more I became aware of animals as fellow beings rather than as commodities for me to make use of. It was as if the elimination of animal products from my diet had allowed me to open my eyes and see the animal kingdom properly for the first time. I felt a softening inside and I slowly started moving from a whole foods, plant-based diet to a whole foods vegan diet. Another veil lifted; I knew I was on a path towards meaning and life.

Veganism is so much more than just the food. It is a whole world of beauty and connection with all life forms; it is full of meaning and compassion. It is the key to learning how to really celebrate life.

A New Kind of Politics

"Despite a tiny budget, limited experience and very limited media exposure, almost 100,000 Australians gave the animals in this country their first vote at the September 2013 national election by putting the AJP first on their Senate ballot paper. The AJP had the thirteenth highest vote across all fifty parties standing for election, ahead of thirty-seven. With just a slightly higher overall vote the AJP could have been in the top seven based on primary votes." ▓

—Professor Steve Garlick, Founding President of the Animal Justice Party of Australia.

▓ INTERVIEW WITH
Professor Steve Garlick
Founding President of the Animal Justice Party of Australia

"As I travel through the Australian bush I find myself apologising for being human to all the wildlife I come upon. If you could hear an animal's quiet sobbing, what would you do?" ▓

—Steve Garlick.

▶ Steve Garlick with Dusty and Lambie.

Professor Steve Garlick has professorial positions at two Australian universities. He is a spatial economist and an applied ethicist. He is an academic, advocate, activist and political party leader. His publication record focuses on knowledge systems, human capital, innovation, environmental sustainability, wildlife emotion and behaviour, and trans-species learning. He has undertaken many international reviews of higher education. With wife Rosemary, Steve operates a self-funded wildlife recovery centre for traumatised native mammals. He is founder and president of the newly formed Animal Justice Party of Australia and in 2009 with Rosemary, received the international Shining World Compassion Award for assisting wildlife with trauma...   ∎

Both you and your wife are running a self-funded wildlife recovery and research centre for severely injured wildlife. How did that come about?

About twelve years ago my wife came racing home in the car saying, "Oh no, a terrible thing's happened. I think I've run over an echidna." We went back down the road and picked him up. As it turned out the echidna wasn't badly injured; we contacted an organisation that looked after injured wildlife and took him to them.

That was how we started. Initially, we joined an organisation that cares for injured animals. A little way down the track we formed our own facility. So many people euthanase animals because they don't know what else to do, and we wanted a place where those animals could be cared for and nursed back to health. We work mostly with severely injured animals and specialise in wild mammals such as macropods, wombats and possums. My wife Rosemary is a doctor, and we found that many of our injured animal friends recovered and had a second chance of a full life in a safe place. Quite by chance, we met an excellent veterinarian, and together we've been able to rehabilitate many injured animals successfully. Word gets around and people bring wallabies, wombats, reptiles and birds from all distances now.

Even though you and your wife both have full-time jobs and run a wildlife sanctuary, you've now also spearheaded a political party, the Animal Justice Party. How did that come about?

Four years ago the Australian Capital Territory government decided it was going to kill ('cull') five hundred and fourteen kangaroos that were contained on an old radio transmission station property, a Commonwealth Department of Defence site in Canberra. They must have started off as a small group caught within this fenced area, and over the years the group had grown in number. The site became surplus to Defence requirements and was transferred across to the Territory government at no cost. They saw it as a prime piece of real estate but the kangaroos were in the way and needed to be disposed of.

When we heard about this, several of us, including Ken Henry, the former head of Treasury, put forward an alternative plan to the Department of Defence which involved moving the animals to a safe location on private land outside of the ACT where people with properties were agreeable to having them.

Our efforts were to no avail as the ACT government was in a hurry. The kangaroos were brutally killed, all of which we have on film. Kangaroos suffer incredibly from stress and a disease called myopathy, which results from exertion involving fear. This is exactly what happened. They were rounded up into a very small, enclosed area where they were then given lethal injections. This went on for quite some time – adults, young and joeys still in their mothers' pouches.

People were outraged, of course, but it went ahead. This exercise was condoned by the RSPCA and the Greens, and cost millions. Our proposal to move these animals to a safe location was at minimum cost.

Three years later this land is a housing development with your typical McMansions. An irony that I discovered through Freedom of Information is that the site was a contaminated waste dump, with PCBs, asbestos and many other lasting metals, a fact which had been denied by government for twenty years.

One of their spurious arguments was that the kangaroos were destroying the natural habitat by eating the grasslands of other native animals. But when I uncovered the fact it was a contaminated site, they had a metre or more of topsoil removed – a far greater impact on the other wildlife than the nibbling and foraging of kangaroos.

We realised we could get nowhere from outside government. It became clear the only time politicians take any notice is when there are votes to be gained or lost. We needed a political party.

I researched what was happening in other countries, in particular, the very successful Dutch Party for the Animals, which became an inspiration as to what could be achieved for animals. The Animal Justice Party of Australia was registered federally in May, 2011. Just recently we have also fulfilled the requirements to register the Party in NSW. It is our intention to have the AJP registered in each of the states and territories.

What are the objectives of the party at this stage?

The four basic principles we have agreed upon are respect, kindness, compassion and recognition of individual capabilities, firstly to animals, but also to humans who have no voice in the community.

There is no political party in this country at the moment that is expounding those values, and I include the Greens in that. We've been disappointed with the Greens because if they had an active program of supporting animal welfare there'd be no need for a party like this. Their conservation policies are about the whole of the environment, the whole species, whether it is flora or fauna. They are not talking about individuals. We are concerned that individual animals and people without a voice have some recognition in Parliament because too often decisions are made on the basis of economics, which places an extremely low value on animals.

Kangaroos have been in this country for sixteen million years. You would think that by listening to them and watching them closely we'd learn something about sustainability. To do that we need to have respect, compassion and kindness towards them and the way they have adapted to this great continent of ours, their right to be here, to live full lives, to have fun, to forage, to mate – in other words, to live out their rightful life span.

That's a powerful statement coming from an economics professor.

Yes. I've been an economist for more than thirty years, and I have come to the realisation that our economic practices have caused a disservice to society. I feel I can use my economics background in a very different way now, and I am applying this learning to help the plight of our fellow beings who are not being allowed a voice, let alone a choice.

Why would we not want to help animals in the same way we might want to help humans?

Is the AJP going to take a stand just for the welfare of animals or for the total abolition of animal use?

I am vegan but I'm enough of a realist to know a political party is about numbers. This will be a journey. For example, our website has a policy about diet where we discuss the reasons and ethics for moving away from an animal-based way of eating. We know this will not change people's food choices overnight, but we are committed, through raising awareness, to educating people of the benefits of a vegan diet on a personal and planetary level. When people saw the shocking footage on the cruelty animals suffered as a result of the live export trade on the Four Corners program in 2011, many of them decided not to eat meat anymore. Whether that's short term or long term is yet to be seen but we know it had an impact.

The reality is, animal cruelty is happening every day. We used to say this country's economy was built on the sheep's back. I'm sorry, but *this economy was built on the back of animal cruelty*. The AJP decries this cruelty and espouses the benefits of a plant-based diet and hopefully we can make some inroads into ensuring a kinder, more compassionate world whereby we treat all beings as worthy of a good and happy life.

In a way you are promoting veganism as a way of promoting justice for animals.

We believe we can't do it unless we are able to have some force as a political party. A lot of advocacy organisations are pushing this message and doing a good job. Our role is to push this same message in the political environment.

An issue that failed to be raised in that entire live export campaign was the ethics of animals being slaughtered at all. No one looked at the bigger picture. Our slaughterhouses aren't exactly picnic parlours.

It's hard to believe that anyone who saw those images on the Four Corners program could continue to justify the entire industry. We are not just talking about the treatment these animals are subjected to, but their very lives. How can these people's hearts be so cold? From an economic viewpoint, the income from this industry is minimal and the number of jobs is small.

I worked in the federal government during the Hawke and Keating eras. During that time there was massive restructuring because of the reduction in tariff protection. Tens of thousands of people, low-skilled people in particular, lost their jobs. There was a whole range of labour market retraining programs; a lot of people did well out of all that and took up occupations that were more inspiring for them. That was all done for economic reasons and the AJP's argument is there's no difference here. We're asking for this industry to be restructured and, we would argue, restructured out of existence.

The live export industry was told twenty-five years ago that if it were based on animal ethics and welfare, it would have been closed down immediately. Nothing has changed. The current government view is that all we need is a better monitoring scheme. And guess what? They're going to give the monitoring back to the industry! The industry has had twenty-five years to get it right and it has failed.

Why do you think the government caved in and that basic welfare standards still cannot be guaranteed?

It's not about animal welfare at all. It is about pandering to big business and playing politics. Big properties are owned by big companies these days, they're not owned by individual farmers. These big companies carry weight and the government has dealings with them in other areas as well.

There are so many issues. What would you say to people who wish to join the AJP?

The AJP stands for the wellbeing of and better lives for animals. In economic terms, the return on your investment is much greater – whether that's a return to society, a return to the economy, a return to the environment – if we have a better relationship with the animals in this country.

We need to inculcate kindness, compassion and true welfare for animals into our education systems and into our everyday lives. Education is crucial and it is particularly important that we begin educating young children about animal welfare. We can learn so much more that will benefit not only the animals but we humans as well. I encourage folk to have a look at our website and to have a look at our values.

Why do we need an Animal Justice Party?

We need an Animal Justice Party because our country's economy is largely built on animal cruelty. The attitude of the ordinary person with his/her head in the sand is all pervasive, that it's just a 'natural' part of life. In fact, all levels of government are culpable. We as a nation, we as individuals, we as government, don't stop and think about what we are actually doing when we abuse other living beings. We assume it's fine, you can go about killing animals, making animals' lives miserable for the sake of a few extra dollars.

I am under no illusion that it will take time to change public perception. We are advocating changes in diet, different ways of working, different ways of learning.

Even in the university arena where I work as a professor, the lack of regard for animal welfare is evident in the way they experiment on live animals. I've left some committees in disgust at the way they treat animals purely for human benefit. There are a lot of institutional barriers and political inexperience we are going to have to overcome. And given the fact politics is a dirty game anyway I think this will be a long-term project. But its time has come.

I take the view that learning from animals comes from an ethic of care. It's only in an ethic of care where you can really understand the needs of animals. I suppose that started for me about twenty years ago when my family was involved in a tragic motor vehicle accident. My wife and one of my sons were killed in that accident and my other boy was fortunate to survive but with a lot of disabilities. I looked after my son for many years. He had to learn how to walk again, how to talk, and many other things. He had a severe head injury. When Rosemary came along she came with her incapacitated mother, whom we looked after for five years. So my life changed and I became more involved in caring for the lives of others. When animals came along twelve years ago it seemed like a natural shift. We've learnt so much from them about suffering, perseverance, determination, play and nurturing. Through caring comes the learning.

It's a lot of hard work, but it's incredibly fulfilling. Rosemary and I have rescued about four thousand wild animals. We've helped in the rehabilitation of about seventeen hundred severely injured or seriously ill animals. We build strong bonds with these animals and they build strong bonds with each other.

When they have recovered, we release them to a large property nearby. Every night Rosemary goes down to the property and calls them. Within fifteen minutes she can have thirty or forty animals, mainly kangaroos, skipping around her feet. They know this is the person who helped them. You can't buy that kind of connectivity. They just come, sit, try to put their arms around her and then they go. They come back in large numbers and bring their young with them to show her. That's the kind of return you can get on this investment in caring. While it keeps us tired and poor, to us it's worthwhile.

If you could pick one thing, one powerful thing people could do right now to help animals, what would it be?

The most powerful thing I think is to reflect on the lives of animals in terms of how it might affect you if you were that animal. How would you like it if someone decided they would like to eat you, or how would you feel if they were abusing you? If there was some brutality towards you, how would you feel? In other words, for just a moment, put yourself in an animal's shoes. If people truly do that, they will no longer be able to perpetuate the pain they have caused, albeit it unwittingly.

All animals, including humans, have something to offer, so respect animals as you would expect to be respected by your fellow human animal beings.

Link:

http://www.animaljusticeparty.org/

■ MOVING TOWARDS ENLIGHTENED LEGISLATION
Barry Spurr

Barry Spurr is a member of the Animal Justice Party
and Professor of Poetry and Poetics at The University of
Sydney...   ■

▶ Barry Spurr.

Everyone concerned about animal welfare is increasingly frustrated about the inability, slowness, reluctance or downright refusal of government, at all levels – local, state and federal – to enact humane and enlightened legislation, and enforce it, in the interest of the protection of all animals from cruelty and exploitation. Even when the overwhelming opinion of the people is clearly opposed to an issue of animal welfare, such as the use of wild animals in circuses, government refuses to act or produces lamely compromised legislation, which fails to address the situation effectively. Constant lobbying of government by animal welfare groups has achieved little or nothing in a range of areas that urgently need attention, such as pet farms, the live export industry, jumps racing and factory farming, all of which, again, would be opposed by most electors.

I believe the only way forward is for there to be a political party in Parliament to represent the interests of animals, whose voices are simply not being heard or heeded by the mainstream parties.

Giving Voice to a New Way of Thinking

■ ROWING TO A BETTER WORLD

Dr Jonathan Balcombe

"Veganism is the Holy Grail of personal activism for animals, sustainability and society." ■

—Jonathan Balcombe.

▶ Jonathon Balcombe and Hannah.

Jonathan Balcombe is an animal scientist. He was born in England and raised in New Zealand and Canada. He studied biology in Canada before earning a PhD in ethology (animal behaviour) from the University of Tennessee. He is the author of three popular books on animals, *Pleasurable Kingdom: Animals and the Nature of Feeling Good; Second Nature: The Inner Lives of Animals;* and *The Exultant Ark: A Pictorial Tour of Animal Pleasure.* Balcombe is the Animal Studies Department Chair for Humane Society University. In his spare time he enjoys nature watching, biking, piano, vegan cooking and trying to understand his two cats… ■

When I was eight I climbed into an aluminium rowboat with the elderly director of a summer camp north of Toronto. He rowed a quarter mile out into the shallow bay and we spent the next two hours fishing. The water was like glass in the calm summer evening. It was my first time in a small boat, and floating on this vast expanse of dark water was exhilarating. I remember the excitement I felt as the sudden jerk of my primitive fishing pole, a stripped sapling with a line and hook, signalled that a fish had struck the bait.

I caught sixteen fishes that day. Some were released, but several others, larger bass and perch, were kept for breakfast the next morning. Mr Nelson did all the dirty work, baiting the barbed hooks with writhing earthworms, twisting the wire out of the fishes' lips, plunging his knife into their skulls to kill them. His face contorted strangely as he performed these tasks and I wondered if he was feeling revulsion or if he was merely lost in concentration.

As a sensitive, highly-strung boy with a soft spot for animals, a lot of what went on in that rowboat disturbed me. I fretted privately about the worms. I wondered if the fishes felt pain as the reluctant hook was extracted from their bony faces. I worried the 'keepers' may have survived the knife and were slowly dying in the wire basket dangling over the side. But this kind man sitting at the bow didn't seem to think there was anything wrong, so I rationalised it must be okay.

I never took a shine to fishing, soon losing interest when it came time to bait my own hooks and remove them from fish. I couldn't help seeing things from the fishes' perspective.

But like the great majority of humans, I grew up eating and wearing anonymous animals. I ate pigs, cows, sheep, lambs, chickens, turkeys and many kinds of fish. I loved meat. I couldn't get enough of it. I used to sneak into the kitchen after breakfast to eat leftover bacon rinds. I drank gallons of cow's milk, and I enjoyed dipping narrow slices of toast into soft-boiled eggs.

Gradually but inevitably, I began to question my eating habits. At age twenty-four I took a year off from my biology studies to travel. I wanted to experience a non-Western culture. I chose India. The film *Gandhi* had recently been released and I was captivated that a nation had gained independence behind the leadership of a skinny, half-naked lawyer who spun his own cloth and preached nonviolent non-cooperation. Before I left I decided to join the dietary ranks of India's half-billion Hindus and swear off meat.

I saw things in India that dampened the idealism the *Gandhi* film had instilled in me. On one occasion I happened upon an ugly scene in a fishing village in which several men were severely beating a dog with a shovel. I stepped into the fray and narrowly avoided being beaten myself. But India's marvellous rail system, colourful culture and nature, and countless vegetarian restaurants more than made up for these deficits, and I returned home three months later fully committed to a plant-based diet.

Nearly thirty years on, my childhood love of animals has become a career in animal protection. Though they don't pay me, I see animals as my clients. I never tire of watching animals. Today at the airport I watched a toddler beaming with delight as she took some of her first steps, and it gave me the same feeling I get when I watch animals playing. The innocence and the sublime purity of their emotions are deeply rewarding and inspiring.

The more I observe animals the more they reveal of themselves. It was while waiting at a traffic light that I first noticed how starlings, foraging in the grass, open their beaks like tweezers then look inside to see what's there. It was in a colleague's kitchen that I noticed fruit flies prying and squeezing their way through pinholes to escape a dish of peaches that had been covered with perforated cellophane to trap them. It was under the floodlights of an Ontario park that I discovered red bats eavesdrop on the hunting calls of other red bats pursuing large moths and try to intercept them. That particular discovery was published in 1988 as part of my Master's degree in biology.

These are exciting times in the study of animal behaviour. Scientists are making discoveries on animals' inner lives that would have been deemed fantasy a generation ago. Male mice sing ultrasonic courtship songs to females. Reef fish line up to await their turn for a spa treatment by cleaner-fish, while onlookers compile 'image-scores' to decide which cleaner to team up with. Prairie dogs have a special call for 'man with gun'. Parrots name their babies. Dogs stop cooperating when they receive fewer treats than another dog for performing the same task. Vampire bats help a friend in need. Roosters share food to earn sexual favours from hens. Pigs quickly master mirrors. Caged birds become pessimistic and free ones optimistic. Baboon mothers grieve the loss of an infant and seek therapy by expanding their social networks. Calves have 'eureka moments' when they solve a problem. Chimps outscore humans on spatial memory tests. Octopuses hold grudges, gorillas make up jokes and rats laugh.

Discoveries like these help confirm what may seem obvious to anyone who has lived closely with animals: that they are individuals with thoughts and feelings, that they have rich inner lives that matter and are worth living.

Animals are sentient. And let no one deny it – sentience is the bedrock of ethics. The foundation of moral systems is that individuals can feel pain and suffering, pleasure and joy. The basis for moral consideration is not the ability to write, to vote or to cook pasta. The basis for moral consideration is the capacity to feel. Evolution is indifferent. She doesn't play favourites based on species membership. A mouse's genes are as important as a human's genes. A mouse's pain is as important to the survival of a mouse as a human's pain is to the survival of a human. The idea that the intensity of an individual's pain is proportional to brain size or intelligence is, in the words of biologist John Webster, "a pathetic piece of logic."

In April 2001, while bird watching in Virginia, I had an epiphany that steered my life in a new direction. Two crows landed on a billboard, one sidled up to the other, bent over and offered his neck feathers, and the other preened him. The deliberateness of the soliciting crow's action clearly indicated he wanted to be preened, and that it felt good. The idea that animals can feel pleasure is hardly a revelation. But I realised at that moment that in all the years I had studied biology, animals' capacity for pleasure had essentially gone unmentioned.

This was a gaping void in scientific discourse and in the public's understanding and appreciation for the nature of being an animal. That void set me on a mission (Balcombe 2006 & 2010). I began to notice animals in a new light. Behaviours I had previously seen only through the lens of evolution and ultimate adaptation I now saw through the proximate lens of an individual's conscious experience. Monkeys don't consciously forage for fruit to promote their survival, any more than we contemplate our genetic fitness as we bite into a banana. All animals eat to satisfy their hunger and they enjoy the sweet taste of fruit as much as we do. To generalise, animals don't study Darwinian principles. As pleasure seekers like us, they act on their feelings, their impulses, their wants and needs.

The neglect of pleasure is morally consequential. Pleasure's moral significance sometimes exceeds that of pain and suffering. Murder serves to illustrate this. The main reason it is wrong to kill another person is not that it may cause them pain and suffering, although that certainly compounds the crime. If pain and suffering were the sole basis for murder being immoral, then there could be no objection to a pristinely humane killing that the victim never even knew was coming. No, murder is bad because it ends a life that was *worth living*. And it is pleasure, not pain, that makes life worth living.

An animal threatened with death behaves as we would: she flees, struggles, bites and claws desperately to escape. Henry David Thoreau said it well, "The squirrel that you kill in jest, dies in earnest." I find it deeply ironic that we place the highest value on the sanctity of human life while simultaneously discarding animals' lives as if they had no value at all. An American doctor is imprisoned for assisting a dignified suicide, while three hundred unwilling chickens are legally slaughtered each second. That is a failure of empathy and a stark reminder of the profound gulf we have placed between our species and all others.

Animals are sentient. And let no one deny it – sentience is the bedrock of ethics. The foundation of moral systems is that individuals can feel pain and suffering, pleasure and joy. The basis for moral consideration is not the ability to write, to vote or to cook pasta. The basis for moral consideration is the capacity to feel. Evolution is indifferent. She doesn't play favourites based on species membership. A mouse's genes are as important as a human's genes. A mouse's pain is as important to the survival of a mouse as a human's pain is to the survival of a human. The idea that the intensity of an individual's pain is proportional to brain size or intelligence is, in the words of biologist John Webster, "a pathetic piece of logic." ∎

The surest, most immediate way to bridge the gulf is to do what Gandhi did with animals: he stopped eating them. Vegetarianism, ideally veganism, is the Holy Grail of personal activism for animals, sustainability and society. The best thing one can do for animals is to stop eating animals. The best thing one can do for the environment is to stop eating animals. The best thing one can do for personal health is to stop eating animals. When I speak to audiences, I give them a homework assignment: eat a plant-based diet for thirty days. It's short enough not to be daunting, but long enough to have an effect on their food preferences. Of those who try it, some contact me later to say it is the best decision they've made. They are right.

References

Balcombe J (2011). *The Exultant Ark: A Pictorial Tour of Animal Pleasure*. (University of California Press)

Balcombe J (2010). *Second Nature: The Inner Lives of Animals*. (Palgrave Macmillan).

Balcombe J (2006). *Pleasurable Kingdom: Animals and the Nature of Feeling Good*. (Macmillan).

■ TELLING IT AS IT IS

Gary Yourofsky

"Never be afraid to do what's right, especially if the wellbeing of a person or animal is at stake. Society's punishments are small compared to the wounds we inflict on our soul when we look the other way." ■

—Martin Luther King Jr.

Gary Yourofsky is a dynamic and hard-hitting speaker whose commitment and dedication to improving the lives of animals is unquestionable. Yourofsky has spoken to more than sixty thousand students in one hundred and seventy schools and universities nationwide in the USA. His extensive knowledge of the facts behind the meat and dairy industries, combined with footage from slaughterhouses, serves to spread the message that we need to be kind to animals and ultimately, to go vegan.

▶ Gary Yourofsky and Katie.

In 1997, Yourofsky liberated 1,542 minks from the Eberts Fur Farm in Ontario. In freeing the animals from a certain and painful death, this act and others led him to be banned in five countries. Despite the controversy surrounding his approach, the one thing that cannot be aimed at Yourofsky is that he lacks passion, honesty and a deep and abiding love for animals and their welfare… ■

My stepfather used to be a clown in The Shrine Circus. He took me backstage when I was twenty-three. I saw three elephants chained to the cement floor in the warehouse of the Michigan State Fairgrounds. Sadness, hopelessness and fear were emanating from their eyes, their bodies. They were swaying neurotically from side to side. A monkey was screaming in his cage, grabbing the bars of his prison. Two tigers were pacing neurotically in their tiny cages. Cruelty was staring me in the face. I knew something was wrong.

If you pay attention to energy, you can tell when a fellow being is in peril. The 'slave show' I witnessed made me question where my food and shoes came from and what truly went on in animal research laboratories.

I went to the Thorn Apple Valley pig slaughterhouse in Detroit for six weeks straight. I kept going back because my mind wouldn't let me grasp the horror I was witnessing. I couldn't believe my eyes. My heart hurt. Their fear was palpable; the screams impossible to brush aside. I knew I had to make a choice. Was I going to be their friend or their enemy? Was I going to be hypocritical or ethically consistent? At first, like every meat-eater, I chose hypocrisy. I was stubborn, addicted and emotionally stunted from more than two decades of consuming abused, tortured and murdered corpses. I can't believe I only condemned the abuse of elephants in the circus but not the murder of animals in a slaughterhouse. Finally, after a two year battle with my idiocy and selfishness, the hypocrisy was too much to deal with. I went vegetarian in 1995.

When I became vegan on 24 July 1996, and finally understood that animals had an inherent right to be free and live completely unfettered by human domination, I wondered why it took more than twenty-five years to attain this nonviolent awakening. I began to ask, "Who taught me animals were put on this Earth for food? Who taught me to disrespect animals and view them as mere commodities? Who stole my compassion, my empathy and my conscience? Who lied to me? Who instilled that vicious mindset of human-to-animal exploitation as standard operating procedure?"

If every meat-eater logically and compassionately re-evaluated their beliefs, they would understand why veganism is the only ethical and acceptable way to live. Isaac Bashevis Singer, the compassionate Jewish humanitarian who escaped Nazi-occupied Poland, once condemned every meat-eater by stating, "What do they know – all these scholars, all these philosophers, all the leaders of the world? They have convinced themselves that man, the worst transgressor of all the species, is the crown of creation. All other creatures were created merely to provide him with food, pelts, to be tormented, exterminated. In relation to them [animals], all people are Nazis; for the animals it is an eternal Treblinka."

Veganism still wasn't enough for me. My experiences at the circus, the slaughterhouse and other places of torture I visited stirred the revolutionary blood that was in me, that's in all of us. In my desire to do more, I founded ADAPTT (Animals Deserve Absolute Protection Today and Tomorrow) in 1996. I started running the gamut of activism by engaging in demonstrations, legislative efforts, leafleting and editorial writing as well as civil disobedience and direct action, resulting in five country banishments and thirteen arrests.

On 30 March 1997, I was part of a mink liberation effort at the Eberts Fur Farm in Blenheim, Ontario. (Hilma Ruby, my lone, upstanding compatriot out of the five, spent sixty days in prison. The three others bargained, pleaded, apologised and/or agreed to cooperate with the authorities in order to save their own asses.) We released one thousand five hundred and forty two mink from their cages that glorious night but were apprehended shortly thereafter. That action made me one of America's most outspoken and spirited animal rights activists.

For my random act of kindness and compassion on behalf of the tortured and doomed mink, I spent seventy-seven days in prison. Canadian Judge A Cusinato sentenced me to six months in the Elgin Middlesex Detention Center in London, Ontario. A deportation parole was issued, though, and I returned to Michigan after serving seventy-seven days at the maximum-security lockup. Before being carted off to prison, I was able to address the judge.

"I stand before this court without trepidation and without timidity because the truth cannot be suppressed today and the truth will not be compromised.

Mohandas Gandhi, one of the most benevolent people to ever grace this earth, once said, 'Even if you are only one person the truth is still the truth.' The dilemma we face today is whether this court chooses to acknowledge the truth. The following statement is for everyone's edification.

"One day every enslaved animal will obtain their freedom and the animal rights movement will succeed because Gandhi also proclaimed, 'Throughout history the way of truth and love has always won. There have been murderers and tyrants and at times they have seemed invincible, but in the end they always fall. Always!' The true devoted humanitarians who are working towards the magnanimous goal of achieving freedom for animals cannot be stopped by unjust laws. As long as humans are placed on a pedestal above non-humans injustice to animals will fester because without universal equality one type of equality will always create another type of inequality. There will be no compromise here today because the truth cannot be compromised. My presence in this courtroom today is paradoxical. I ask this court: *If it is NOT a crime to torture, enslave and murder animals, then how can it be a crime to free tortured, enslaved and soon-to-be-murdered animals?* Humankind must climb out of its abyss of callousness, its abyss of apathy and its abyss of greed. Enslaving and killing animals for human satisfaction can never be justified. And the fur industry must understand that the millions of manual neck-breakings, anal and genital electrocutions, mass gassings, drownings and toxic chemical injections can never be justified. The snaring of millions of free-roaming animals in steel jaw leghold traps, who die slow, horrific deaths, is unjustifiable. There will be no compromise, for the truth cannot be compromised. The schism this court has created among the five co-accused has been sealed. Now that I have been convicted, through my volition and in a symbolic protest of the unjust conditions that animals endure, a hunger strike will begin at seven thirty tomorrow morning. For every mink that ever languished in a tiny cage and was savagely murdered at the Eberts Fur Farm, I will go hungry. And for the forty million other animals worldwide who have the skin ripped off their backs in a disgusting display of barbarity, in the name of vanity, I will go hungry. And if this court expects me to experience an apostasy, meaning an abandoning of my beliefs, it is sadly mistaken. In April 1997, when I was incarcerated for ten days in a Chatham jail, I briefly experienced, vicariously, what a caged animal goes through. And thanks to that ten-day bail hearing, my empathy for every mistreated animal intensified. No matter what I go through during my incarceration and hunger strike, nothing will be compared to the everlasting torture that innocent animals endure on a daily basis. And if this court is alarmed by my honesty, let me close with a quote from slave abolitionist William Lloyd Garrison: 'I will be as harsh as the truth and as uncompromising as justice. On this subject, I do not wish to think or speak or write with moderation. I am in earnest. I will not equivocate. I will not excuse. I will not retreat a single inch. And I will be heard. The apathy of the people is enough to make every statue leap from its pedestal and hasten the resurrection of the dead. My influence shall be felt in coming years, not perniciously but beneficially, not as a curse but as a blessing, and posterity will bear testimony that I was right.' There will be no compromise here today because the truth cannot be compromised."

During my seventy-seven day incarceration, I felt lifeless, moribund and enervated. Not from any sort of punishment or correction the system thought it doled out, but from the lack of public compassion and activism for animals. Apathy is a bittersweet plague, which leads to nihilism. And nihilism is the father of inertia, which results in the death of one's emotions. I feel the majority of people submersed in the aversion of revolution have destroyed their humanity. If we can't feel, see, or understand the preciousness of this earth and all of its inhabitants, then why should we be blessed with the gift of existence? This planet could be the most beautiful place imaginable, a place where humans view animals with awe and respect. What a pathetic life I must have led before I heard the cries of the enslaved and the tumult of the animal kingdom. Activism engulfs me. My life is this struggle. From liberator to educator, I continue to fight for interspecies justice.

In the spring of 1997, while on bail for the mink liberation, a few teachers invited me to speak at Canton High School in Michigan. This planted the seed for educational activism and it blossomed wonderfully. I spoke to seven hundred students that day and received a standing ovation. A few weeks later the teachers informed me that one hundred students decided to become vegetarian/vegan. I realised then that education was the most effective form of activism.

Nowadays, I average around two hundred lectures a year! As of 1 January 2014, I've given a total of two thousand four hundred and ninety-five lectures in thirty states at one hundred and eighty institutions to nearly sixty thousand students. Professors tell me I have around a fifteen percent conversion rate, which is remarkable since I walk into every classroom with zero support. They also tell me that fifty to sixty percent of the students drastically reduce their animal product intake. My honesty and genuineness are appreciated by dozens of professors who invite me back year after year. The animals and the students are the only things that matter.

Almost all of my lectures are in private college classes for ethics, philosophy, composition, women's studies, public speaking and sociology students. I never request money from students nor charge professors for the lecture, as I don't believe people should have to pay to learn the truth. I am definitely not a salesperson, marketer, fundraiser or politician. Professors also tell me I bring to life the writings of Peter Singer and Tom Regan. My lecture tour remains the only one of its kind on the planet. Besides the tour, my main focus is compiling an uncompromising amount of vegan information on my website.

Since the information I offer is free, my tour is a money-taker and not a money-maker. Sadly, the animal rights movement is more concerned about image than substance, politics than activism, and fundraising rather than giving freely. Oddly enough, from 2008 to 2011, my tour sponsor was a generous meat-eating philanthropist from California. I mention this because the state of the animal rights movement is fucked up. A meat-eater should not be sponsoring a vegan crusade. But as long as politics is more important than the truth, grassroots activists like me will continue to struggle.

One more thing that keeps hindering animal liberation is the focus on animal welfare instead of animal rights/freedom/liberation. In the book *Dominion*, Matthew Scully explains that people have to choose between being radically kind or radically cruel. This illuminates the hypocrisy of the meat, dairy and egg-eating animal welfare movement, which seeks to regulate the enslavement and killing of billions of animals via 'humane slaughter' laws. By definition alone, slaughter is radically cruel and can never be humane. If cows, pigs, chickens and turkeys go into slaughterhouses alive and come out chopped up into hundreds of pieces, how could anyone claim that animals aren't being mistreated, abused, tortured, terrorised and savagely murdered in these places? How in the world could slaughtering billions of innocents be done with love, humanity and concern? Killing animals via so-called 'humane slaughter' laws doesn't exonerate killers from the killing.

> If every meat-eater logically and compassionately re-evaluated their beliefs, they would understand why veganism is the only ethical and acceptable way to live. Isaac Bashevis Singer, the compassionate Jewish humanitarian who escaped Nazi-occupied Poland, once condemned every meat-eater by stating, "What do they know – all these scholars, all these philosophers, all the leaders of the world? They have convinced themselves that man, the worst transgressor of all the species, is the crown of creation. All other creatures were created merely to provide him with food, pelts, to be tormented, exterminated. In relation to them [animals], all people are Nazis; for the animals it is an eternal Treblinka."

There is no such thing as humane slaughter just as there is no such thing as humane rape, humane slavery or humane child molestation. Buying meat, milk or eggs from free-range, cage-free, grass-fed, organic, local or antibiotic-free facilities, doesn't exonerate the consumer from complicity either. From the animal's point of view, the killers and the consumers are the same.

As an ethical vegan, it is logical to proclaim the only nice slaughterhouse is an empty slaughterhouse. To deny every animal's inherent right to fly, swim and run freely is cruel and dishonest. If given an option, no animal would choose pain or death.

Links:

GaryTofu@earthlink.net

www.adaptt.org

■ THE PRICE OF LIBERTY
Ronnie Lee

▶ Ronnie and Dennis Pickles.

Ronnie Lee describes himself as an 'eco-socialist animal liberationist'. He was a founding member of the Band of Mercy – which later became the Animal Liberation Front – in England in 1973. Ronnie was ALF's press officer from 1978 until 1986.

He spent a total of almost nine years in prison for animal liberation activities. After his release in 1992 from his last prison sentence, he became involved in public education, doing street information stalls on various animal protection issues. Between 2003 and 2011 he was co-ordinator for the greyhound protection organisation, Greyhound Action.

Ronnie now divides his time between vegan outreach work, animal protection campaigning and involvement with the Green Party of England and Wales, where he was founder of the Greens for Animal Protection group...   ■

People often ask me what it was that drove me to risk my liberty for the cause of animal protection. The answer is, quite simply, anger. Raging anger at the arrogant and selfish tyranny of the human species over all the other creatures on this planet. To me it was a war of liberation, a war to free non-human animals from the yoke of human oppression. And as a warrior for those animals, I was quite prepared to risk my freedom in order to win theirs.

This anger grew in me after a friend persuaded me to become vegetarian at the age of nineteen, which led me to discover the full horror of animal exploitation and to become vegan two years later. It was an anger that very quickly caused me to become involved with direct action, first of all with the fox-hunt saboteurs and then as a founder member of the Animal Liberation Front; an anger that led me to spend a total of more than nine years in prison for animal liberationist actions.

Forty years since that anger first exploded inside me, it is still burning just as fiercely, still fuelling me as I drive forward in the battle for animal liberation. But now I harness the energy and determination it gives me more carefully and more thoughtfully and with more of a view to tactics and to strategy. So, although I am still a warrior for the animals, my war is fought for the hearts and minds of ordinary people, through vegan campaigning.

■ DISCOVERING CARNISM
Dr Melanie Joy

"All truth passes through three stages. First, it is ridiculed. Second, it is violently opposed. Third, it is accepted as being self-evident."   ■

—Arthur Schopenhauer.

Melanie Joy, PhD, EdM, is a Harvard-educated psychologist, professor of psychology and sociology at the University of Massachusetts, Boston, celebrated speaker, and author of the award-winning book *Why We Love Dogs, Eat Pigs, and Wear Cows*, soon to be published in nine languages. Dr Joy was the eighth recipient of the Institute of Jainology's Ahimsa Award (past recipients include the Dalai Lama and Nelson Mandela), which she was presented with in the House of Commons in London. She also received the Empty Cages Prize, presented in Milan, Italy.

▶ Melanie Joy with rescued pig at Farm Sanctuary, USA.

Dr Joy's work has been featured in media venues around the world, including National Public Radio, PBS, the BBC, Radio Canada, Germany's ARD, ABC Australia and *The New York Times*. Dr Joy has given her critically acclaimed carnism presentation across the United States and in sixteen other countries. She is also the author of *Strategic Action for Animals*, and she has written a number of articles on psychology, animal protection and social justice. Dr Joy is the founder and president of the Carnism Awareness and Action Network...   ■

Learning to Kill

Traumatic memories are unique. They are immune to the passing of time and remain eternally present, evoking images and feelings as clear and powerful as when the event took place. Perhaps this is why, after more than forty years, I can recall in such detail the time I killed my first and last animal. And perhaps this is also why I found myself on the path toward veganism at such an early age.

I was around four years old, enjoying a typical summer day with my parents on my father's fishing boat. My child-sized fishing pole was in its usual place, in a holder on the side of the boat next to my parents' larger ones, the lines gracefully dragging along the water as we cruised slowly forward. I was meandering around the deck, when suddenly my line became taut. Without missing a beat, my father sprang to the throttle to turn off the engine and then both my parents rushed to grab my straining pole, cheering and calling me to their sides. Holding the pole, I remember being surprised that it felt so heavy; the line was so unyielding that I couldn't pull it in on my own. My father stood behind me, his strong hands steadying my pole and cranking the reel as I yanked with him. And with his help, I pulled a blackfish out of the water, flung her onto the blinding white deck of the boat, and stared as she flopped wildly and helplessly, gasping for breath. My parents applauded me and yet I felt numb, guilty, and confused – how was I supposed to celebrate that I had just killed someone?

Of course, at the time I couldn't comprehend – let alone express – the complex dilemma I was in, wanting to believe in and please my parents and yet feeling a deep aversion to killing animals. So my aversion disguised itself, expressing itself in more subtle ways. My father's boat, once an oasis to me, became a source of distress; on our outings I would cry whenever someone caught a fish and beg my father to throw him or her back in. And fish, which had been my favourite food, suddenly became disgusting to me; the smell was sickening and I threw up when I was coaxed into eating it, so that eventually my parents gave up trying to serve it to me. Unbeknownst to me, by the time I was just five years old, I had eliminated the first group of animal products from my diet. And I had had my first experience of *moral disgust*, an issue I would spend years researching and one that would play a critical role in shaping my theory of carnism.

Learning to Love

Another experience that shaped my veganism and my activism was my relationship with my companion animals, the first of whom was my dog, Fritz. My parents adopted Fritz when he and I were both babies, and we grew up together; Fritz was a part of our family until he died at the age of thirteen. During his life, Fritz and I were inseparable: we played together, we napped together, and we were even punished together when, for example, I would be caught slipping him my food under the dinner table.

Fritz was my first dog, my first sibling, my first friend, and my first heartbreak. My relationship with Fritz had a profound influence on me; it taught me, among other things, that authentic and lasting bonds can and do form between human and non-human beings, that love need not – should not – be limited by arbitrary boundaries such as species. Indeed, my relationship with Fritz, and later with my other companion animals, helped preserve my natural empathy and compassion for non-human beings, qualities all children harbour toward other animals but which the dominant, meat-eating culture breeds out of us as we become 'mature' adults. These qualities, the emotional counterparts to my rational conception of justice, were integral in leading me along the path to veganism.

Learning to Eat

Despite the natural connection I felt with my companion animals, and the fact I considered myself an 'animal lover', it was another decade before I realised that loving someone meant not eating them. It was 1989, and I had recently awoken to find myself hooked up to intravenous antibiotics at Beth Israel Hospital in Boston after having eaten what turned out to be my last hamburger. According to my doctors, and to the Department of Public Health, I had contracted campylobacter from consuming tainted meat at the diner I'd made the mistake of patronising several days earlier.

Contracting campylobacter was one of the worst experiences of my life; I had never been so ill and I truly felt I could die from the pain. But contracting campylobacter was also one of the best experiences of my life; it was a turning point for me. Before getting sick, I had been increasingly uncomfortable with the idea of eating meat, having witnessed on a handful of occasions the horrors of animal agriculture. But I hadn't been ready to allow the truth about how animals are turned into food to penetrate my consciousness; I couldn't take in the reality of animal agriculture until I was ready to make the behavioural changes that would inevitably follow. You could say I was like a vegan living in a meat eater's body. But the campylobacter really lit a fire under my butt, so to speak; after getting sick I never wanted to touch another burger, or any meat, again. So I didn't. And over time, I discontinued eating and wearing all products procured from the bodies of animals.

And as my behaviour shifted, so did my paradigm – I didn't see different things; I saw the same things differently. I became increasingly open to learning the truth about animal agriculture, and the more I learnt, the more I felt compelled to share that information with others. My veganism evolved into activism. I thought, perhaps naively but quite understandably, that if everyone just knew 'The Truth' about animal agriculture, the world would be vegan. But of course, the facts don't sell the ideology. Not even close.

And so I began to ponder this odd phenomenon. When it came to eating animals, I wondered, how was it possible for rational, caring people like myself, in the words of psychiatrist and social activist Robert Jay Lifton, to 'just stop thinking?' This question was to lay the course for a journey of exploration that transformed the way I understood and related to the issue of eating animals, a journey that was to become my life's work.

Learning to Think

I spent nearly two decades seeking answers to the question of how people could 'just stop thinking' when it came to eating animals, how humane people could participate in inhumane practices without realising what they were doing. This investigation ultimately culminated in my doctoral dissertation on the psychology of eating meat. For my research, I interviewed vegans, vegetarians, meat eaters, meat cutters, butchers and people who had raised and killed their own animals for food. And what I found was that there was much more to the picture than simply individual attitudes and behaviours toward animals. Individual beliefs and practices don't exist in a vacuum and they don't come out of nowhere. The practice of eating animals, I discovered, stems from an invisible belief system that conditions people to shut down their awareness so that corpses are perceived as cuisine. This belief system I came to call *carnism*.

Carnism is a dominant, violent belief system, or ideology, that operates very much like other dominant ideologies – such as sexism, racism and classism – whose tenets run counter to core human values. Carnism uses a set of social and psychological defence mechanisms so that caring, rational people unwittingly enable brutal, illogical practices. The primary defence of the system is invisibility, and the primary way the system remains invisible is by remaining unnamed – if we don't name it, we won't see it and if we don't see it we can't question or challenge it. The invisibility of carnism is why eating animals is seen as a given rather than a choice and it's also what empowers the other defences of the system. Imagine, for example, how much less power the Three Ns of Justification (which teach us that eating animals is *normal, natural* and *necessary*) would have, were they exposed as carnistic myths, rather than embraced as objective facts and universal truths.

Carnism conditions us to disconnect from the truth of our experience, psychologically and emotionally. It distorts our perceptions such that we don't think of the meat on our plate as a dead animal and therefore we don't feel disgusted by it. And disgust, it turns out, is a moral emotion. Disgust arises when we are confronted with eating (or smelling) something we find morally offensive. My research on disgust was what finally gave meaning and words to my early aversion to eating fish and other aquatic life; though my young mind was unable to grasp the moral implications of killing an animal, some deeper part of me recognised and responded to my internal conflict. The disgust I felt helped to protect me from further violating my morality.

So, through extensive conditioning and continued reinforcement, carnism blocks our thoughts and feelings when it comes to eating 'edible' animals, thereby enabling us to consume them. Carnism, essentially, teaches us not to think or feel.

Learning to Take Action

After spending years buried in my doctoral studies, I emerged with a theory but without a clear understanding of how to *use* that theory, how to apply what I'd learnt in order to actively bring about change for farmed animals and ultimately to work toward animal liberation. The last thing I wanted was for my dissertation to be relegated to the back shelves of the University of Michigan Archives, the storeroom (and often the burial ground) for all US theses. And as I pondered ways to construct a strategy from my theory, I realised that strategy in and of itself was essential to the success of the animal liberation movement – that the most important contribution I could make was to support those who were already doing the crucial work of creating positive change for animals. So I put my work on carnism on hold and focused all my attention on putting together a comprehensive strategic approach to animal liberation, to empower the courageous activists and advocates on the front lines of the movement. This effort materialised into my first book, *Strategic Action for Animals*.

Learning to Listen

During the course of writing *Strategic Action for Animals*, there came a turning point that again shifted the trajectory of my activism and my life. My publisher decided I should remove the chapter I had included on carnism, as he felt it wasn't a fit for the book. I was discussing this restructuring of my manuscript one night with a dear friend and colleague, who said to me, "Melanie, you need to turn that chapter into a book on carnism. That's the work you're meant to be doing now. I've always known it; it's just taken a while for you to figure it out."

And my friend was right. From the moment I realised my purpose was to raise awareness about carnism, life unfolded in the way it only seems to when we're truly following the path we're meant to be on. As soon as *Strategic Action* was in press, I began writing my book on carnism, *Why We Love Dogs, Eat Pigs, and Wear Cows*. People who would become critical to the success of the book – including my editor, agent, publisher, publicist and a variety of others whose paths crossed mine at just the right moment and in just the right way, emerged with little or no effort on my part, sometimes even seeking me out without even knowing I was working on a manuscript. This is not to say the process of writing a book isn't arduous, painstaking, and lengthy! But I found myself surrounded by support and guidance and yes, luck, every step of the way, enabling me to push through what sometimes felt like overwhelming challenges, both personally and professionally.

Learning to Live

The publication of *Why We Love Dogs...* was of course not the end of my journey as a vegan activist, but another turning point along the way. It has given me a platform from which I can more effectively raise consciousness about the violent system that is carnism. It has enabled me to help weaken the system by exposing it, and by empowering vegans through giving them a new frame with which to understand it and new tools with which to challenge it. It has enabled me to remain inspired in the midst of a world replete with animal suffering, as I have the opportunity to connect with vegans around the world, the unsung heroes of a movement that will no doubt be looked back upon as having brought about one of the most important social transformations in the history of humankind.

And so I began to ponder this odd phenomenon. When it came to eating animals, I wondered, how was it possible for rational, caring people like myself, in the words of psychiatrist and social activist Robert Jay Lifton, to 'just stop thinking?' This question was to lay the course for a journey of exploration that transformed the way I understood and related to the issue of eating animals, a journey that was to become my life's work. ∎

I owe my veganism and my activism to my companions and compatriots, to my non-human friends who helped teach me the true meaning of kindness and justice, and to my human friends who remind me, daily, that beneath and beyond the labyrinthine fortress of carnism lies a truth that cannot be destroyed: *we care.* Meat eaters care, which is why they feel compelled to turn away from the atrocity that is carnism; and vegans care, which is why they feel compelled to speak out against the atrocity that is carnism. We care about the truth, about justice, and about the other beings with whom we share the planet. Our caring can be dimmed but not extinguished; it can be hidden but not abolished.

◼ THE ABOLITIONIST APPROACH TO ANIMAL RIGHTS AND VEGANISM AS THE MORAL BASELINE

Professor Gary L Francione

"Nonhumans will continue to be exploited until there is a revolution of the human spirit, and that will not happen without visionaries trying to change the paradigm that has become accustomed to, and tolerant of, patriarchal violence." ◼

—Gary L Francione.

▷ Gary L Francione with Stratton, Emma, Robert, Stevie and Chelsea.

Gary L Francione is Board of Governors Professor, Distinguished Professor of Law, and Nicholas deB Katzenbach Scholar of Law and Philosophy at Rutgers University School of Law in Newark, New Jersey. Professor Francione received his BA in philosophy from the University of Rochester and his MA in philosophy and his JD from the University of Virginia. He studied philosophy in Great Britain as a Phi Beta Kappa Scholar. He was articles editor of the *Virginia Law Review*. After graduation, he clerked for the late Judge Albert Tate, Jr, US Court of Appeals for the Fifth Circuit, and for Justice Sandra Day O'Connor of the US Supreme Court. He practised law in New York City before joining the faculty at the University of Pennsylvania Law School in 1984, where he was tenured in 1987. He joined the Rutgers faculty in 1989.

Professor Francione has been teaching animal rights theory and law for more than twenty-five years. He has lectured on the topic throughout the United States, Canada and Europe, and has been a guest on numerous radio and television shows. He is well known throughout the animal protection movement for his criticism of animal welfare law and the property status of nonhuman animals, and for his theory on animal rights.

He is the author of numerous books and articles on animal rights theory and animals and the law. His most recent book, *Eat Like You Care: An Examination of the Morality of Eating Animals*, (with Anna Charlton), was published in 2013. His other books include: *The Animal Rights Debate: Abolition or Regulation?* (with Robert Garner, 2010); *Animals as Persons: Essays on the Abolition of Animal Exploitation* (2008); *Introduction to Animal Rights: Your Child or the Dog?* (2000); *Rain Without Thunder: The Ideology of the Animal Rights Movement* (1996); *Animals, Property, and the Law* (1995); and *Vivisection and Dissection in the Classroom: A Guide to Conscientious Objection* (with Anna Charlton, 1992).

Professor Francione is the co-editor, with Professor Gary Steiner, of a series, *Critical Perspectives on Animals: Theory, Culture, Science and Law*, published by Columbia University Press. He has also written in the areas of copyright, patent law, and law and science.

Professor Francione and his colleague, Adjunct Professor Anna Charlton, started and operated the Rutgers Animal Rights Law Clinic from 1990-2000, making Rutgers the first university in the

US to have animal rights law as part of the regular academic curriculum and to award students academic credit, not only for classroom work, but also for work on actual cases involving animal issues. Professor Francione and Professor Charlton currently teach a course on human rights and animal rights, and a seminar on animal rights theory and the law. He also teaches criminal law, criminal procedure, torts and evidence…   ∎

Animal Use and Animal Treatment

We've got to get people to the point where they see that it's the *use* of animals that's morally wrong and that it's not just a matter of whether the *treatment* of animals is 'humane'. If we cannot justify the use of animals, then any amount of suffering and killing, even if painless, is morally objectionable.

There is a crucial distinction between my views and those of Peter Singer and it focuses precisely on this distinction between use and treatment. One of the fundamental premises of the animal welfare movement is that animals can suffer, and their interest in not suffering is morally relevant, but they don't have an interest in continued existence. Therefore, using and killing animals for human purposes is acceptable as long as we do not impose 'too much' suffering in the process.

If you look at the history of the animal welfare movement, which started in Britain in the late eighteenth/early nineteenth century, you see the recognition that animal suffering matters morally and the acceptance of an obligation owed directly to animals to take their suffering into consideration. We have an obligation to treat them 'humanely'. It is at this time when the welfarist approach became politically and legally popular and, throughout the nineteenth century, you see the emergence of laws that were intended to provide for animal welfare. If you read Jeremy Bentham, who was one of several important spokespersons for the animal welfare position, he makes it clear that although animals can suffer, and that their suffering matters morally, they are different from us as a cognitive matter. They are not self-aware in the way that we are. They don't have an interest in continuing to live so it is morally acceptable to use them as long as we treat them in a way that respects their interest in not suffering. According to Bentham, the cow doesn't care *that* we kill and eat her, she only cares about *how* we treat her while she is alive, and how we kill her. She doesn't care about the ending of her life because she has no sense of the future and we are not harming her by depriving her of future existence.

Peter Singer, whose views are derived directly from Bentham, maintains that most of the animals we routinely exploit do not have a sense of the future, and that if they don't have a sense of the future, they are not reflectively self-aware, and if they are not reflectively self-aware they don't have an interest in their lives, and so killing them is not per se harming them. As long as we provide them with a reasonably pleasant life and a relatively painless death, our use of animals as human resources is morally defensible. So for welfarists, it's just a matter of whether or not the treatment of animals involves too much suffering. Although Singer more recently appears to think that more of the animals we routinely exploit *may* have 'some' sense of the future, he has thus far failed to recognise that they have the same kind of morally significant interest in continued existence that he accords to humans, nonhuman great apes, marine mammals and elephants, and that would make veganism a moral baseline in a way that would prevent him from supporting campaigns for 'happy' exploitation.

My view is that that is wrong as a philosophical matter. That involves a speciesist notion of self-awareness.

Because you and I are animals who use language, or symbolic communication, my guess is that our sense of consciousness and our self-awareness are probably different from the sense of self-awareness that a nonhuman animal has. Our cognition is a function of the concepts we employ in our language. But so what? The rescued dogs who share our home are self-aware, but they are just self-aware in a different way, that's all. You can't jump to the conclusion that, as a factual matter, they do not have a preference, a desire, or a want to continue to live because they may not be able to recognise themselves in mirrors (although some animals clearly do) or they don't wear wrist watches or plan vacations.

The notion that nonhuman animals do not have an interest in continued existence – that they do not have an interest in their lives – involves relying on a speciesist concept of what sort of self-awareness matters morally. I have argued that every sentient being necessarily has an interest in continued existence – every sentient being values her or his life – and that to say that only those animals (human animals) who have a particular sort of self-awareness have an interest in not being treated as commodities begs the fundamental moral question. *Even if*, as some maintain, nonhuman animals live in an 'eternal present' – and I think that is empirically not the case at the very least for most of the nonhumans we routinely exploit who do have memories of the past and a sense of the future – they have, *in each moment*, an interest in continuing to exist. To say that this does not count morally is simply speciesist.

Singer is *the* philosopher of the animal welfare movement. I would say that most of the large animal organisations buy into Singer's notion that killing an animal per se is not harming an animal. There are many animal advocates who are horrified by the fact that PETA takes in a large number of animals at its shelter in Norfolk, Virginia, and they kill approximately ninety-five percent of them. These advocates say, "How could PETA do that?" I think it's fairly clear that they accept Singer's notion that killing an animal is not harming the animal per se as long as you kill the animal in a painless way.

The welfarist tradition, of course, fits very well with the idea that humans were created in God's image and that animals exist for our use. In any event, many people assume that it's all right to use animals and think it's just a question of treating them 'humanely'. Many people are aware of what goes on in slaughterhouses and, indeed, what goes on throughout the life of the animal and they recognise on some level that it is not good. But they have this hope – unfounded in my view – that it can be made better and, because they think the use of animals is, as a general matter, morally acceptable, the question becomes only one of treatment. So they continue to consume animals and animal products but they support efforts – usually in the form of a donation to some large organisation – to make treatment more 'humane'. This involves a certain amount of self-deception, a certain amount of culture and tradition, and this overarching belief that we are closer to God than are nonhumans. But then, you could make the same observation about sexism, racism, homophobia and other forms of human discrimination. For example, we have a religious and cultural context in which white, straight males have been privileged over women and gays. The discriminatory thinking is similar to what goes on with animals. People are increasingly uneasy about some human discrimination (but not all) so we're making some changes, but not nearly enough and not quickly enough.

The Principle of 'Unnecessary' Suffering

Why are some of us more sensitive? Why are some of our sensibilities different? I have no idea. I think that some of it has to do with taking morality seriously. In many ways, a characteristic of our time is that many people are moral nihilists; they reject moral realism, the notion that moral statements can be, and at least some are, objectively true. We don't talk in terms of moral concepts anymore. We talk about religion, but religion and morality are not necessarily the same thing. We have lost the concept of realism. Morality is for many people really no different from being an aesthetic matter, similar to asking whether classical music is better than rock music. This does not mean that these people necessarily act immorally; it means only that they do not have a framework within which to analyse moral problems when they are confronted with those problems.

I am very much a realist and I believe in the existence of moral facts. One of those moral facts is that, other things being equal, it is wrong to inflict suffering or death on a sentient being unnecessarily. I have never met anyone who disagreed with that. People can disagree with what constitutes necessity, but we all agree that inflicting unnecessary suffering and death on sentient beings, human or nonhuman, is wrong. If 'necessity' means anything in this context, it means that we cannot inflict unnecessary suffering and death on nonhuman animals for reasons of pleasure, amusement, or convenience. But yet, 99.9% of the use of animals that we engage in can be justified only by reasons of pleasure, amusement, or convenience. For example, we don't eat animals and animal products because we have to. On the contrary, no one maintains seriously that animal foods are necessary for optimal health; indeed, mainstream health care people are increasingly of the view that animal foods are killing us. And animal agriculture is an ecological nightmare. We eat them because we enjoy the taste; we eat them because animal foods are convenient. But pleasure and amusement cannot suffice as a moral matter.

In 2007, an American football player named Michael Vick was arrested because he had a dog fighting operation at a property he owned in Virginia. He ended up going to prison for several years. He is now out of prison and is playing football again. But people are still angry with Vick because of what he did with and to those dogs. It was pretty horrific. But Vick's case provides an excellent example of the delusional way in which we think about nonhuman animals. I often begin public lectures by talking about Michael Vick. It goes something like this:

"Let's focus on Michael Vick for a second. What he did was a bad thing, wasn't it?"
"Yes. Absolutely. He is a terrible person."
"Why is he a terrible person?"
"Because he tortured and killed those dogs."
"But we accept that it is sometimes morally acceptable to inflict great pain and death on dogs—for instance, in research intended to find a cure for serious human illnesses." [Note: I do not believe that any vivisection is morally justifiable; I just use this approach to get a general audience involved intellectually in the discussion.]
"But what Vick did was not like that; it was wrong."
"Why was it wrong?"
"Because he was just doing it because he enjoyed it. There was no reason for hurting those dogs. He did it just because he enjoyed it."
"So it was wrong because Vick inflicted suffering and death on animals only for reasons of pleasure and amusement. But how, then, can we justify eating animals? We kill fifty-six billion animals a year for food, and that does not include fish. Why are we doing that?"

A discussion ensues and we quickly get to the bottom line: We have no better answer than Michael Vick had. He liked sitting around a fighting pit watching dogs rip each other apart; we like sitting around the summer barbeque roasting the corpses of animals who have probably been treated worse than the animals that Mike Vick fought.

We then have a further discussion that can often last for hours and always – and I mean always – ends in at least several people telling me that they never thought about the issue that way and they are going vegan. But the bottom line is that this really is not rocket science; most of our animal use is transparently frivolous. Most of our animal use violates a moral principle that we all claim to accept: that the imposition of unnecessary suffering and death is morally wrong. I regard all vivisection as morally unjustifiable but it is our *only* use of animals that is not transparently frivolous.

Moral schizophrenia is the notion that schizophrenia as a psychiatric or psychological concept involves a delusional way of thinking, and I honestly believe that when it comes to animals we act in literally delusional ways. We can get so horribly upset about what Mike Vick did and at the same time be sitting around a dinner table eating hamburgers or steaks or fish or ice cream, talking about what a bad guy Michael Vick is. I work with rescue groups because I think it's a good use of time to try to get animals out of these shelters and into homes. I believe that their lives have value and I don't believe that killing them is an acceptable solution. A lot of these rescue people are not vegetarians or vegans. These are sincere and committed people who have jobs and families but spend every minute of their spare time trying to get animals out of shelters; trying to save dogs and cats at the same time they are eating chickens and pigs and cows and eggs, and dairy, etc. I deal with this all the time, every day of my life. It is a delusional way of thinking but it's fairly common. So much for humans being rational animals!

I think it is important to take morality seriously. And if we took seriously the one principle with which we all agree – that it's wrong to inflict unnecessary suffering on animals – we would be committed on an individual level to stop eating, wearing, or otherwise using nonhuman animals. And if enough of us stopped demanding animal products, we could have a major impact. I should also say that although I think we can get to a position of no exploitation based only on rational argument, the bottom line is that if someone does not care, rational argument is not going to work. Caring is a different matter. I think that has a spiritual component. Notice that I did not say 'religious'. I said 'spiritual'.

Shifting the Paradigm: Creative, Nonviolent Vegan Education

In my view, the key to change is creative, nonviolent vegan education. It's really important how you get the message across. If people sense that you are judging them and condemning them, then they will shut down. I've learnt as a teacher that the way to get a student to understand something is by working with the student where the student is. Belittling someone in any educational context is a prescription for disaster. When I'm talking with people who do animal rescue, I don't say to them, "You're a terrible person because you eat meat." They're not terrible people; they are people who, in my judgment, are not thinking in a clear way, but who are doing an enormous amount of good to help animals. What I'm trying to do is get them to see that there's no difference between the dog they're trying to get out of the shelter before the shelter kills the dog or the chicken that they're eating tonight at dinner.

But our vegan education should be clear and consistent. We should never be promoting the false idea that there is a moral distinction between flesh and dairy or eggs; or between fur and wool or leather; or between eating animals or wearing them. That just confuses people. And it should confuse people. Those distinctions make no sense. If we talk with an omnivore about why she should go vegan, and she cares and wants to change, but is not ready to go all the way immediately, she will take whatever incremental steps she wants to take. We should, however, never promote the idea that some forms of animal exploitation are morally acceptable or different from other forms of animal exploitation.

In the 1980s I was trying to move the 'movement' in the direction of vegan education and it just didn't work. I argued that we ought to take all of our resources, all of our time, all of our energy, and put it into creative, nonviolent, vegan education. We ought to shift the paradigm. As long as people are eating, wearing and using animals, they're never going to find their moral compass. Forget about anti-fur campaigns, forget about veal crates; just focus on one thing: veganism. Once people get the vegan idea everything else changes. Until people get the vegan idea, nothing changes. But the 'movement' opted for characterising veganism as difficult and instead, chose to promote single-issue campaigns, which I regard as useless.

A case in point: the anti-fur campaign. I have been in this movement now for almost thirty years. As a matter of fact, the fur campaign was going on before I got involved. The fur industry is stronger now than it's ever been. More people wear fur than used to be the case. At least when you went to London people didn't wear fur. Now you see fur in London again. Another case in point was the veal campaign. For a while a lot of people were not eating veal but now they're being told by all these large organisations that veal is more 'humane'. Veal consumption is going up again. We need to reject the insidious notion that there is a morally right way of doing this. There is no morally right way to do any of this; it is all wrong.

We need to shift the paradigm. We don't sit around and say that we ought to have rules to make child molestation 'compassionate', or that we ought to have 'humane' child molestation. No one would have a discussion like that; indeed, most people would find it offensive. But we have these discussions when it comes to animals.

One of the things I hear frequently is that animal exploitation is pervasive and so we need to take 'baby steps' with regard to welfare reform. I have two replies. First, child molestation is pervasive; so is rape. But we don't sit around and say "How can we have humane rape?" or "Let's try to achieve more compassionate child molestation." No, we say "You shouldn't have any rape and you shouldn't have any child molestation." Even though these are pervasive problems we don't seem to think that the solution is to regulate them and make them 'better'. We agree that the solution is to advocate for their abolition and that's what we ought to do with animal exploitation.

Second, a central thesis of my work has been that because animals are considered as chattel property – they are economic commodities – we will generally protect animal interests only when we get an economic benefit from doing so. This means the standard of animal welfare will always be very low (as it is presently, despite all of the 'happy' and 'compassionate' exploitation nonsense) and welfare reforms will generally *increase* production efficiency; that is, we will protect animal interests in situations where treatment is economically inefficient and welfare reforms will, for the most part, do little more than correct those inefficiencies. For example, the use of gestation crates for sows is economically inefficient; there are supposedly more 'humane' alternatives that actually increase production efficiency. Similarly, using controlled-atmosphere killing with chickens is more economically efficient than electrical stunning.

Animal welfare reforms, apart from being morally inadequate, do nothing practically. Indeed, they make the public feel more comfortable about continuing to exploit animals. We've had animal welfare for two hundred years and we're exploiting more animals now in more horrific ways than at any point in human history. So animal welfare doesn't work. *The only way things are going to ever change is if the paradigm shifts.* The only way the paradigm will shift is if we stop thinking about animals as resources. The only way to stop thinking of them as resources is to move away from the *treatment* issue to the *use* issue and recognise that animal use – however 'humane' – is wrong. No matter how nicely they're treated, it is wrong to use and kill them. No matter how nicely you treat slaves, slavery is a bad idea. No matter how gently you rape someone, it is a bad thing to do. No matter how kind you are to a child that you molest, it is wrong. No matter how well you treat animals you use as resources – although, as I discussed above, I don't think you'll ever treat the animal very well, particularly in a mass distribution system – it is wrong to use them for your own pleasure, amusement or convenience. We need to shift from concern about treatment to rejection of use. We need to move away from welfare towards what I call the abolitionist approach. Abolition as a social matter must begin with the individual embracing veganism as her personal acceptance of abolition, her personal rejection of the notion that animals are things, property, resources for us to use.

Veganism is the moral baseline for the abolitionist approach to animal rights; and abolitionist theory, as I have developed it, rejects violence. I see it as a nonviolent movement; violence is not an answer to anything. I hear some animal advocates say that it is morally acceptable to inflict violence on 'animal exploiters'. But in a society in which virtually everyone exploits animals, everyone is an animal exploiter. If you are willing to inflict violence on a vivisector, you have to see as justifiable the infliction of violence on your non-vegan parents, spouse, children, or friends. In any event, human history is a history of violence. If violence were a solution to anything, we'd be living in a Garden of Eden now. Violence doesn't work; it only begets more violence.

Conclusion

I think we're facing a profound spiritual and cultural crisis. God is no longer dead, as Nietzsche declared, but the God who has been resurrected is not a particularly kind, compassionate or loving one. The emerging religious movements have tended towards serious intolerance and have departed in many ways from the people who were involved in establishing those traditions. When I look at the right wing Christian movement in the United States, for example, I see *no* similarity between it and the teachings of Jesus Christ. On the other hand, as I mentioned above, moral discourse is rapidly vanishing and is being replaced by a sort of moral relativism, which, I think, leads to a lot of mischief. We are increasingly violent. We have disrupted the ecology in a dramatic way.

Maybe I am not being realistic but, despite it all, I have not lost my optimism. Yes, human beings are often irrational, spiritually bankrupt, and violent. But it does not have to be that way. We are capable of great achievement. It is sad, however, that we put so much of our creativity into building harmful things rather than into building peace.

■ DEAD COW WALKING
Marc Bekoff

"Who we eat is a serious moral question and it's incredibly easy to change who goes in our mouth."   ■

—Marc Bekoff.

▶ Marc Bekoff and Bessie.

Marc Bekoff, PhD, is Professor Emeritus of Ecology and Evolutionary Biology at the University of Colorado, Boulder, and co-founder with Jane Goodall of Ethologists for the Ethical Treatment of Animals. He has won many awards for his scientific research including the Exemplar Award from the Animal Behaviour Society and a Guggenheim Fellowship. Marc has published more than nine hundred articles, numerous books, and has edited three encyclopedias. His books include the Encyclopedia of Animal Rights and Animal Welfare, The Ten Trusts (with Jane Goodall), the *Encyclopedia of Animal Behavior*, the *Encyclopedia of Human-Animal Relationships, Minding Animals, Animal Passions and Beastly Virtues: Reflections on Redecorating Nature, The Emotional Lives of Animals, Animals Matter, Animals at Play: Rules of the Game* (a children's book), *Wild Justice: The Moral Lives of Animals* (with Jessica Pierce), *The Animal Manifesto: Six Reasons For Increasing Our Compassion Footprint, Ignoring Nature No More: The Case For Compassionate Conservation, Jasper's Story: Saving Moon Bears* (with Jill Robinson), Ignoring Nature No More: The Case for Compassionate Conservation, *Why Dogs Hump and Bees Get Depressed: The Fascinating Science of Animal Intelligence, Emotions, Friendship, and Conservation,* and *Rewilding Our Hearts: Building Pathways of Compassion and Coexistence.* In 2005 Marc was presented with The Bank One Faculty Community Service Award for the work he has done with children, senior citizens, and prisoners. In 2009 he was presented with the St. Francis of Assisi Award by the Auckland SPCA...   ■

Our relationships with nonhuman animals ('animals') are frustrating, challenging, paradoxical, and all over the place (Bekoff 2007, 2010; Bekoff and Pierce 2009). We are continually challenged by our interactions with other animals and in many ways they help us come to terms with who we are – big-brained, big-footed, overproducing, overconsuming, arrogant and invasive mammals. We can and do wreak havoc all over the planet, but we also do many wonderful things. There's nothing to be gained by bashing our species, and being positive about who we are and what we can do has benefits for other animals who depend on our goodwill and concern for their lives.

Everyone matters and makes a difference. In my work with Jane Goodall's *Roots & Shoots* programs we concentrate on empowering members to realise that each and every individual counts and each of us can make positive differences for all animals, nonhuman and human, and that we must work together as a cohesive community to make this happen globally. We stress that kids are ambassadors for social change including our attitudes toward animals.[1]

Considering *who*, not *what* we choose to eat can make a huge difference. Mass media and others conveniently mask the fact that a hamburger, for example, is really a dead cow on a bun and since it isn't called a cowburger there are people who don't know they're eating a being who used to moo. Likewise, when people eat bacon, lettuce and tomato sandwiches, they're really eating Babe, lettuce and tomato sandwiches, and you can be sure that the cow or pig who provided the meal into which you're sinking your teeth suffered immensely during his or her journey to your bun. The plate on which this unnecessary meal is sitting is a platter of death and as unpalatable as this might sound, you're eating misery.[2]

This might sound harsh but those are the facts even if the cow was one of a very lucky few who walked up Temple Grandin's purportedly humane 'stairway to heaven.' Dr Grandin is famous for making the living conditions of cows more humane *but only an incredibly tiny fraction of a percentage of cows who contribute to the more than fourteen billion hamburgers eaten yearly in the United States benefit from these superficial niceties*, and their lives are still filled with misery and untold pain and suffering before they're killed and on their way to your mouth. A 'better' life on a factory farm isn't close to being marginally 'good'.[3] Surely, nobody would choose to send his or her dog to a factory farm.

Cows are sentient mammals who are very intelligent. They worry over what they don't understand and have been shown to experience 'eureka' moments when they solve a puzzle such as how to open a particularly difficult gate. Cows communicate by staring and it's likely we don't understand their very subtle ways of communicating. They also form close and enduring relationships with family members and friends. They don't like to have their families and social networks disrupted, nor do they like being subjected to the reprehensible conditions to which they are exposed during their transport to the factory farm or concentrated animal feeding operations (CAFOs) and their short stay at these filthy and inhumane facilities. They also suffer not only their own pains but also the pains of other cows who are their short-term roommates on the way to your plate (Bekoff 2013, 2014). Because cows are sentient one should really ask, "*Who's* for dinner?" not "*What's* for dinner?" Who we eat is a serious moral question.

Pigs, chickens and other food animals also experience deep and rich emotions; we've recently learnt that chickens are empathic and feel the pain of other chickens.[4] Fish too are now viewed differently based on solid scientific research. Fish are not stupid or unfeeling, but rather sentient beings who don't like being hooked and cooked.[5] The same is true for many other animals who previously were thought to be unfeeling objects suitable for consumption.[6]

Each of us can make more ethical and humane choices about the food that – or more correctly *who* – formerly sentient and feeling beings – end up in our mouths. Excuses such as "Oh, I know they suffer, but don't show me because I love my burger," adds cruelty to the world because you're eating animals who do really care about what happens to them and to their family and friends. Indeed, as one of my friends who works 'in the industry' has told me time and again, when you're eating meat you're eating misery. And, most likely, you're also eating filth and disease.

You still can go to most burger joints and order a healthy vegetarian or vegan meal and know you're not only saving cows and the planet but also adding compassion to a severely wounded world. By replacing mindless eating with mindful compassionate eating, each of us can make a positive difference that will benefit ourselves and future generations, our children and theirs, who depend on our goodwill, as they will inherit what we leave in our wake. It's easy to expand our compassion footprint (Bekoff 2010) so let's all do it now.

We must also be nice to the people we want to reach. Fighting fire with fire doesn't work so no matter how difficult it is, engage others with kindness, compassion and understanding and show them – don't tell them or make them feel inferior or stupid – that they can easily make a positive difference for animals and the environment.

So, no more lame excuses. It's easy to reduce unnecessary cruelty on out planet. Respecting and loving animals is a panacea for the future as is working with kids. Their unbridled enthusiasm is inspiring and contagious, so teach the children well. Let's not let down future generations, as they will have to survive the decisions we make.

References

Bekoff, M. 2002. *Minding animals: Awareness, emotions and heart.* Oxford University Press, New York.

Bekoff, M. 2007. *The emotional lives of animals.* New World Library, Novato, California.

Bekoff, M. and Pierce, J. 2009. *Wild justice: The moral lives of animals.* University of Chicago Press, Chicago.

Bekoff, M. 2010. *The animal manifesto: Six reasons for expanding our compassion footprint.* New World Library, Novato, California.

Bekoff, M. 2013. *Why dogs hump and bees get depressed: The fascinating science of animal intelligence, emotions, friendship, and conservation.* New World Library, Novato, California.

Bekoff, M. 2014. *Rewilding our hearts: Building pathways of compassion and coexistence.* New World Library, Novato, California.

Endnotes:

[1.] (http://www.rootsandshoots.org/)

[2.] (http://www.psychologytoday.com/blog/animal-emotions/201012/dead-cow-walking)

3. (http://www.psychologytoday.com/blog/animal-emotions/201002/going-slaughter-should-animals-hope-meet-temple-grandin)

4. (http://www.psychologytoday.com/blog/animal-emotions/201103/empathic-chickens-and-cooperative-elephants-emotional-intelligence-expands-its-range-again)

5. (http://www.psychologytoday.com/blog/animal-emotions/201101/do-fish-feel-pain-redux-interview-the-author-who-shows-course-they-do)

6. (http://www.psychologytoday.com/blog/animal-emotions/201006/vegans-and-oysters-if-you-eat-oysters-youre-not-vegan-so-why-the-question)

■ THAT'S WHY WE DON'T EAT ANIMALS
Ruby Roth

> *"By changing what we eat, we can change our minds and the world we live in. By making vegan choices, we activate our personal agency and influence the public realm, reaching every major industry and every corner of the earth. In our commitment to the wellbeing of others, we practise the embodiment of love and herein lies the tremendous transformative power of veganism."* ■

—Ruby Roth.

Ruby Roth is the author of *That's Why We Don't Eat Animals: A Book About Vegans, Vegetarians, and All Living Things* and *Vegan Is Love: Having Heart and Taking Action…* ■

▶ Ruby Roth. Photo credit: Jacob Rushing www.macandcob.com.

When my second children's book *Vegan Is Love* was released in April 2012, major media outlets picked up the news. Not in celebration of a new resource for a new generation, but because inviting children into an honest dialogue about meat and dairy was deemed outrageous and controversial.

While a slew of media talking heads judged my book to be propaganda, dangerous, brainwashing, and even child abuse, healthy vegan families had a good laugh. After a child psychologist on television called *Vegan Is Love* "the most disturbing children's book" he'd ever seen, I received a note from a ten-year-old vegan girl who had seen the segment and asked, "Why is that expert so ignorant?" The following day an even younger girl asked me, "What's so scary about your book? It just tells the truth!" It will forever amuse me that grownups have such a hard time with something children understand so easily.

To this day I have never known any child to be overwhelmed by the information or illustrations in my books – only adults. In this way, the media outrage over *Vegan Is Love* revealed the power of the invisible forces that shape public thinking about children, food, health and animals. If the public were aware of the level of disease and abuse caused by eating animals, outrage would be directed at the industries, not at a children's book about choices alternative to the status quo. As I experienced the media's repetitive concerns over veganism and the nutrient deficiency they are so confident is inherent to the diet, the successful advertising work of an organised network of colluding government institutions and big agricultural industries became tangibly clear. It is one thing to know it intellectually and another to experience it first hand. The anchors' recurring questions alone were enough for me to determine the public has been officially brainwashed.

Though nations of people have thrived on plant-based diets for centuries, the idea of veganism is still relatively new to the mainstream. Most people haven't yet realised that veganism is not simply the standard food pyramid minus meat and dairy (which would leave nothing upon nothing), but in fact an entirely different arrangement of food groups and recommended micronutrients, many of which meat-eating populations are highly deficient in – such as magnesium, required for calcium absorption, and vitamin B12. Everyone's health may improve from exploring the vegan pyramid and its recommended nutrients. The public desperately needs a reality check about whose diet is indeed dangerous, brainwashing, propagandistic and even child abuse.

It has become clear to me that those of us who discover the level of disease and abuse in the meat and dairy industries find enough motivation to change our eating habits – such that most people, including conventional nutritionists, doctors and psychologists, have nary the slightest notion of what they are eating, of our corrupted food systems, of the relentless brutality they participate in, nor the cognitive abilities of animals. In most every interview I had, the question of animals utterly disappeared, leaving me with a profound sense of our bias towards anthropocentrism, the belief that humans are the centre of all reality. Perpetuated in adulthood, it is this outlook which I believe is precisely the root cause of the health and environmental crises we find ourselves in today and which validates the very need to educate children early on about the effects of our choices on the public realm. Our naive supremacy is a miseducation that begins in childhood – on our plates and at the zoo.

Unlike adults, children respond to the revelation of meat and dairy production with curiosity, insight and reflection rather than fear of judgment and defensiveness. The difference in reactions from children and adults is the difference between regret and remorse; the former is a feeling, which exists without an explicit admission of responsibility, while the latter implies a sense of guilt, personal pain, or anguish. If adults react negatively to veganism, it is often because deep down we know that what is done to animals on our behalf is hidden and violent, but can't admit it or figure out what happened to make us so uncaring as we aged. Outrage over veganism only exposes the willful ignorance most parents feel content to impose on their children. On the other hand, the regret and diplomacy with which children consider the facts is a profound mark of emotional intelligence – something that seems harder to implement as we grow up, something we seem to lose as we gain ego. That children love and recognise animals with a profound curiosity that transcends barriers of language or species makes early education about veganism *key* to unlocking the potential we have to reverse the devastation we systematically inflict on animals and the environment.

The path to a greener future lies in engaging our children in new ways of thinking, eating and living. I believe any ambivalence involved is more about adults' willingness to change than it is about kids' abilities to learn. It is important to remember that kids are capable of much more than our societies give them credit for. We tend to shelter them from the 'adult' world, catering to a concept of childhood that reinforces a fragility we imagine children inherently require. But there is no universally accepted concept of childhood. Notions of what is and isn't appropriate for children vary throughout history and the world. Kids are more competent and sturdy than we think. By sugarcoating or avoiding truths, we hinder what our children are capable of, psychologically, spiritually and morally. We hinder our progress as a society.

If the public were aware of the level of disease and abuse caused by eating animals, outrage would be directed at the industries, not at a children's book about choices alternative to the status quo.

But what if a child feels upset or saddened upon discovering the use and abuse of animals? These are perfectly healthy responses to confronting the violence we inflict upon the earth and other living beings. We will be doing a world of good for the health of humankind if we help children learn to manage their feelings, instead of avoiding triggers to begin with. The most important lesson to instil while engaging children in veganism and animal rights is that we do not have to fear anything we have the power to change. By making vegan choices, we activate our personal agency and influence the public realm, reaching every major industry and every corner of the earth. In our commitment to the wellbeing of others, we practise the embodiment of love. Herein lies the *tremendous* transformative power of veganism. By changing what we eat, we can change our minds and the world we live in. Kids need but little evidence to motivate them to love deeply, think critically and act responsibly. It is we adults who have something to learn ... or rather, recall from childhood.

Link

www.wedonteatanimals.com

The Law Has a Say

■ A LAWYER FOR ANIMALS
Nichola Donovan

▶ Nichola Donovan and Pippa Malo.

I am a volunteer refugee lawyer and the honorary president of Lawyers for Animals Inc. LFA is a legal policy think tank committed to alleviating the suffering of animals. I choose to work in animal law because I have become aware that animals are the most persecuted beings on Earth and yet the most kind. Like human groups who have been persecuted throughout history – slaves, women, children or those with mental or physical impairments – I believe animals need to acquire a legal voice in order to be protected. I am very lucky to experience empathy with animals. Sometimes when I am with dogs, horses, humans or dolphins, I feel empathy flowing both ways. I regard this as 'love'. I think most young children feel an empathy with animals, but they learn to suppress it so they can conform with the dominant adult paradigm of speciesism. When I look at the world through a non-speciesist lens, I feel that I see it much more clearly and truly appreciate the majesty of nature. I also recognise my own miniscule place in the ecosystem. Like most, I am a selfish being and should certainly do more. When you discover a vital truth of which few others are aware, I think you are compelled to share it.

Link

nichola@lawyersforanimals.org.au

■ WHY ANIMAL LAW?
Mariann Sullivan

"A vegan world. It sounds ridiculous. But, as we all know, it's not ridiculous at all. It's a world where there are no animals suffering in agribusiness, where environmental degradation is diminished, climate change is slowed, and where everyone is so much healthier and we all have enough to eat. Not ridiculous at all, but kind of a big goal."   ■

—Mariann Sullivan.

▶ Mariann Sullivan.

Mariann Sullivan is a lecturer in animal law at Columbia Law School and an adjunct professor of animal law at Cardozo Law School. She is also the Program Director at *'Our Hen House'*...   ■

My path to teaching animal law started, without question, with a dog. His name was Calhoun and I loved him in ways I can't explain, or even try to describe. He wasn't an extraordinarily bright dog, and while he was certainly cute, he wasn't especially beautiful. He was exceptionally sweet, but that hardly sets him apart from a lot of other dogs. But he was my dog.

It was only after I got Calhoun, and got to know and love him, that I started to wake up about animals. I guess it started with dogs and cats, but it wasn't long before it all started to come together. One day an acquaintance mentioned he had stopped eating animals because of the way the animals are treated. It's not like I didn't know before that meat was made out of animals, but somehow I'd managed to avoid thinking about it. But because of Calhoun, that comment was finally able to slip by the wall of denial I had been building up for more than forty years.

After I found out what was really happening, there was no way out. I had to stop eating them. That was the easy part. But that was hardly going to accomplish anything. I also needed to do whatever I could to end this travesty – this utter nightmare we have created out of our world. I tried to avoid thinking how big the problem was, and tried to think just about what I could do.

Since I was a lawyer, that's what I focused on. I joined a bar association committee, did some writing and started teaching animal law. Law isn't the only path to change the world. If I had had a different career, my path would have been different, but the goal would have been the same: a vegan world.

A vegan world. It sounds ridiculous. But, as we all know, it's not ridiculous at all. It's a world where there are no animals suffering in agribusiness, where environmental degradation is diminished, climate change is slowed, and where every-one is so much healthier and we all have enough to eat. Not ridiculous at all, but kind of a big goal.

As I came to find out, the law can do only so much when it comes to changing the world for animals and getting us closer to a vegan world. In fact, it's hard to make any kind of change through the law, and the changes that are possible are woefully small.

But it doesn't have to be that way. The law doesn't exist in a vacuum – it largely reflects, and sometimes enforces, the values of society. So the law won't change until people's hearts and minds change. That's why my partner, Jasmin Singer, and I founded *Our Hen House*, which is a multimedia hub of opportunities to change the world for animals. It's designed to help everyone who has awakened to the nightmare to find ways to make change, regardless of where they are, who they are, what they do or who they know. Because if we all work together, doing what we can, we can make those changes in hearts and minds. Ours changed, and so can everyone else's.

■ GROWING UP WITH ANIMAL LAW: FROM COURTROOMS TO CASEBOOKS
Bruce A Wagman

"Animals cannot speak, but can you and I not speak for them and represent them? Let us all feel their cry of agony and let us all help that cry to be heard in the world." ■

—Rukmini Devi Rundale.

Over the past thirty years, there has been a dramatic increase in our understanding of animal intelligence and behaviour and a broad acceptance that animals are sentient beings that have a right to live free from suffering. This has led to the recognition that the existing legal system has failed to provide animals with access to justice[1]. As a result animal law has found its way into the mainstream and although still a young discipline it is growing rapidly.

Bruce Wagman, a partner with Schiff Hardin LLP, has a nationwide animal law practice representing many animal protection groups, as well as individual clients. His work includes litigation in state and federal courts, consulting, legislative efforts and teaching. He is the co-editor of the first casebook used in law schools, a book on international animal law, and a frequent lecturer

▶ Bruce A Wagman with Rafiki, Nzuri and Tatu.

on the subject. He covers cases that include animal hoarding, horse slaughter, dangerous dog defence and evaluation, cruelty, exotic and wild animal issues (including wild horse protection), biomedical research, farmed animals, complex injury cases, dog bite litigation and defence, animal ownership, veterinary malpractice, pet custody and animals in entertainment. He has been teaching animal law courses in law schools since 1996.

A vegan and guardian to his own eight animal companions, he lives and works in the San Francisco Bay Area. This is his story…   ■

During the past twenty-two years I have had the rare privilege of riding on the waves of intellectual, legal and academic development in the field of animal law. I started by incorporating isolated bits of pro bono work into a civil litigation practice and in 1996 I began teaching animal law. Since late 2005 my work has consistently been more than ninety percent animal law. I have had the honour of teaching full semester animal law classes more than twenty-five times at four Bay Area law schools, guest lecturing and speaking at conferences and classes in other schools across the nation, and co-authoring *Animal Law: Cases and Materials*, originally published in 2000 and now in its fourth edition, and *A Worldview of Animal Law*, published in 2011. Each day I am grateful for the gift of this practice, the result of a truly providential mix of coincidence and circumstance. My path as a lawyer for the animals, and as an animal law professor and lecturer, has paralleled the incredible growth in the field. During my tenure in animal law's thrall it has become a rapidly growing, vital social justice movement. It has developed much like environmental law, its natural older cousin, which attracted so many in the 1960s and 1970s. Given that animal law and I have grown up together, I have been asked to write this article, which will discuss our mutual path in practice and academia.

Puppyhood

Roughly two decades before I graduated from Hastings Law School in San Francisco in 1992, those who helped found the field of animal law had already taken the crucial first steps. With a limited number of dedicated lawyers doing the work, and with the law schools basically devoid of regular animal law classes, in 1992 the field was still just a feisty but undeveloped kitten's meow, with clear promise to turn into a big cat. I was working for judge doing a federal clerkship in San Francisco that year when the American Bar Association's convention came to town.

I am neither religious nor prone to revelations or sudden conversions, and I had the only one of my life in a small seminar room at the Marriott Hotel in San Francisco at that convention. I had no expectations for the session on Animal Rights Law, but I was curious and my wife Deborah was interested as well – and it was an afternoon out of chambers. Although I had no intention to use my law degree to work for animals, law school had triggered my desire to change some of the problems I perceived in our society. In particular, Brian Gray's Native American Law class made me seriously consider working in that field. I never went further with that pursuit, mainly because of what happened at that ABA seminar. But it is a fact that Professor Gray uncovered in me the drive that from that point forward kept me on the path I still travel.

Deborah and I walked in wholly unprepared for what we were about to hear and learn. There was a celebrity panel, but two stand out still. William Kunstler was one of those iconic civil rights attorneys who had represented scores of activists and social objectors, including the protesters at the 1968 Democratic convention in Chicago. He died in 1995 but in his final years he turned his attention to animal issues. Then there was Joyce Tischler, a woman who would play a significant role in my career. Joyce was one of the founders of the Attorneys for Animal Rights, which by that time had become the Animal Legal Defense Fund.

At the time I considered myself an animal lover. I lived with five or six companion animals and one wife, but I had limited knowledge about the treatment of the majority of animals in America, and how they were impacted by the institutions and industries that use them. I was a meat-eating, milkshake-loving barbequer with leather boots. I don't think I had heard the phrase 'animal rights' and I surely had no idea what the law had to do with animals, aside from the fact that like most Americans I incorrectly assumed the anti-cruelty laws I heard about were keeping the country's animals safe and free from harm. When I found out that day how wrong I was, I decided to try to help right that wrong with my law degree.

I cannot tell you today what anyone in particular said at that session, but I know the speakers objectively described a crushing list of tragedies and holocaust experiences for billions of animals in America. They exposed the ignored instances of legal (and illegal) cruelty occurring at every level of society. I learnt about individual and institutional acts (many fully sanctioned by the law) that indisputably cause an unimaginable level of pain and suffering to innocent animals. Somehow, for the first time I saw the faces of the cows and pigs and chickens being slaughtered and tortured for my food, and I realised that in all the ways that matter they were the same as the dogs and cats sleeping in my house. I realised my personal choice to eat one and feed the other was arbitrary and capricious, and I felt that I personally, and the law, were contributing to their suffering. From what I remember the program was presented in a very unemotional and academic context. Perhaps most important for the topic at hand, interspersed with the discussion of the animals' treatment was the fascinating notion that lawyers were taking up their keyboards and applying their brains to make a change. Legal advocacy for animals was a viable means of effecting change. As lawyers, we could not change the world for every animal. But for each animal we helped to save, or whose life we improved, we would change her world completely.

My path was set that day. For some reason I remember what happened when we left the room at the Marriott. Stunned into sadness, the tears from what we had heard and seen still drying on our cheeks, the distance to the escalator seemed endless. I know I turned to Deborah and the only words I could say were, "It's over, isn't it?" Deborah knew what I meant and simply nodded. We changed our diet that day…really, it had just begun.

[1.] Voiceless, *What is Animal Law?*, accessed 15 June 2011, http://www.voiceless.org.au/Law/Misc/What_is_Animal_Law_.html

■ INTERVIEW WITH
Bruce A Wagman

Since then Bruce has spent more than two decades as a legal advocate for animals and has gone through the highs and lows of having an animal law practice. I was fortunate enough to interview him in May 2011, to find out more about his experiences since the day he and his wife attended the ABA convention in 1992.   ■

What exactly is an animal rights lawyer?

I call myself an animal lawyer as opposed to an animal rights lawyer. 'Animal rights' is a highly charged term that I think throws people off track. My practice ranges from dangerous dog cases to dog bite cases to veterinary malpractice cases to the big picture cases involving animals in entertainment, farmed animals and animals in biomedical research. So, given the breadth of my practice as well as my feeling that saying 'animal rights' just gets people thinking the wrong thing sometimes, I'm an animal lawyer.

What actually brought you into the line of work when other avenues could have been more profitable to you?

It's a calling more than a profession. It's not a job. It's like going into the priesthood I suppose. There's nothing else I would rather do or would do or could think of doing. Once I discovered there was a way to use my legal career to help animals, my focus was to get to the point where I was doing that all the time.

What was it about your relationship with animals that called you to it?

I went to a conference in 1992, a session at an American Bar Association conference and I heard about how animals were treated by industries for food, research and entertainment, and decided I couldn't stomach being a part of that anymore. I wanted to be part of the solution and the way to change.

How does the law permit the atrocious cruelty perpetrated on farm animals, particularly when there are animal cruelty laws?

Well, that unfortunately is easy to answer. There are exemptions under most laws for standard farm animal practices or agricultural practices and those include all the atrocious and torturous treatments that animals suffer in America and in Australia, with the Australian codes of practice and the American laws perpetuating and permitting the cruel practices. We human beings differentiate between *animals we feed and animals we eat* and somehow we are able to make that distinction in general as a society without any recognition of the horrible hypocrisy of that decision.

Who are your clients?

My clients range from individuals in dog bite cases where I represent a family trying to get their dog off death row because the dog has been in a fight or bitten another dog or somebody, to the animal welfare organisations around the country and around the world. They range from small groups, such as dog rescue groups, to sanctuaries, to the bigger animal protection groups that everybody is well aware of.

I believe a lot of your work is pro bono.

I do a fair amount of pro bono work but I do run a commercial practice, a profitable practice doing this. One hundred percent of my work is animal law. I work for a law firm that supports me in an incredible fashion but also appropriately requires I bring in money to stay in the firm, and I am glad to be a part of the firm and to receive its valuable and consistent support.

Could you give me an overview of some of the cases you are working on?

Currently, I have a case involving one hundred and sixteen horses who were abused by a man in a Midwest state. I am assisting with the criminal side and also on the civil side where the clients are trying to recover the costs of care for the horses by animal protection groups since the day they were seized from him. I am also involved in a case in which the National Meat Association is trying to strike down a law in California that requires immediate euthanasia for animals who are too sick or injured to stand in slaughterhouses. A law has been passed in California to prevent the inhumane treatment of what we call 'downed animals' or non-ambulatory animals, so they would immediately be euthanised and at least be given a humane death at that point. The meat industry wants those animals taken to slaughter so they can continue to profit from them. Our effort is to save those animals from further suffering after they've gone down.

I am also involved in a case concerning the welfare of egg-laying hens and the amount of space needed for each hen to perform certain behaviours deemed necessary for the chickens. I've got a dog custody case involving a business that has taken my client's dog and refuses to return it. I've got a couple of veterinary malpractice cases. Those are the ones I've been most active on.

In one of your articles you also talked about the drugging of dolphins.

Yes, that was something I learnt about early on in one of my first cases while challenging a Swim with the Dolphins program. That was fifteen years ago and I haven't done a lot of work with those cases since that time but I can't imagine the treatment has changed. The experts at that time talked about the dolphins being drugged in order to enable them not to go crazy while being in the Swim with the Dolphins programs.

With these kinds of issues, Bruce, how do you survive emotionally doing this work?

I have a handful of tools I use to make sure I stay something short of a basket case because it is very challenging. So I always think about who I'm fighting for and what it would mean if I stopped fighting for them. I think about their eyes and how they feel and how I could possibly help, and that keeps me going. I also stay in physical contact with my eight animals at home which gives me an inter-species contact, which is very important to me and makes me continue to be reminded of how sensitive, conscious, sentient, intelligent and emotional other species are. Then I run every morning and I walk every afternoon on the beach and try to cast my sorrows out into the sea, if you will. I do a lot of reflection that way. I also listen to a lot of music, which is my other temple besides the beach to take me away and give me something to hang on to.

You are doing amazing work and we know how incredibly hard it is emotionally but given that you are constantly in contact with some of the toughest things it must be very difficult. What would be the worst-case scenario you've dealt with?

They are all the worst-case scenario. There are degrees of suffering so some cases are worse than others but with respect to the animals I am trying to help, from their perspective their case is the worst every time. It's hard to evaluate someone else's pain and suffering. The things that are done to downed animals in slaughter houses and actually all the way from the farm to the slaughterhouse certainly seems to be some of the worst cruelty that goes on anywhere, as is the standard treatment of farm animals. But if you ask the elephants in the zoo who are stuck on concrete for their entire lives or the elephants in the circus who are chained and carted by railroad car from one circus to another and whose feet are so painful that they have to live their entire lives in excruciating pain; or if you ask the dogs who are living in their filth and excrement and barely being fed and starving and living in conditions no one could imagine living in; or if you ask the chimpanzees who are taken away from their mothers at day one and beaten and abused so they will cower and be frightened so they can appear on television and movies. If you asked them they would all say, "mine is the worst case." So those are all the worst cases. The dog bite cases do not involve that kind of cruelty but there are an awful lot of cases that do. Then you have the scenario of, is it worse to be a battery-caged hen stuck in a cage for your entire life or an animal who is treated badly in a slaughterhouse but at least dies quickly? I don't know.

What can we do to reverse the fact that the law permits such cruelty to be perpetrated on farm animals?

Well, there are a lot of ways to do it. It is a multi-fronted war I suppose and so there's education, there's litigation and there's legislation and we have to do it all, I think. Some of the best education is what happened to me, maybe like that T-shirt I have that says, "If slaughterhouses had windows you'd be vegetarian before you finished reading this t-shirt," I think when people are exposed to the horrors some of them don't want to know about it because they think "I like my hamburgers" but some of them say, "I can't participate in that any more." Another way is trying to fit the treatment of animals into the law and demonstrate the illegal nature of it. Then also affecting the bottom line: if the market supports the mistreatment of animals then mistreatment of animals will continue, but if consumers vote with their wallet and say, "I am not going to buy this any more," then the response from the industry may be a change in practices.

Are we making progress?

That's a good question. It's interesting because over the years I've always said "no" but of late when I find myself at conferences with my colleagues who have also always said "no", I'm starting to say "yes". We are not making huge progress. The world is not turning vegan, the world is not even turning vegetarian, but people are talking about these issues. People are agreeing on them to some degree. It is still an incredible battle between industry and those of us who would like to make things better for animals. Is it going to change to the point where people like me and you would be happy in our lifetimes? I don't think so. But if I can make life better for a pig in a sow stall or a chicken in a battery cage, or even better, if I can make life better for millions of them, then I will feel like it's getting better. We are fighting against a large and powerful commercial industry as well as thousands if not millions of years of human civilisation in which we discount and discard animals as something not worthy of anything except our exploitation and use.

So everything starts with one small step doesn't it?

Yes, animal law is about forty years old and that is pretty young and it is still pretty small, so if you think about it in the context of how short a time we have been going in a devoted, dedicated sense and how much has changed already, then we are doing good. There is no question there has been significant change. Are we happy with what we've done? Yes and no, because we wish we'd done more. Are there animals still suffering by the billions around the world? Yes. But there has been some change and I think it is important going back to the question you asked about being able to look at the progress we've made so we don't give up. It is very important to see the value we have made, as opposed to dwelling on the losses and how much there is still to do.

That's so terribly important and my hope is that you are getting a lot of people interested in animal law and lawyers being trained.

Yes, there is no question about it. There are more than a hundred courses around the country. I teach at three law schools and there are lots of young lawyers out there who want to practise animal law. There is not work for them because there is nobody paying for them all, but there is plenty to be done, that's for sure.

Bruce A Wagman is the author of *Growing Up With Animal Law: From Courtrooms to Casebooks*, Journal of Legal Education, Vol. 60, No 2 (Nov. 2010).

Spiritual Awakenings

■ A SPIRITUAL JOURNEY: EMBRACING ALL BEINGS INTERVIEW WITH
Scott White

Scott White is a physiotherapist and yoga teacher in Western Australia...   ■

▶ Scott White with Chester and Rex.

What motivated you to adopt a vegan lifestyle?

What I eat today has been, and still is, a process of evolution. I came to the understanding I have today simply by adopting a discerning mentality. However, this decision to discern and discriminate was motivated by the suffering caused by physical injury, my desire to overcome suffering, and subsequently recognising the link between the pain I felt and the pain all other creatures are susceptible to.

In 2006 I was twenty-two years old, and the strongest I had ever been. As an avid runner and weight trainer I followed a strict schedule of weights, sprint training, boxing, and ate a mainly animal-based, low-fat, high-protein diet. I had also recently graduated from university as a physiotherapist. I had an active social life and physically was one of the fittest and healthiest people I knew. However, in December 2006, I sustained the beginnings of an injury that would take years to heal. While training at the local surf club with the beach sprint team I tore an adductor (groin) muscle. Over a period of several months this injury eventually progressed into severe osteitis pubis (inflammation of the pubic bone). This had the effect of essentially flooring me. By June 2007, I was unable to exercise. As a conventionally trained physiotherapist I followed the standard medical treatment for the condition, which was a CT guided cortisone injection. This gave no relief, and the only options the physicians suggested were more injections. So I had three injections in total and by the third, my condition had deteriorated significantly. By now I was unable to walk without a major limp, and was restricted to distances of no more than a few hundred metres before having to sit. I was subsequently referred to a surgeon, and based on my symptoms was given a poor prognosis for surgery, but was scheduled for an operation anyway given the lack of other options.

However, I decided to put the surgery on hold and investigate alternatives to treat the condition. This led me to acupuncture, cupping, massage, specialist physiotherapists and interstate trips to see pelvic specialists. None of the treatments was able to resolve the issue. By now I was strongly entrenched in the chronic pain cycle. Trying to move and stretch my body hurt, but lack of movement was causing other major problems such as major atrophy, major stiffness and deconditioning.

By this stage I was willing to try anything. It was now March 2008, fifteen months after the initial injury, and I had spent well over two thousand dollars on medical costs. This is when I decided to take some risks with my body and potentially aggravate the pain further. I had a copy of the book *Light on Yoga* by BKS Iyengar. This book, which is now regarded as a classic, was published by an Indian man in Pune in 1966. I decided to start the course he outlined in the back of his book. To begin with I was so stiff I had to stay on the week one poses for three months, and the first few weeks of starting were very trying, to the point of being unable to talk after a session because of the pain.

A cause of my own pain and sorrow resided in the flesh of my muscles and joints. A turning point for me was a spearfishing trip with a close friend, about a year into my yoga practice. Physically, I was significantly improved, but my body was still very temperamental, and I didn't have the strength to pull myself back in the boat from the water. So my job for the day was to stay on the boat, bag any speared fish, and cut up any baitfish and throw them back in the water to attract more fish. A contradiction seemed blatantly obvious for me at this point. I was expending so much energy in attempting to rid my own body of pain and return my body to a state of wholeness. Yet I was contributing to pulverising the bodies of these animals. Having known what it feels like to have a torn muscle, I was slicing up these bait fish and chucking their mangled bodies back into the water. I couldn't seem to reconcile this discrepancy. I selfishly aimed and strived to have a body that worked properly, yet I was maiming others. From a purely intellectual point of view I could have argued those actions of killing fish wouldn't impact at all on my physical recovery. That, if I kept working hard, eventually my body would heal. And that's probably true, as you definitely don't need to be vegetarian to overcome injury. However, my concern was more at the philosophical level. If I want to experience healing, I should stop harming others.

"... Moreover, you have to want everyone to be healthy if you want to become healthy. Nature's law mandates that you get back whatever you put out. You receive health only if your activities and attitudes promote, or at least do not interfere with, the health of those around you. Like disease, health is contagious; it can be passed from one person to another, again and again." Dr Robert Svoboda, *Prakriti: Your Ayurvedic Constitution*, p120.

The Sanskrit word for Karma simply means action. It also implies its inherent reaction. I felt I wanted to emancipate myself from the cycle of action and reaction that involves harming others. It was the last time I went fishing.

What does being vegan mean to you in its fuller context?

I view veganism and to a lesser extent vegetarianism as having parallels with the yogic concept of ahimsa (non-violence). Ahimsa, being the first constituent of yoga, represents non-violence on multiple levels: physical non-violence, intellectual non-violence, and non-violence of speech.

For me personally it represents an attempt to avoid actions that harm other beings at all levels, not just restricting this view to food intake. The brutalisation of animals for all purposes should be shunned. Subsequently, lifestyle choices I make reflect this. Given the society we live in, one is only able to do so much, but I believe if the endeavour is there then it all helps.

You went through mainstream academia. How much did your own values diverge from what you were taught?

Mainstream academia has a lot of positives, and there is no doubt this has helped me shape a scientific way of viewing things. However, I also recognise it takes a lot of will power to hold values that fall outside the commonly accepted norm when studying. The easiest way to pass the degree is to conform, and generally not question things. If you start raising questions about this or that, then it's almost like you're earmarking yourself for scrutiny among the lecturers and examiners. Not everyone has the capacity to tolerate this added pressure.

I think what is needed is a paradigm shift. The current model of education is reductionist. It moulds a highly developed intellect, but fails to address existential questions. Consequently, this leaves people prone to spiritual alienation. Perhaps this contributes in a way to the moral decline evident in the world today, especially among professions that are populated with highly educated people, such as in politics and the sciences.

What is it you understand about our nutritional needs that has given you the confidence to go vegan?

At least anecdotally, I see examples of vegans and vegetarians whom I revere as demonstrating the best examples of health and longevity. Whilst a vegetarian or vegan diet is no guarantee of longevity, it is interesting to note that Krishnamacharya lived to more than one hundred years old, his student Indra Devi lived to one hundred and two and his other student BKS Iyengar is still alive and at the time of publication (2014), was ninety-five. These people are also amazing examples of energy and vitality, right up to their final years.

How do you view animals in the context of our planet and their place alongside humans?

The Bhagavad Gita explains that a human life is "as transient as a drop of water on a lotus leaf." I think very often it is sheer forgetfulness of this that can cause us to tolerate killing without contemplating our own mortality. For me it's difficult to make that separation between animals given the common fate of death we all share. Yoga philosophy views all beings as manifestations of the same spirit, so it follows that any demarcation between humans and animals is illusory. Subsequently, moral and ethical codes of conduct that we apply to humans should equally be extended to the animals we share the planet with.

■ CORPORATE OMNIVORES TURNED VEGAN YOGIS
Natasha Cuculovski and Luca Padalini

▶ Natasha and Luca with rescued hens at Animal Liberation Victoria.

We met at primary school, age ten. We recall that Natasha copied Luca's math homework and thought he was too tall to be her boyfriend! Many years later we married and set up our home in inner-city Melbourne, Australia. Natasha had careers in radio and corporate communications, while Luca worked as a business banking manager. We were overworked, stressed, unhealthy, unhappy and lived a toxic lifestyle focused on wealth creation and consumerism.

The end of a long stressful working week was spent on the couch eating hotdogs in white buns with fries, drinking a bottle of scotch and coke, watching brain-numbing television until the early hours of the morning. Weekday evenings after work were often spent in the doctor's waiting room followed by the pharmacy next door – we were always sick.

We also each had unresolved personal issues that were seriously impeding our relationship, our mental, emotional and physical health. Our life lacked passion and fun; we were boring and contributing little to humanity. We were on a downward spiral and on the brink of divorce. In our darkest hour we found comfort in the words "Leap and the net will appear" – we had to regain control of our lives and make changes. We sought help from a wonderful hypnotherapist who was able to get to the root of our individual problems. The healing process had begun.

We 'un-plugged', left our jobs, packed up the house and took one year off to travel and heal.

What started as an extended holiday became a year of journalling, reading, deep self-enquiry, soul therapy, remembering and reconnecting. We began with a bungee jump in France – a therapeutic and symbolic way to release a whole lot of mental tension and emotional pain. Our travels took us around the world, experiencing so many wonderful things, meeting endless people; it was our 'bucket list'. The last three months of that year were spent living in the Sivananda Ashram in Kerala, India.

The ashram is where our personal and spiritual growth blossomed. It was there we discovered the peace of Yoga, our heartfelt joy for chanting, our spirits ignited whilst giving to others in selfless service (Karma Yoga), and the need to change our lives on all levels – including what we ate.

Let us be honest here and say we were raised as meat-eaters and loved it. We ate animal foods every single day of our lives, and there was a huge emphasis on eating meat in particular. We thought there was something wrong with people who considered salad a meal; that wasn't normal, that wasn't 'real food'. So it was a new frontier for us to live in an ashram where the diet was vegetarian. Initially we resisted and fully intended to return to our meat-eating diets upon leaving India. However, six weeks into our stay the ashram screened the film *Diet for a New America*, based on John Robbins' famous book. At the end of the film there was a rapturous applause from the audience of hundreds – perhaps we were the only meat-eaters there? We remember looking at each other with utter dread, both knowing there was no way we could return to a diet of meat. This was the first time we had ever seen a film like this, we had never been exposed to images or information about where our food came from. Yet once we'd seen the film, we could no longer plead ignorance. We recall feeling shocked and angry – because we'd been kept in the dark our whole lives, and now that we'd been shown the film, had to deal with our consciences! We so wanted to erase the film from our minds, put our heads back in the sand and return to our 'normal' way of eating. Yet at same time we knew that was not possible. We returned to our room that night and talked about how we instantly 'got it' and could never eat meat again. We didn't know how to explain this to our family and friends, or how to re-integrate into the Australian culture we'd been raised in, but we just knew a new path was shining in front of us. We will never forget the feeling of joy, tingles on our skin, our hearts beating and tears in our eyes at the moment we agreed to no longer eat meat. It was as though our souls were screaming "Yes! Finally, you are making connections."

Needless to say, when we left the ashram and returned to Australia, we were completely different people and no longer fit into the narrow-minded box we once lived in.

Black suits, ties, cufflink shirts and high heels were all replaced with Ali Baba Yoga pants and flip-flops.

Our marriage was back on track, our health improving and we had a new spark for life, we longed for more self-creation.

After only four months in Melbourne we sold our belongings on eBay, re-packed our bags and headed off for another adventure. We spent the next two and a half years living in Thailand and traveling through Asia and South Africa. One of the most life-changing experiences of this journey was our practice of Karma Yoga. We worked as volunteers with abused and abandoned children, street kids, disabled adults and blind children at the Father Ray Foundation in Pattaya, Thailand, and cared for orphaned babies at The Pattaya Orphanage. We also taught *English at a secondary school for underprivileged children in rural Thailand and* volunteered in Durban, South Africa, with abandoned HIV/AIDS babies. The heart chakra was really opening now.

We felt a strong calling to teach Yoga and so completed our Yoga Teacher Training. From there we went on to work at renowned Yoga retreat centres in Thailand, India and Spain as Yoga teachers, meditation guides, Reiki practitioners, detox consultants, guest liaisons and kitchen hands.

We continued to share vegetarian information with our students until we came across a one-hour video from animal rights activist Gary Yourofsky from www.adaptt.org.

Gary presents lectures to high school and college students about veganism. "Well," someone might as well have whispered in our ears, "Your life is about to change in just one hour." We watched his lecture and we got it. We made the total connection and saw all the things we were still doing as vegetarians, that we were harming animals, the environment and ourselves. Sometimes you just need someone to give you a little shake and say, "Hey, wake up, don't get comfortable, the journey isn't over, it's just begun!" The lecture showed footage of a calf being beaten on a dairy farm in Ohio and we were in tears, it was very difficult to watch.

This was our turning point – we finally saw how violent and destructive dairy was, as well as eggs and bee products. Just like in the ashram, we had that feeling of knowingness, that what we were currently doing was not okay, it was not enough and it was time to wake up – again!

And that was all it took – a one-hour lecture that was filled with so much passion and information it was impossible to ignore. We were left with Gary's words ringing in our ears, something along the lines of, "Enough. Now you know, you can't claim ignorance any more, this isn't a game, stop already." Up until that point, we had stopped eating meat but increased our consumption of dairy and eggs. We thought this was okay and that we were doing enough by abstaining from meat. Since watching Gary's lecture, we haven't touched a single animal product.

Once we made the full connection and became vegan, we experienced radiant health, intense spiritual growth, a deep connection with nature and all beings, and felt a strong purpose to bring this message to others. We realised that Yoga and veganism are teaching the same thing: non-violence and compassion. Thus we created "Move Me – Yoga, Food, Life".

Now, as World Peace Diet Facilitators, we are dedicated to planting seeds of compassion in our students around the world - it's how we intend to be a turning point for others.

Link:

www.movemeyoga.com.au

◼ SPIRITUAL AWAKENING
Dr Will Tuttle

> *"By harming and exploiting billions of animals, we confine ourselves spiritually, morally, emotionally and cognitively and blind ourselves to the poignant, heart-touching beauty of nature, animals and each other. To be free, we must practise freeing others. To feel loved, we must practise loving others. To have true self-respect, we must respect others. The animals and other voiceless beings, the starving humans and future generations, are pleading with us to see: it's on our plate."* ◼
>
> —Dr Will Tuttle, *The World Peace Diet*, p65.

Will Tuttle, author, educator, pianist and composer, has lectured and performed widely throughout North America and Europe. Author of the acclaimed *The World Peace Diet*, he is a recipient of the Peace Abbey's *Courage of Conscience Award* and is the creator of several wellness training programs. His PhD from the University of California, Berkeley, focused on educating adults in intuition and altruism and he has taught college courses in creativity, humanities, mythology, religion and philosophy. A former Zen monk and Dharma Master in the Korean Zen tradition, he is devoted to cultural healing and awakening and has created eight CD albums of uplifting original piano music. A vegan since 1980, he travels full-time with his spouse Madeleine in their solar-powered RV, and presents more than one hundred and fifty lectures, retreats, workshops and concerts annually... ◼

▶ Will Tuttle.

I was born into a typical heavy meat and dairy-eating family in New England in the early 1950s, but fortunately discovered vegetarianism when I was just twenty-two. Right after graduating, my brother Ed and I decided to go on a pilgrimage in search of spiritual understanding. We ended up walking for many months with no money from New England and eventually reached Alabama.

When we reached Tennessee we stayed for several weeks in a place called The Farm, a relatively newly formed spiritual community of about nine hundred people, mainly from San Francisco. One of the things that intrigued me about The Farm was it was a vegan community, not for health reasons, but for ethical and spiritual reasons. The experience absolutely sealed my commitment to vegetarianism and was worth the months of walking to get there. Close to a thousand people, mostly living as married couples with kids in self-built homes, they had created a thriving community on a large piece of beautifully rolling farm and forest land.

The Farm had its own school, telephone system, soy dairy, publishing company and a blossoming outreach program called Plenty, which provided vegan food and health-care services both in Central America and in the ghettos of North America. The spiritual leader, Stephen Gaskin, was a student of Zen master Suzuki Roshi, founder of the San Francisco Zen Centre.

The plant-based food was delicious and the atmosphere was unlike anything I had ever experienced. People were friendly, energetic and bright, and there was a powerful sense of purpose, of working to create a better world. The soy dairy made tofu, soymilk, soy burgers and 'Ice Bean', the first soy ice cream, and the school-house for the children served all-vegan meals. The kids, vegan from birth, grew tall, strong and healthy. Gardens, fields and greenhouses provided food with people working on various crews, building, cooking, farming, teaching and together making The Farm remarkably self-reliant.

I was deeply touched by the loving attentiveness people showed each other and by the courage the whole community displayed in running almost completely contrary to the values of the larger society. The people there, like myself, were all raised in a culture of domination, which killed and abused animals for food, clothing, entertainment and research, and which emphasised competition, private property, consumerism, limited liability for large corporations, and viewing the earth, animals and even people as commodities to be used by the market for self-centred profit.

The Farm was a living example of veganism emphasising gentleness, compassion and respect for all creatures. It exemplified a life of voluntary simplicity and appropriate technology, sharing resources and finding happiness through strong, healthy family and social relationships, helping others, spiritual growth and creative expression, rather than through personal aggrandisement. To me it seemed these people were going much farther toward actually living the teachings espoused by Jesus than mainstream religions were. The lived ideal was that all life is sacred and the attempt was to consciously create a community and lifestyle that reflected this ideal, which in turn would be an inspiration to others and be a model for sustainable living.

Needless to say, banking, corporate and government institutions were extremely hostile to The Farm and though it is still going strong, it's smaller and somewhat less radical than it was in its heyday in the 1970s and early '80s. It was fascinating to discover in talking with my spouse Madeleine, whom I met 15 years later, that in the same month of 1975 while at The Farm when I gave up meat forever, she also made a decision as a young woman in Switzerland never to eat meat again.

Though my brother and I seriously considered exploring the possibility of joining The Farm, we eventually received intuitive guidance to walk farther south to Huntsville, Alabama, where we discovered the local Zen centre. Here we were able to focus on our meditation practice, sitting for about eight hours daily and helping with the upkeep of the centre. Over the next several years I continued living in Buddhist meditation centres in Atlanta and then in San Francisco, but loosened up somewhat on my vegan diet, since most people at these centres ate eggs and dairy products and I was at that point unaware of the extent of the cruelty involved in these foods.

In 1984 I had my second opportunity to live in a vegan community. This time it was an ancient Zen monastery in South Korea. I travelled there and participated as a monk in the summer's three-month intensive retreat. We rose at 2.45am to begin the day with meditation, practising silence and simplicity.

We ate vegan meals of rice, soup, vegetables and occasional tofu, and retired after the evening meditation at nine o'clock. The meals were eaten in silence with each of us using a set of four bowls, three for the rice, soup and vegetables and the fourth for tea which we used to clean our bowls and then drink, so that not even a single grain of rice would go to waste.

The community consisted of about seventy monks, with some lay people who helped with certain tasks. The vegan roots there were old and deep, extending back six hundred and fifty years. In that temple, people had lived the same way for many centuries, meditating and living a life of nonviolence. There was no silk, leather or wool in any clothing and though I was there in the summer mosquito season, it was absolutely not an option to kill one – or any creature. We simply used a mosquito net in the meditation hall. Through the months of silence and meditation, sitting still for seemingly endless hours, a deep and joyful feeling emerged within, a sense of solidarity with all life and of becoming more sensitive to the energy of situations.

When after four months I returned to the bustle of American life, I felt a profound shift had occurred, and the veganism I'd been practising for a few years felt like it had grown roots that extended to the centre of my heart. Until then, I had mistakenly thought my daily vegan purchases of food, clothing and so forth were my personal choices, like options. Now I could clearly see that not treating animals as commodities was not an option or a choice, for animals simply are *not* commodities, and it would be as unthinkable to eat or wear or justify abusing an animal as it would be to eat or wear or justify abusing a human being. The profound relief and empowerment of completely realising and understanding this in my heart has been enriching beyond words.

There seems to me to be nothing more essential, vital and noble than coming to this Earth, freeing ourselves from the shackles of violence and delusion forced on us from infancy and helping others to do the same. For me it continues to be an inner and outer adventure that is challenging and heartbreaking at times, but overall is profoundly satisfying. There are enormously inspiring examples of organisations working selflessly to bless others. Two that stand out for me are the Supreme Master Ching Hai International Association, a grass-roots spiritual community with more than two hundred vegan Loving Hut restaurants worldwide and the SMTV online television network, and Food Not Bombs, a grass-roots activist community which directly feeds vegan food to hungry people around the world and educates for community empowerment and sustainability. And there are many more!

It seems to me the vegan tide is just beginning to come in and we will be seeing vast positive changes happening in our world as increasing numbers of us make the journey to vegan living. It is the essence of both spiritual and cultural transformation and presents us with the ultimate inspirational challenge: to be, as Gandhi said, the change we'd like to see in the world.

■ FINDING MY GOOD HEART
Beth Lily Redwood

"To live, serve and give thanks for this precious life arising through all of us is simply the expression of our own true nature: seeing all beings as unique and complete manifestations of a universal, loving intelligence, to be honored, respected, learnt from and celebrated."   ■

—Will Tuttle, *The World Peace Diet.*

A graphic designer, digital artist, photographer and writer, Beth Lily Redwood has been an ethical vegan since 2005. Her artistic work seeks to awaken in the viewer a deep appreciation for and recognition of the sacred soul, beauty and individuality of animals. In so doing, her goal is to increase compassion and respect for animals and to help end their suffering. Beth's photography and digital art has been featured in galleries, exhibits, and magazines, and she was interviewed by 'Our Hen House'.

Beth is the publications manager for Melanie Joy's Carnism Awareness and Action Network (CAAN). She has designed materials for animal advocacy groups and individuals, including The Prayer Circle for Animals, Animal Outreach of Kansas, Veganpalooza, and Daniel Redwood's animal rights album, 'Songs for Animals, People and the Earth'. To view Beth's photography and digital art, go to bethlilyredwood.com...   ■

▶ Beth Lily Redwood and Karuna Bell.

My fortuitous meeting with Will Tuttle was a true experience of "when the student is ready, the teacher will appear." My husband Daniel and I met Will and his artist wife, Madeleine, at a potluck at a friend's home in Virginia Beach. That weekend, Will was speaking during the worship service at a Unity church in Richmond.

Daniel and I attended the service and little did I know it, but after that day, life as I knew it would never be the same. Until that day, I had failed to make the basic connection between my consumption of animal products and the painful, mortal consequences to the animal who was being consumed. Without realising it, I was negating my efforts to be the kind of person I wanted to be – loving, compassionate, non-harmful, nonviolent and peaceful – by engaging in the opposite behaviour through my daily meal choices.

Though the information had been readily available, I had not learnt about the experiences of farmed animals mostly because I was afraid it would be too upsetting. But the sad irony is that by walling myself off emotionally, I was perpetrating the very actions I found too disturbing to contemplate. In *The Great Compassion,*

Norm Phelps writes, "Make no mistake, when you purchase a piece of meat, you are placing an order for an animal to be killed. You are responsible for the killing. The animal was killed for you."

Albert Einstein challenged us to open our hearts to our fellow beings, both human and non-human, "A human being is part of the whole called by us universe, a part limited in time and space. We experience ourselves, our thoughts and feelings, as something separate from the rest, a kind of optical delusion of consciousness. This delusion is a kind of prison for us, restricting us to our personal desires and to affection for a few persons nearest to us. Our task must be to free ourselves from the prison by widening our circle of compassion to embrace all living creatures and the whole of nature in its beauty."

I believe someday we will look back upon the abuse, killing and eating of animals with horror. In *The Animal Kingdom: A Spiritual Perspective*, the Ageless Wisdom teachings predict, "The time will come when the attitude of man to the animal kingdom will be revolutionised, and the slaughter, ill-treatment and that form of cruelty called 'sport', will be done away with."

The practice of veganism is the everyday blessing of the joy of expressing a loving heart, the wholeness of making my actions consistent with my beliefs, the peace of living in harmony with all beings. My energy feels lighter, brighter and I'm more aware of my oneness with the beauty and blessings of life. It's as though something that had been broken is now healed and I've awakened to a new life – a life in which I've come home to my true self.

Excerpt from *The Missing Peace: The Hidden Power of Our Kinship with Animals* by Judy Carman. © 2009 Beth Lily Redwood.

■ ANIMALS AND THE AFTERLIFE
Kim Sheridan

"The greatness of a nation and its moral progress can be judged by the way its animals are treated." ■

—Mahatma Gandhi.

Kim Sheridan has degrees in Psychology, Clinical Hypnotherapy and Naturopathy. She is a filmmaker, lecturer and workshop leader. A popular guest on radio and television, Kim is also the founder of EnLighthouse Entertainment™, Compassion Circle™, Healthy Chick®, and Go Green Already!™. She has been listed in *Who's Who in Executives and Professionals, 2000 Notable American Women* and *Great Minds of the 21st Century.*

She co-authored *UnCooking with Jameth and Kim* and is author of *Animals and the Afterlife: True Stories of Our Best Friends' Journey Beyond Death…* ■

▶ Kim Sheridan and Kristin.

I think we all have certain key moments in our lives that we see as pivotal. For me, one such moment took place when I was in college and went fishing with my boyfriend at that time. I had previously joined him on several afternoon trips to a nearby creek where he enjoyed catching crayfish, which he intended to cook for dinner. He collected them in a bucket of water and I quietly helped them back to safety whenever he had his back turned. He thought they kept escaping on their own; little did he know I was their guilty accomplice.

Having had little success at crayfish hunting, he had now purchased his first fishing pole and decided to become a 'real' fisherman. I had no intention of actually joining him in his new hobby – I merely went along for the peaceful scenery and the relaxing ride in a rowboat. It seemed like a nice way to spend a sunny Sunday afternoon. However, all illusions of tranquillity quickly vanished for me when I found myself face-to-face with the struggling, terrified victim of my boyfriend's new source of 'relaxation', who was dangling from his fishing hook.

As I looked into the fish's eyes, I literally *felt* the terror – and understood the excruciating pain this helpless creature was now enduring, having been violently pulled out of his world and into the foreign, suffocating world of what must have appeared to him as monsters or aliens who had no mercy. It was one of those moments when my direct connection with an animal was undeniable – and completely overwhelming. The fish was asking me – *begging* me – for help.

I began to cry and scream to my boyfriend to please let the poor creature go. For the first time, I really understood how unnecessary such suffering was. My boyfriend wasn't intentionally abusing an animal, of course; he was simply unable to hear that animal's cries. But I heard them loud and clear and I've never forgotten them. After much struggling, the fish's life reached a tragic end and I understood – for the first time, perhaps – the meaning of the phrase, 'Ignorance is bliss'.

Up until that point, it hadn't fully registered what an incredible amount of suffering takes place to land any animal on our dinner plates – not only a cow or a chicken or a lamb – but also a fish. It was then that it first fully hit me that all animals are sentient beings worthy of our compassion; and when we choose to eat them, a tremendous amount of suffering takes place, whether we are the ones who do the killing or not.

Our human-crafted devices of killing – whether they be hooks or nets or slaughterhouse production lines – are so outside the laws of nature, so outside the laws of compassion, that if a human were to be subjected to any one of them, the perpetrator would undoubtedly receive maximum punishment.

I began to think about humanity and our bloody history here on Earth. I began to wonder if perhaps we were missing the lesson, over and over, and were repeatedly being given the opportunity to do things differently – to expand our minds and our hearts to love unconditionally. The animal kingdom provides us perhaps with an even bigger opportunity to get the lesson of love, for the animals we oppress don't have the means – or the voice – to fight back. It's entirely up to us to speak up for them.

To love that which is different comes naturally to some people, but for humanity as a whole this has been perhaps the hardest lesson of all. Human history demonstrates this in a most dramatic way. Slavery, the Holocaust, the so-called holy wars and the oppression of Native Americans, women and countless other groups are but a handful of examples of this. The ongoing and often widely accepted oppression of non-human animals in our world is evidence we have a long way to go yet. We as a species still have a lot of growing up to do.

Perhaps the animals are here to teach us. What better examples of unconditional love do we have than our companion animals? Humans are capable of tremendous acts of hatred, so perhaps it is we who must learn to commit commendable acts of love – and even to develop our own souls and earn a place in Heaven – because of the love of an animal.

Interestingly, many of the wisest teachers, philosophers, geniuses and gurus throughout history have made compassion toward animals a core element of their teachings. Unfortunately, this is very often overlooked or downplayed, but it is there loud and clear, whether we choose to pay attention or not.

Many great spiritual leaders have promoted compassion for animals. In fact, a vegetarian diet is often considered a logical step on the spiritual path. Gandhi, St Francis and Jesus were all strongly opposed to animal 'sacrifice'. St Francis and Jesus both actually *rescued* animals from sacrifice, and they certainly didn't gain any popularity by doing so. For more information on this, I highly recommend *Peace to All Beings: Veggie Soup for the Chicken's Soul* by Judy Carman.

Spiritually inclined people often proclaim we are not human beings having a spiritual experience, but rather, we are spiritual beings having a human experience. I wholeheartedly agree with this statement. If we are indeed spiritual beings having a human experience, then it could equally be said that animals are spiritual beings having an animal experience. The logical conclusion: We are *all* spiritual beings.

Note: Excerpts taken from pages 347-348 and 390-393 of *Animals and the Afterlife*.

■ MAKING POSITIVE CHOICES
Kathy Divine

▶ Kathy Divine with rescued lamb.

Kathy Divine is author of *Forever 21: the empowering guide to reclaiming your youth, beauty, health, happiness and spirituality*, *Vegans are Cool* and *Plant-powered Men* ...   ■

I never imagined I would become a vegetarian, let alone a vegan. The turning point and ultimate commitment for me came when I read a small green booklet called *The Key of Immediate Enlightenment* by Supreme Master Ching Hai. The section, Why We Must Be Vegetarian, laid out clearly and simply why being a vegetarian was great for health, increased compassion towards animals, was good for the environment and essential for spiritual cultivation. My goal at the time was to find a way to connect with God in a deep and profound way. When I read that being vegetarian was conducive to good meditation practice, I realised I must become a vegetarian at least, if not a vegan. I intuitively knew that everything in this booklet was correct and from that moment it became my serious goal to follow its principles so I could expand my compassion for all beings and come to know God more profoundly.

A healthy, nutrient-rich vegan diet has enabled me to reverse serious fibromyalgia, which I had for several years. There are many medical conditions, such as diabetes and heart disease, which can be reversed by following a healthy vegan diet. Untold suffering can be avoided to ensure greater quality of life and longevity by simple changes to the diet. I am happy to have been able to experience the immense health benefits of a healthy vegan diet, as I am now able to help many people who are suffering in the same way I was.

Being vegan is the best thing we can do to ensure our health is optimised, the planet is in balance and our beautiful animal friends live in peace and harmony. The vegan diet, particularly an organic vegan diet, has the lightest eco-footprint when compared to other diets such as animal-based diets, so for all reasons and in all ways, the vegan diet is the way to go!

Link:

www.vegansarecool.com   www.kathydivine.com

■ COMPASSION ENCIRCLES THE EARTH FOR ALL BEINGS EVERYWHERE
Judy Carman

Judy Carman, MA, is a former counsellor and program director for mental health clinics. As an author and activist for animal rights, environmental protection, and world peace, she has helped establish organisations both for adults and children over the years. Most recently she has co-founded Animal Outreach of Kansas and the Worldwide Prayer Circle for Animals, and is also a Peace Representative of the World Peace Prayer Society. She is part of an animal rescue network and has been deployed to several disaster areas to help animals and their people.

▶ Judy Carman and rescued sheep at Farm Sanctuary, USA.

Her books include *Born to Be Blessed: Seven Keys to Joyful Living* and *Peace to All Beings: Veggie Soup for the Chicken's Soul.* She is co-author with Tina Volpe of *The Missing Peace: The Hidden Power of Our Kinship with Animals.* Her *Peace to All Beings* was judged one of the best spiritual books of 2003. In it Judy introduced the concept of *Homo ahimsa* (ahimsa is the Sanskrit word for nonviolence and loving kindness) to describe the new compassionate human we will become if enough of humanity awakens in time.

Judy is featured in *Vegetarians and Vegans in America Today.* She contributes articles and essays to newspapers, books and magazines. Some of her articles appear at peacetoallbeings.com, along with excerpts from *Peace to all Beings.* She has been a keynote speaker and workshop leader at many conferences… ■

The following is an excerpt from Chapter Twelve of The Missing Peace, *by Tina Volpe and Judy Carman, with a postscript addition.*

God's Lambs by Judy

I, like most young children, was shielded from the violence of the world initially. The majority of children's storybooks bear witness to that. It is almost as if the adults who write them are saying, "No, really, Earth is a paradise where animals and people live together in harmony, and horses and cows and pigs come into the house with the dogs and everybody is happy." I have yet to find a children's book that ends with pictures of the beloved animals lying slaughtered and bleeding.

Yet eventually this fantasy crumbles and the truth about what human beings really do to animals (not to mention other people and nature) can no longer be kept from the children. Though we may not remember it, the loss of that belief in a paradise affects us with a deep and penetrating grief about which few of us speak.

It is at such a point in our young lives that we feel the need to ease this vague and untitled pain and find inner peace. It is a longing to reconnect with animals and nature and feel again that precious kinship. It is a longing to find the paradise we thought existed here, and for some, it becomes a lifelong goal to create that kind and peaceful world, regardless of the odds against it.

The beginning of the disconnection is well illustrated in this example. A four-year-old I know whose father hunts birds once explained to me that the birds are 'bad'. When I asked him why, he said, "Well, Daddy hates them, so he kills them." In order to make sense of the fact that his gentle, adoring dad would do such harm, he decided on his own that the birds must be really bad.

Looking back on my life, I think my lost paradise came into sharp focus with the lambs. I was ten years old when every kid's dream came true for me. My family moved to the edge of town onto seven acres with a pasture. A pasture! That meant we could share our lives with more animals and that sounded just perfect to me.

When the sheep arrived to live with us and have their babies, I fell in love with them, of course. In my naïve imagination, we would always be together. I spent as much time as I could with them. They were so perfectly innocent and they loved to be hugged and cuddled. Each one had his or her own special personality. Holding them was like holding a little piece of Heaven. I loved to look at the picture of Jesus holding a lamb in his arms, and it gave me a sense of the sacredness of these precious beings and their mystical connection to divine love.

Then one day, as you have already no doubt guessed, I came home from school to an empty pasture. No lambs. No warning. No chance to save them. Where had they been taken? Yet my tears at their loss were nothing in comparison to the next shock I was to experience.

It was dinnertime and the table was filled with the usual meal over which my mother had faithfully laboured. The big hunk of meat was, as usual, the center-piece of the meal and, somehow, a symbol that we were prospering and well fed. And then it happened. Someone – I don't recall who, but someone who knew, spoke glowingly of the delicious lamb we were eating.

There it was, for me, as for so many of us, the sudden overwhelming realisation that meat comes from the animals we love, animals we see in books, animals in pastures, animals whom we know personally; animals whose eyes once shone brightly with the joy of living. I might as well have discovered I was eating my dog. I was inconsolable. What kind of world was I living in where friends ate friends; where innocent, defenceless animals were taught to trust and then be taken away without goodbyes, brutally killed and devoured?

Such things are called the loss of innocence in children. It is also the loss of innocents, the terrible loss of billions of innocent beings. And historically, both losses have taken an immense toll on the soul of humanity.

From that point on, I did not want to eat meat. (It took me many more years to learn about the suffering inherent in milk and eggs.) However, this was the fifties in Kansas. My father was a hunter. My uncles ran the stockyards and slaughter-house. I had never heard of vegetarians; perhaps my parents hadn't either. I became known as 'woolly minded' for not wanting to eat animals. I guess I was, since it was the woolly lambs themselves who transformed and renewed my mind. So I ate very little meat and fed a lot to the dogs under the table.

It was confusing. There was so much pride about such a brutal thing. We occasionally would eat at the Golden Ox, a restaurant built on the edge of the stockyards. The Kansas City steaks were famous, I was told. The stench of dead and dying cows outside the restaurant was horrific, but inside everyone seemed happy. As I flashed back to the storybooks in which kids and cows were friends, it all blurred together for me in a confusing mess. As kids, we can't articulate it, but what we are feeling is, "This isn't the way the world is supposed to be. What is going on?"

Meanwhile, to add to the confusion, my father was a big-game hunter. Our home décor included a dead polar bear made into a rug (shot by him in Alaska), a dead zebra made into a rug (shot by him in Africa), and numerous animals' heads looking down at me from the walls. Dad didn't hate these animals. He simply thought he had the right to kill them (including entire families for museum displays).

Dad killed hundreds of animals, including wolves from a plane, many mammals and beautiful birds, and uncounted fish. Favourite guests in our home included many a hunter and fisherman who loved to share their stories over glasses of bourbon and scotch. The air of respect and admiration that filled the house for Dad and these folks was palpable. Indeed, many, like my father, were medical doctors and other professionals who made great contributions to the human community.

For this and other reasons, I remained puzzled and wondered if something was wrong with me because the juxtaposition of admired men and ruthless killing didn't make any sense to me.

That state of mind led me on a lifelong search to find meaning in life, an explanation for all the violence, and to find my own way and purpose. Somehow, my quest to do what I could to stop the suffering of others and find my own peace became a tandem journey.

Finally, in my twenties I began hearing about vegetarianism and learning how to live in that way. As my journey has continued, we have all become more aware of the atrocities, and some reforms and some liberations have taken place. With the help of the information that came out from the many animal rights groups that formed, I began to learn his was not just about avoiding the eating of animals. This was about changing the entire world-view of humanity toward nature and all life.

This was not just a new way to eat; this was indeed a spiritual, intellectual, ethical and moral revolution. Realising this, I felt compelled not only to leave off eating animals, but also to speak out for them and for the new paradigm of living in harmony with all.

In a way, it is ironic to think one could find peace and joy when confronted with an endless litany of abuses committed by people against innocent and help-less animals, and, of course, people and nature as well. But compared to where I was as a clueless child and a young adult, I have found a peace and joy that is with me always. How can this be?

I hope the many stories in this book show how this can happen (*The Missing Peace* is a collection of stories from hunters, farmers, psychics and many others who found that becoming vegan gave them an inner peace they had never known before). Perhaps it seems a stretch to say that living a vegan life can bring us peace and joy. But let us look at the broadest definition of veganism. The foundation of such a life includes doing the least harm possible in all our actions and living a life of service, nonviolence, loving kindness and kinship with all beings. Is it any wonder then that so many people find such precious peace by living in this way? For by giving peace, they receive exactly that in return.

As we have learnt throughout *The Missing Peace*, veganism is much more than a diet. It is a spiritual makeover of extraordinary proportions. It involves question-ing absolutely everything we've been taught by our culture, de-programming our minds, finding friends who are learning to live this way, practising being mindful and treasuring each moment instead of listening to our egos' regrets and fears.

And I have to say to you all, that sounds like a lot, but with each step, our spir-its become more liberated and more joyful. And if I did it, anyone can, absolutely anyone. I certainly have not reached some pinnacle of perfection, but every day is more entrancing than the one before, and God's peace is always with me. There is just something so spirit lifting about knowing that at each meal we are saving the lives of people and animals, and in so doing, we are demonstrating love and peace.

By doing the absolute least harm possible, we are set free to participate in the celebration of life; to look into the big eyes of a cow and know she is our friend, not our food; to feel the ecstasy of our oneness with all life; to sing praises with the crickets and frogs; to greet the fly in our house and carry her gently outside; to pray for and with the ones we cannot save; to know we are creating a better world, a new culture, with our love. That is the treasure – the missing peace found at last.

I came full circle a few months ago when I visited Farm Sanctuary in Watkins Glen, New York. There I was able to snuggle with lambs once again and bask in their sweet and peaceful presence. They were as I remembered them. Like dogs, they gathered among us asking for hugs and caresses. They looked at me so trust-ingly as my lamb friends had done so long ago. But the innocent trust of these lambs will not be betrayed.

May all lambs be safe from harm. May all beings be free. May all human beings awaken to universal love and ahimsa.

Postscript: Several years have passed since I wrote *God's Lambs*. My inner peace remains my constant companion, and I continue to meet new people who have experienced the same serenity and joy as a result of living a nonviolent, vegan life. Of course, there are moments and sometimes days when news of yet another unbelievable atrocity toward animals comes into view on the news or the internet. Anger and outrage are normal reactions to the relentless cruelty we witness. And yet from the vantage point of a nonviolent life, while the anger ripples the surface of our lives, it need not drag us down to despair.

From the place of peace within our hearts there is a steadiness and a sense of purpose. Those who have passed through the doorway of denial, witnessed the warfare against animals and chosen to refuse to participate in it have seen not just the cruelty, but also the miracle of human transformation. Because we have transformed, we know it is possible for all humanity to give up domination and begin to live in peace with all beings.

We are teaching and living the ultimate peace – a peace not just for people but for all beings everywhere. It is no wonder that peace comes back to us to fill our lives. A few days ago I had such a good example of that. I live in the country, and my walks take me by pastures, hay fields and prairie flowers. There is one pasture where the cows are often near the fence. I like to stop and sing to them when they are close by, and they like to crowd up to the fence and watch me and listen. They are such good listeners. They don't even wince when I hit a wrong note.

In the past they have backed up a step or two if I get too close to the fence, but on this day something was different. I took a step forward while singing, and they did not move back but instead pushed even closer to each other and the fence. I took another step and still they did not retreat. Finally I was within a couple of feet of them. Then, to my great joy, each one took turns stretching out their necks toward me to sniff my hair and face. I was so close to their big wet noses and their huge, beautiful brown eyes and long, long eyelashes, it brought tears to my own eyes. Two of them actually licked my cheek with their tongues – a little slobbery, but so precious I could not refuse what I like to believe were cow kisses.

The animals are reaching out to us in many ways these days, trying to tell us who they really are. May every human being find his or her own animal teacher and experience the joy of our sacred interconnectedness and communion. Peace to you and to all beings.

Links:

www.peacetoallbeings.com

www.circleofcompassion.org

www.animaloutreach-ks.org

www.elephantfreedom.com

www.worldpeace.org

■ INSPIRING A KINDER HUMANITY
Supreme Master Ching Hai

"If the lion is to lie down next to the lamb peacefully, humans must do it first." ■

—Supreme Master Ching Hai.

▶ Supreme Master Ching Hai with avian friend.

This article was compiled with assistance from Supreme Master Ching Hai International Association members.

Very few individuals living today have inspired the transition to a vegan lifestyle in more numbers globally than Supreme Master Ching Hai, a world-renowned humanitarian, artist, poet, author and spiritual teacher.

Respected US author and inspirational speaker Dr Will Tuttle wrote about Supreme Master Ching Hai as follows:

"The worldwide followers of [Supreme Master] Ching Hai, a noted Vietnamese spiritual teacher with students numbering in the hundreds of thousands, have set up vegan restaurants in many cities and contribute vegan food, clothing, shelter and aid to disaster victims, prisoners, children and the elderly in countries around the world. …in less than twenty years she has been the proximate cause of hundreds of thousands of people's transition to veganism." *The World Peace Diet: Eating for Spiritual Health and Social Harmony*… ■

Born in central Au Lac, Vietnam, Supreme Master Ching Hai studied in Europe and worked for the Red Cross. Through her experiences, she realised that suffering existed in all corners of the globe, and her yearning to find a remedy became the foremost goal in her life. She embarked on a journey to the Himalayas in search of spiritual enlightenment and eventually received divine transmission of the inner Light and Sound, which she later called the Quan Yin Method, a method she introduces to her students.

As a modern-day spiritual teacher, Supreme Master Ching Hai has given lectures around the world free of charge upon the invitation of governments, the media and various organisations including the United Nations. Her students, all vegans, are remarkably diverse, coming from all corners of the world, and from all religious and non-religious backgrounds.

Supreme Master Ching Hai says, "Through meditation, I have realised the sameness of all beings and the inner connection between all of us. We came from the same essence – many people are too busy to hear what their animal friends are telling them. There's no end to what an animal can and will do for the near and loved humans."

The Supreme Master Ching Hai emphasises that we must adopt a plant-based diet as the first step towards reawakening the love power we already have within us. This, she says, is the same as what past enlightened teachers have taught for millennia through concepts such as ahimsa, compassion and karmic retribution, or 'as you sow, so shall you reap.' She says that a plant-based lifestyle is the noble way of living, and animals are our 'co-inhabitants'.

As an internationally recognised humanitarian, Supreme Master Ching Hai has donated tens of millions of dollars to various charities and disaster relief efforts from her independent income as an accomplished artist, fashion and jewellery designer. Many of her beneficiaries include animal companion shelters, farm animal sanctuaries, and victims of disasters both wild and domestic. She has also contributed large donations to animal protection organisations such as People for the Ethical Treatment of Animals, the Humane Society of the United States, Physicians' Committee for Responsible Medicine and the Sea Shepherd Conservation Society.

Since the early 1980's she has also been one of the planet's most dedicated ecological pioneers, promoting environmental protection. She has been invited to many climate change conferences and media interviews, where she emphasises the fact that livestock raising is the most significant cause of global warming, and that an organic vegan diet and organic vegan farming are the key priorities needed to reverse the urgent planetary crisis. Two slogans she created, that have become known worldwide, are 'Be Veg, Go Green 2 Save the Planet!' and 'Be Vegan, Make Peace'.

For years, Supreme Master Ching Hai has emphasised that to end the suffering of humans and animals, as well as protect our fragile environment, we must adopt a compassionate plant-based diet.

In 2006, she forsaw the pandemics that would sweep the Earth if the meat-eating habit persisted. To encourage the global adoption of a plant-based lifestyle, she created the *Alternative Living* flyer explaining the nutritional benefits of plant-based proteins. The flyer has been distributed worldwide and enabled many people to feel confident in eating a vegan diet.

She was the inspiration for Supreme Master Television, an international, non-profit television station dedicated to programs that promote peace, healthy and eco-friendly living, vegan living and the beauty and intelligence of our animal co-inhabitants. It aired live from 2006 through 2012, and reached hundreds of millions around the world via fourteen satellite platforms, on more than seventy-five cable and IPTV networks in more than sixty languages. It continues to be available online, where thousands of hours of free content are available to viewers, as well as the most recent videos of her talks.

Loving Hut, which has become the world's largest vegan restaurant chain, is another organisation established on the foundation of her teachings to help humanity transition more quickly to a compassionate lifestyle. She and her followers have helped raise awareness of the importance of eating a vegan diet for greater environmental stewardship, personal health and compassion for animals, helping to make the vegan diet and lifestyle trendy. And Supreme Master Ching Hai's vision 'World Vegan World Peace' is in the making.

Link:

www.godsdirectcontact.org.

■ A NEW FORM OF COMMUNICATION INTERVIEW WITH
Sharon Callahan, Animal Intuitive and Healer

"Much of my work is with companion animals, including cats, dogs, rabbits and birds, but I feel we really need to shift our thinking so we consider each and every animal down to the tiniest insects as our companions on the path. If we do that, the world will change." ■

—Sharon Callahan.

Sharon Callahan is a writer, photographer, internationally recognised animal communication specialist and leading pioneer in the use of flower essences for the treatment of animals.

Although Sharon's ability to communicate with animals has been with her from childhood, a near-death experience in 1987 enhanced her ability to communicate with animals telepathically, giving her a deep understanding of the role of animals in the spiritual lives of human beings. This experience led to the creation of Anaflora flower essences for animals, the first flower essences made exclusively for the animal kingdom. Anaflora flower essences and essence formulas are now endorsed by veterinarians and widely accepted and used by animal health care professionals throughout the world… ■

❱ Sharon Callahan.

Could you give one or two examples of how your work has helped people and their companion animals?

I largely work on a spiritual level helping people understand the animal's spiritual purpose in their life and how that animal is attending to and helping them on their path to awakening or enlightenment. For example, someone might call me about a cat who's not using a litter box or a dog with allergies and the consultation evolves from whatever the presenting challenge is into something far more glorious than the caller ever imagined.

For example, bees are dying off in great numbers throughout the world and as they're one of the prime pollinators it's a very distressing situation. I worked with several beekeepers back east and communicated with their bees. The bees indicated they wanted the insides of the hives to be made out of a kind of fibrous material, and round, as they would make them in nature. The bees are now thriving, producing beautiful bounteous honey and because these hives are built with love and attention, the honeybees are no longer dying off like those in the commercial hives.

In many ways bees are more evolved than human beings because they give over their energy to the good of the hive rather than having that energy go into an ego or individual self. There is much that can be learnt from animals such as bees.

Not only are they one of the major pollinators but they are an incredible example of how we can live together in a cooperative way for the good of everyone.

In this instance, the bees themselves were able to tell us what would help them. Scientifically, it is believed they are dying off because of a mite that affects their trachea and their ability to breathe. This may be, but the bottom line is we are destroying their habitat through abuses of all kinds, including deforestation and pesticides. The way I look at it is the animals are leaving simply because we don't love them enough for them stay. We don't love them enough to house them properly or to leave their environments alone. Basically it comes back to lack of love.

Much of my work is with companion animals, including cats, dogs, rabbits and birds, but I feel we really need to shift our thinking so we consider each and every animal down to the tiniest insects as our companions on the path. If we do that, the world will change.

How do you perceive your relationship with animals?

I don't tend to think in terms of relationship because that suggests relationship of one being toward another. I tend to feel a oneness, a togetherness or connection, with all beings and things so there isn't even the separation of relationship if that makes any sense. I don't even know what to say about what I do any more because I don't feel I'm really the doer. Communion would be a better word. Communion is still a kind of separation but it's more of a working with, rather than a relating to, so it comes a little bit closer.

What are some of the greatest lessons from this work for you?

The greatest lesson the animals and the work have taught me is to simply get out of the way and to relinquish any sense of my little self and to allow whatever needs and wants to come through me as a channel for the Divine to move through unobstructed by any personal need or label or thought about who I am.

There's a beautiful poem (Shams-ud-din Muhummad Hafiz) that says,

"I am a hole in a flute that the Christ's breath moves through, listen to this music."

I'm not the flute player, I'm not even the flute. I'm simply the hole in the flute the universal breath moves through. That can be the Christ breath, the Buddhist breath. I am simply the hole in the flute.

What led you into this work?

It happened more than twenty-five years ago when my life as I knew it was falling apart. I'd been in a very challenging relationship. My father had committed suicide some years before and then my twenty-five-year-old daughter mysteriously disappeared and was never found. I was also getting very physically sick from Lyme Disease which wasn't diagnosed at that time. Something inside me gave me the courage to leave the marriage and I walked out of the house with just a backpack and my cat, Haiku. I simply left the house and walked downtown. I sat in a coffee shop and asked God to help me. He sent along a lovely older hippie woman, who took Haiku and me back to her home where she let us live for a year.

It was the combination of occurrences: depression over the marriage, the loss of my daughter, the suicide of my father and the breakdown of my body – the universe was conspiring to break me down so that I literally almost died and was reborn. I use the word 'conspire', which is actually a wonderful, wonderful word. We tend to distort it in western culture, we think of it as a negative, but conspire means to breathe with. So in some magical way the universe conspired to bring me close to death literally. I had a near-death experience and when I came out of that I was like a child again. I had amnesia for a while, I did not know who I was or who my friends were, those wonderful friends who had helped me, and it was out of that childlike state that the work arose. I found myself making flower essences and I began to communicate with plants and animals. As I recovered people started to ask me for help with their animals or to speak with the animals for them. It sounds almost unbelievable but it really did arise like that, not from me but through me from the very beginning, from that childlike state where I was literally experiencing flowers and plants on the level of friendship. I was able to hear the animals, to listen to them and to communicate what they said to their humans.

One really important thing for people to realise is that nothing in life that happens to us is bad. If I told my story out of context, they might think it was a tragic story. But it isn't. I was shattered on every level, emotionally, physically, mentally – and out of that arose a newer different being, a newer different me, not an ego self but more a wiping of the slate clean, which has enabled me to simply be that hole in the flute.

I recently read an article in an interspecies communication magazine where many of the animal communicators were interviewed about their dietary habits. Some were strict vegans and others still ate meat. I wondered if you could talk about where you stand on this issue and why.

It's quite a spectrum isn't it? I wouldn't venture to judge anyone else but I would simply ask a question back which would be, why would animals talk to you if you ate them? And I think I'd probably leave it at that.

So what do you really think is at the bottom of our mistreatment of animals? I know you said before that we're just not loving them enough, but why not?

For me it's more that we've forgotten who we are. We've forgotten we are Divine beings, that we needn't prey on one another or animals, that we don't need to harm anything or anyone to be healthy and whole. We've simply forgotten who we are and the animals would say the same thing. If you remember who you are you will do no harm to any other living creature. So it is vital you remember who you are.

I know you believe animals have souls and that they're spiritual beings. If you were able to change the way our world related to animals right now, today, what would that change be?

Can I go back one step? I like to think of it not that animals or people or other creatures have souls but that we are literally living souls and if anything, the soul isn't in us or in the animals, we're actually in the soul, the one great soul, so I feel that animals, people, plants are living souls.

This brings up objections that come from people who say plants are living things too and we eat plants so it's all right to eat animals.

Plants are alive, absolutely. I think collectively human beings are in a state of evolution that could be very rapid if we would just get out of our own way. I really do believe that food is way too big an issue. Why do we think about it so much? My feeling is we can move from not harming or eating animals to eating vegetables to living on fruit and nuts and eventually living on light. Food in itself is such a story we tell ourselves. Existence is simply different levels of densification of light so we move more and more towards the subtle. I don't know how this would be described properly in scientific terms.

For me it's more that we've forgotten who we are. We've forgotten we are Divine beings, that we needn't prey on one another or animals, that we don't need to harm anything or anyone to be healthy and whole. We've simply forgotten who we are and the animals would say the same thing. If you remember who you are you will do no harm to any other living creature. So it is vital you remember who you are.

When I had a near-death experience in that period of amnesia, what never came back was anything I'd ever learnt in school, so from a scientific perspective I don't know how to describe it but I perceive everything as light. For a period after my illness I literally saw everything as light but then things became more solid and I began to be able to identify and label things again. Now it is clear to me that everything is light.

The great saints, sages and holy people of the past, and those who are living, would say that what we consider as savagery and predation in animals is simply an out-picturing of human consciousness. We're the greatest predators on the planet and in my view, as we move into a position of non-harming we will find literally overnight that animals won't feed on each other either.

Expanding Religious Perspectives

■ ADDRESS AT WESTMINSTER ABBEY AT THE SERVICE IN CELEBRATION OF ANIMALS

Sunday 2nd October 2011
Reverend Andrew Linzey

> *"The truth is that we are spiritually blind in our relations to other creatures, as blind as men have been to women, whites have been to blacks, and straights have been to gays. We think God is only interested in the human species. This is the fault line that runs through almost all historical and contemporary theology."* ■

—Reverend Professor Andrew Linzey

▶ Reverend Professor Andrew Linzey.

My text is from John Henry Newman, "Cruelty to animals is as if a man did not love God"[1].

I have been involved in the animal cause for more than forty years. And what has changed for animals during these years? Sometimes it appears that sensitivity to animal suffering is increasing. It is certainly true that the past forty years have seen significant strides in the United Kingdom.

Hunting and coursing have been banned; fur farming prohibited, veal crates, sow stalls and battery cages are being phased out, testing for cosmetics has been effectively discontinued, and the use of great apes in experiments has been curtailed. The Animal Welfare Act of 2006 introduced for the first time a 'duty of care' for domestic animals.

Underpinning these legislative changes has been a dramatic increase in philosophical work on the moral status of animals, almost all of it critical of existing practices. This, in turn, has been buttressed by

scientific data demonstrating that all mammals at least experience not just physical pain, but also mental suffering, including fear, foreboding, shock, trauma,
stress, distress, anticipation and terror, all states previously regarded as exclusive
to human beings[2].

Yet animal abuse is like a multi-headed hydra. As one is cut off, another grows.
Having seen a progressive reduction in the number of experiments in the early
nineties, they are now back to the levels of the 1980s, with more than 3.7 million
in the UK alone in 2010[3]. And many of these experiments are due to the massive
growth in genetic manipulation, of which animals have been the prime victims.
Having dismantled the worst aspects of factory farming, we now face the emergence of 'mega-dairies' in which up to eight thousand cows are to be kept perma-
nently inside factories devoid of natural light and pasture. Only a few days ago,
we heard of plans for 'mega-piggeries' to house no less than thirty thousand pigs[4].
More than ever, we are turning animals into food machines.

And the underbelly of cruelty to animals shows no sign of diminishing. Com-
plaints of cruelty investigated by the RSPCA have risen year on year from 137,245 in
2007 to 159,686 in 2010[5]. Is this because people are more sensitive or because they
have become more callous? The jury is still out, but the overall trend is disquieting.

Why is it that we cannot as a society see that animal cruelty, like cruelty to
children, should not be tolerated?

Part of the answer is sheer political sluggishness. The government has done
nothing to thwart plans for 'mega-dairies'. Despite overwhelming support for a
ban on 'wild' animals in circuses, the Department for Environment, Food and
Rural Affairs and the Prime Minister obfuscate. The government still manoeuvres
to bring back hunting with dogs. The previous government was at least preparing
to examine the links between animal abuse and human violence, but the current
government has shelved all that. Despite scientific evidence that killing badgers is
ineffective, even counter-productive in reducing bovine tuberculosis, the government now proposes yet more of the same. I am still waiting for an answer from
Caroline Spelman, the Secretary of State for the Environment, who appears unable
to provide answers to my specific questions about its scientific validity.

Instead of frustrating reform, the government should celebrate the fact that
Britain has led the movement for the protection of animals and lament the fact
that it is so falling behind, as it should vigorously support the initiatives of the
RSPCA to make Britain a less cruel country.

And then we come to the churches. Where are they? The answer is they are
nowhere in this debate. With a few honourable exceptions – and I mean a *very*
few – English archbishops and bishops haven't even addressed the issue in the
past decade or more. Almost all church leaders, who are normally loquacious
in lamenting regressive social policies, can't even register animal cruelty as a
problem. They talk airily of environmental responsibility, but when it comes to
confronting our specific duties to other sentient creatures, they fall silent. What
is true about the church's teaching is even more true of the church's liturgy. A
prayer for the welfare of God's other creatures is nowhere to be found in its

liturgical offerings. And why is it that those Christian pioneers, like Arthur Broome who effectively founded the RSPCA, are not remembered in such hallowed places as this?

All this represents not just a failure in moral perception, but a fundamental failure in theology, much deeper and much more profound than is commonly appreciated. Ludwig Feuerbach famously argued that Christianity is nothing other than the self-aggrandisement, even deification, of the human species[6]. Christian theology needs animals to save itself – and ourselves – from idolatry. By 'idolatry', I mean the attempt to deify the human species by regarding the interests of human beings as the sole or exclusive concern of God the Creator[7].

To avoid this charge, theology needs to show that it can provide what it promises – namely a truly Godward (rather than a simply anthropocentric) view of the world. Its obsession with human beings to the exclusion of all else betokens a deeply unbalanced doctrine of the Creator.

Christians haven't got much further than thinking the whole world was made for them, with the result that animals are only seen in an instrumental way as objects, machines, tools and commodities, rather than fellow creatures. We just haven't grasped that the God who meets us in Jesus is also the Logos through whom, and for whom, all creatures exist. To think that animals can be defined by what they do *for* us, or how they meet *our* needs, is profoundly un-theological.

The truth is that we are spiritually blind in our relations to other creatures, as blind as men have been to women, whites have been to blacks and straights have been to gays.

We think God is only interested in the human species. This is the fault line that runs through almost all historical and contemporary theology.

When I was a theological student in the 1970s, I loved reading John Macquarrie's majestic book *Principles of Christian Theology*[8] – an attempt to marry humanistic existentialist thought with traditional theology. At the time I remember thinking to myself how his whole edifice would collapse if he saw that God had interests beyond the human species. And what is true of Macquarrie is true of almost all theology.

Later, when I did my PhD on Karl Barth's doctrine of creation, I was astonished by how he defines without a blush creation *as* anthropology, "… in practice the doctrine of creation means anthropology – the doctrine of man." Again, "He who in the biblical message is called God is obviously not interested in the totality of things and beings created by Him, nor in specific beings within this totality, but in man …"[9]. Such crassness, from someone who is probably the greatest theologian of all time, takes one's theological breath away.

Now, I know all the usual responses.

"We have been given dominion over animals," it is countered.

Well, dominion does not mean despotism. For centuries, it needs to be admitted, Christians have interpreted Genesis 1 as meaning little more than 'might is right' – a view that has influenced the largely secular view of animals today. But modern scholarship has made clear how wrong we were. The priestly theology of Genesis is not that of man the despot, but rather of humanity as the species commissioned to care, under God, for the creation. And in case this appears like liberal revisionism of an ancient text, there is internal evidence in the text itself. In Genesis 1.26-9 humans are made in God's image, given dominion, and in the subsequent verse (29-30) given a vegetarian diet. Herb-eating dominion is hardly a licence for tyranny[10]. Our power over animals is a power to care, not to exploit.

"We humans are made in the image of God," it is often said.

But the God in whose image we are made is a God of love, mercy, justice. It is difficult to see how being made in *that* image can justify the infliction of pain, whatever the motives. Indeed modern scholarship reveals that 'image' and 'dominion' go together: humans are to represent God's own benevolent care for other creatures. If one truly believes that God is benevolent and that humans are made in God's image, then our obligations are clear: we also must be benevolent not just to other humans but to the whole of God's creation. Humans are uniquely responsible to God for how they exercise their authority. What emerges from Genesis chapter 1 is that God creates humans with God-given capacities to care for creation as God's own representatives on earth. We are to be not so much the 'master species' as the 'servant species'[11].

Frequently, religious people speak of the specialness of human beings, how we are made in the image of God, or blessed by the Spirit, but so often they fail to point out the equally biblical truth that humans are also the most unlovely species in the world, the species capable of degrading themselves beyond that of any other creature. Unique we may be, but unique also is our violence, our wickedness, our capacity for evil. Alone among all beings in the universe, we are capable of the best – and also the very worst. It is not for nothing that God says in Genesis 6.6 that he "was sorry that he made man on the earth."

"But the Bible is preoccupied with the salvation of human beings," it is often said.

Well, from my perspective, so it should be. Humans need saving from their wickedness and violence. That animals will be redeemed strikes me as rather obvious – after all they are morally innocent or blameless, not sinful, violent and wicked like human beings. The real question is not whether animals will be in heaven, but whether any humans will be there as well.

I am getting rather fed up with the way in which the animal cause is so casually dismissed.

"We should care for children rather than animals," it is claimed.

Well, this rather overlooks the fact that it was members of the RSPCA who helped found the National Society for the Prevention of Cruelty to Children, and that the leading lights of the RSPCA – Wilberforce and Shaftesbury to take only two examples – worked equally hard for suffering children as they did for suffering animals. They saw, as we need to see, that the cause of cruelty was indivisible. A world in which cruelty to animals goes unchecked is bound to be a less morally safe world for human beings[12].

"We shouldn't indulge animals when humans are starving," it is claimed.

Well, as we all know, there would be more food to eat in the world if we all became vegetarian or vegan. Animals are protein machines in reverse, since grain fed to animals could be used to directly feed hungry humans. But in fact, as a rule, we don't indulge animals. Some companion animals may be lavishly treated, but the RSPCA has to live daily with the thousands who are abused, neglected and treated as fungible, disposable items. The RSPCA and other animal organisations have the unenviable task of rescuing creatures from those who, far from indulging them, do not even given them the basic rudiments of care.

"But human suffering comes first," it is argued.

Well, in my book, all suffering is suffering. It is all part of the great conceit and hubris of the human species to suppose only human suffering really matters or matters most. What after all is most pitiable about the suffering of young children, especially infants? It is surely that they cannot represent themselves, they cannot give or withhold their consent, they cannot fully understand, they are defenceless and vulnerable, and especially that they are morally innocent or blameless. But all these factors are equally true in the case of animals[13].

John Henry Newman argued, "Cruelty to animals is as if a man did not love God." The point was made even more strongly by that Anglican divine Humphrey Primatt in his great work *The Duty of Mercy and the Sin of Cruelty* in 1776. This was the book that influenced Arthur Broome and which he subsequently helped revise, after Primatt's death, for its second edition. Primatt wrote, "We may pretend to what religion we please, but cruelty is atheism. We may make our boast of Christianity, but cruelty is infidelity. We may trust to our orthodoxy, but cruelty is the worst of heresies"[14]. Without any disrespect to atheists (after all, I was once one myself), this has to be said from a Christian perspective. And how do we know this is true? We know it is true because of the generosity of God in Jesus Christ. Here we reach the decisive consideration from a theological perspective: our power or lordship over animals needs to be related to that exercise of lordship seen in the life of Jesus Christ. Jesus provides us with what I have called a 'paradigm of inclusive moral generosity' that privileges the weak, the vulnerable, the poor, the marginalised and the outcast. As Primatt goes on to say, "… a cruel Christian is a monster of ingratitude, a scandal to his profession, and beareth the name of Christ in vain …" But if costly generosity really is the God-given paradigm then it ought also to be the paradigm for the exercise of human dominion over the animal world. The doctrine of the incarnation involves the sacrifice of the 'higher' for the 'lower', not the reverse. And if that is the true model of divine generosity, it is difficult to see how humans can otherwise interpret their exercise of power over other sentient creatures.

When we speak of human superiority, we speak of such a thing properly only and in so far as we speak not only of Christ-like lordship but also of Christ-like service. There can be no lordship without service and no service without lordship. Our special value in creation consists in being of special value to others[15].

Let me conclude, then, in this way: we worship a false God when we worship ourselves, or when we think only human beings matter to God, or when we think our power over animals is its own justification, or when we regard cruelty to any creature as a small, insignificant matter, or even worse, when we think God condones any infliction of suffering.

Let me also be frank about the implications of this: we shall not stop cruelty simply by doubling the number of RSPCA inspectors (highly desirable though that is) or by conducting more campaigns (essential though they are) or even by more education (vital though that is too). We shall only change the world for animals by changing our ideas about animals and how we think about animals. We have to change our mental furniture, our whole mental outlook. We have to move from the idea that animals are just things, tools, commodities, resources here for us, to the idea that all sentient creatures have intrinsic value, dignity and rights. And that is why Christian theology is so important. It has shaped our thinking, both positively and negatively, and continues to do so. We need a new theology freed from naïve anthropocentrism and able to confront the selfishness of our own species.

The Anglican priest, Arthur Broome, set up the RSPCA in 1824 as "a Christian society based on Christian principles"[16]. He saw that Christian charity, if it was to be real, had to extend beyond human beings. Some of us are still striving after that vision and still living that hope.

Endnotes

1. John Henry Newman, *Sermon Notes, 1849-1878* (Longmans, Green & Co, 1913) p113.
2. See, for example, David DeGrazia, *Taking Animals Seriously: Mental Life and Moral Status* (Cambridge: Cambridge University Press, 1996), and Bernard E Rollin, *The Unheeded Cry: Animal Consciousness, Animal Pain, and Science* (Oxford University Press, 1990).
3. See the Home Office figures at http://www.homeoffice.gov.uk/publications/science-research-statistics/research-statistics/science-research/spanimals10/spanimals10?view=Binary.
4. For details of the planning application, see http://www.pigbusiness.co.uk/pig-business-events/foston-june-2011/.
5. Statistics supplied by the RSPCA, September 2011.
6. Ludwig Feuerbach, *The Essence of Christianity* (New York: Harper Torchbook, 1957), Translated by George Eliot, Introduction by Karl Barth, Foreword by H Richard Niebuhr, Section 2, pp 12ff.
7. The point is expanded in Andrew Linzey and Dan Cohn-Sherbok, *After Noah: Animals and the Liberation of Theology* (London: Mowbray, now New York: Continuum, 1997), pp 118-119. My earliest complaint against Christian anthropocentrism can be found in Andrew Linzey, 'Is Anthropocentricity Christian?' *Theology*, Vol. LXXXIV, No. 697, January 1981, pp 17-21.
8. John Macquarrie, *Principles of Christian Theology* (London: SCM Press, 1970).
9. Karl Barth, *Church Dogmatics III/2, The Doctrine of the Creator*, Part Two (The Creature), edited by G W Bromiley and T F Torrance, translated by H Knight, G W Bromiley, J K S Reid and R H Fuller (Edinburgh: T & T Clark, 1960),

p 3, and *Church Dogmatics III/4, The Doctrine of Creation*, Part Four, edited and translated by A T Mackay, T H L Parker, H Knight, H A Kennedy, and J Marks (Edinburgh: T & T Clark, 1961), p 337.

10. I summarise the consensus among Old Testament scholars in Andrew Linzey, *Why Animal Suffering Matters: Philosophy, Theology and Practical Ethics* (Oxford: Oxford University Press, 2009), pp 28-29.

11. See Humans as the Servant Species, Chapter 3, Andrew Linzey, *Animal Theology* (London: SCM Press and Chicago: University of Illinois Press, 1994), pp. 45-61. I have also made these points about dominion and the Imago Dei many times (and in much the same language), see, for example, Animal Experiments: Ethics, Theology and the Possibility of Dialogue, in John H Morgan (ed.), *Foundation Theology 2008: Faculty Essays for Ministry Professionals* (South Bend, Indiana: The Victoria Press, 2008), p 92.

12. Humphrey Primatt, *The Duty of Mercy and the Sin of Cruelty* (Edinburgh: T. Constable, 1776), pp 288, and 288-289. For supporting evidence, see Andrew Linzey (ed.), *The Link between Animal Abuse and Human Violence* (Brighton and Portland: Sussex Academic Press, 2009).

13. These are, I contend, the objective rational grounds for being concerned with animal suffering; see Linzey, *Why Animal Suffering Matters*, Chapter 1.

14. Humphrey Primatt, *The Duty of Mercy and the Sin of Cruelty* (Edinburgh: T. Constable, 1776), pp 288, and 288-289.

15. See Chapter 3 in Linzey, *Animal Theology*.

16. Arthur Broome, Prospectus of the RSPCA, 25 June 1824, *RSPCA Records*, Vol. 11. (1823-1826). © Copyright, Andrew Linzey, 2011. Reproduced with permission.

■ RELIGION: FRIEND OR FOE OF ANIMAL ACTIVISM
Richard H Schwartz and Rabbi David Sears

▶ Richard H Schwartz.

Richard H Schwartz, PhD, is Professor Emeritus, College of Staten Island. He is president emeritus of Jewish Vegetarians of North America, president of the Society of Ethical and Religious Vegetarians, and associate producer of *A Sacred Duty*. He is the author of *Judaism and Vegetarianism, Judaism and Global Survival, Who Stole My Religion: Revitalising Judaism and Applying Jewish Values to Help Heal Our Imperiled Planet,* and *Mathematics and Global Survival*.

Rabbi David Sears is the author of *The Vision of Eden: Animal Welfare and Vegetarianism in Jewish Law and Mysticism* (Orot 2002), among many other works on Jewish thought. He has directed the New York Breslov Center since 1967, and created the Solitude-Hisbodedus website on Jewish meditation with Dov Ben Abraham. He is also an artist, photographer and children's book illustrator... ■

▶ Rabbi David Sears.

Many animal activists regard organised religion as an ideological opponent. Concerning Judaism, this negative presumption is largely due to the misunderstanding of two important biblical verses that, when properly conceived, actually endorse the struggle to improve conditions for animals.

The first misunderstanding is that the biblical teaching that humans are granted dominion over animals gives us a warrant to treat them in whatever way we may wish. However, Jewish tradition interprets 'dominion' as guardianship, or stewardship: we are called upon to be co-workers with God in improving the world. This biblical mandate does not mean people have the right to wantonly exploit animals, and it certainly does not permit us to breed animals and then treat them as machines designed solely to meet human needs. In *A Vision of Vegetarianism and Peace*, Rabbi Abraham Isaac Kook, Chief Rabbi of pre-state Israel and a leading twentieth century Jewish thinker, states, "There can be no doubt in the mind of any intelligent person that [the Divine empowerment of humanity to derive benefit from nature] does not mean the domination of a harsh ruler, who afflicts his people and servants merely to satisfy his whim and desire, according to the crookedness of his heart. It is unthinkable that the Divine Law would impose such a decree of servitude, sealed for all eternity, upon the world of God, Who is 'good to all, and His mercy is upon all his works' (Psalms 145:9), and Who declared, 'The world shall be built with kindness' (ibid. 89:33)."

This view is reinforced by the fact that immediately after God gave humankind dominion over animals (Genesis 1:28), He prescribed vegetarian foods as the diet best suited to humans (Genesis 1:29). This mandate is almost immediately followed by God's declaration that all of Creation was "very good" (Genesis 1:31). Adam and Eve's original vegetarian diet was consistent with the stewardship God entrusted to them and to all humankind.

That dominion means responsible stewardship is reinforced by a statement in the next chapter of Genesis (2:15), which indicates humans are to work the land, but also to guard it. We are to be co-workers with God in protecting the environment.

The second error of some animal activists is the presumption – that the biblical teaching that only people are created in God's image – means God places little or no value on animals. While the Torah states that only human beings are created "in the Divine Image" (Genesis1:27, 5:1), animals are also God's creatures, possessing sensitivity and the capacity for feeling pain. God is concerned that they are protected and treated with compassion and justice. In fact, the Jewish sages state that to be "created in the Divine Image", means people have the capacity to emulate the Divine compassion for all creatures. "As God is compassionate," they teach, "so you should be compassionate."

In his classic work Ahavat Chesed, *The Love of Kindness*, the revered Chafetz Chayim, Rabbi Yisrael Meir Kagan of Radin, writes that whoever emulates the Divine love and compassion to all creatures, "will bear the stamp of God on his person." Rabbi Samson Raphael Hirsch, a leading 19th century Jewish thinker, also discusses this concept, that human beings were created to "serve and safeguard the Earth" (Genesis 2:15). Rabbi Hirsch states that this actually limits our rights over other living things. He writes, "The Earth was not created as a gift to you. You have been given to the Earth, to treat it with respectful consideration, as God's Earth, and everything on it as God's creation, as your fellow creatures – to be respected, loved, and helped to attain their purpose according to God's will ... To this end, your heartstrings vibrate sympathetically with any cry of distress sounding anywhere in Creation, and with any glad sound uttered by a joyful creature."

In summary, as the Lord is our shepherd, we are to be shepherds of voiceless creatures. As God is kind and compassionate to us, we must be considerate of the needs and feelings of animals. In addition, religious vegetarians of diverse faiths believe that by showing compassion to animals through a vegetarian diet, we help fulfil the commandment to imitate God's ways. Critics of religion in the animal rights community may argue, with some justification, that the various religious communities are not doing enough to end the many horrible abuses of animals today, especially in the meat industry. However, this failure should not lead animal activists to scorn and repudiate religion altogether, but as much as possible to enlist the religious world in the common cause of eliminating the cruel misuses of animals.

Judaism clearly forbids any gratuitous display of cruelty toward animals. In Hebrew, this is called tza'ar ba'alei chayim, the biblical mandate not to cause 'pain to any living creature.' This is, in fact, a category for a significant group of laws in the Shulchan Arukh (Code of Jewish Law) and the responsa literature.

By contrast, Psalms 104 and 148 bespeak the worthiness of the animals of the field, creatures of the sea, and birds of the air before their Creator. Psalm 104 depicts God as 'giving drink to every beast of the field', and 'causing grass to spring up for the cattle. Perhaps the Jewish attitude toward animals is best summarised by Proverbs 12:10, 'The righteous person regards the life of his or her animal.' In his explanation of this verse, the Malbim, a nineteenth century biblical commentator, explained that the righteous person understands the nature of the animal, and hence provides food at the proper time, and according to the amount needed. He is also careful not to overwork the animal. Rather, the tzaddik (righteous person) acts according to the laws of justice. Not only does he act according to these laws with human beings, but also with animals.

It would be a tragic mistake for animal activists to dismiss the various religious communities as unconcerned with the plight of animals. Rather, we all should seek ways to transcend our philosophical and theological differences, and find a common ground on which we may stand together for the benefit of animals and humankind.

Link:

www.JewishVeg.com

■ AND WHO IS MY NEIGHBOUR?
Neil Mitchell

▶ Neil Mitchell and Sherry.

Neil Mitchell lives in Johannesburg, South Africa. After teaching English in state schools and Religious Education in Catholic schools, he worked for an NGO developing the capacity of schools and provincial education departments in disadvantaged rural parts of South Africa. During the time of apartheid he was active in church justice and peace organisations and in anti-militarisation movements, including the End Conscription Campaign, which resisted the draft and exposed the atrocities of the South African Defence Force. In 2010 he entered the Order of Preachers, also known as the Dominicans, and began studies for the Catholic priesthood. He seeks to promote a spirituality of nonviolence and compassion which integrates Christian faith, pacifism, veganism, social justice and concern for the environment...   ■

I grew up a white person in apartheid South Africa. Like many white South African families, we had a maid who lived in a single room in the backyard of our home. Our maid when I was little was Anna. Anna would playfully let us climb on her back while she was on her hands and knees polishing our floors. Our house had electricity and water and the rooms had ceilings, but her room had none of these. We had a 'garden boy', Daniel, actually a man getting on in years. Daniel would sing to us as he raked up the leaves and trimmed the edges of our flowerbeds. I had no idea at the time of the dehumanising machinations of apartheid, which reduced black people to being the servants of white people. It didn't occur to me that Anna and Daniel probably had families of their own in the 'location' or the 'homeland' from whom they were separated, or that they actually had their own African names more meaningful to them than Anna and Daniel.

At home we always had pet animals – dogs, chickens, birds, rabbits, hamsters and even a small tortoise that my father brought home one day when he stopped to rescue it from being run over. My brothers and I used to breed finches and budgerigars. I would watch with fascination as the eggs hatched and the tiny chicks emerged. We often had roast chicken for lunch on Sundays, and one day, one of my brothers and I announced to our parents that we would no longer be eating any birds. To do so seemed a betrayal of our budgies and finches. We kept up our boycott for some time. A friend of ours up the road, who also kept budgies, went further. He became a vegetarian. I felt challenged by his action. I felt uncomfortable about eating meat.

When I was about thirteen, at a 'war cry' practice at my all-white high school for sports day, I got into trouble for not singing. I was not singing because it felt stupid. The notion of dominating others in competition just didn't seem okay to me. So I could not drum up any enthusiasm to join in the frenzy of excitement the cheerleaders were whipping up. A teacher hauled me to the front and ordered me to sing on my own. I refused. The whole school jeered. I was told I had 'no spirit'. I felt I was in the presence of some strange force that was trying to brainwash me for its depraved purposes. I was sent for a caning, which is what schools did in those days. I was confused, humiliated and outraged, but some resolve not to surrender my mind to others who wanted to control my thinking began forming in me that day.

This resolve was to get me into more trouble with authority. Every year on 31 May we had a Republic Day ceremony at school with marching cadets and a brass band and the raising of the flag while we sang *Die Stem van Suid-Afrika*, apartheid South Africa's anthem. For the ceremony in my senior year my English teacher selected me to read the Preamble to the Constitution, which began, 'In humble submission to Almighty God ...' I was supposed to regard this as a great honour, but I felt differently. I had by then become more aware of the realities in South Africa. The June 1976 uprising, when students in Soweto protested against inferior education and police responded with teargas and live bullets, had happened the year before. I had had angry and bitter arguments with my classmates about the way blacks were treated in South Africa. I told my teacher that if we humbly submitted to God we would do away with the blasphemous system of apartheid, and said I was not prepared to read the Preamble. I had to explain myself to the school principal. After an angry altercation, he wagged his finger in my face and scowled at me, "South Africa – love it or leave it!"

While a student at the University of the Witwatersrand in Johannesburg I was an active member of the Catholic Students' Society. With resistance to apartheid raging all around us, and the university still largely an all-white institution, it was a very formative time. Some of us used to visit a poor community near Soweto. This brought me face to face with poverty and the ravages of apartheid. We helped people get identity documents, register their children's births, and deal with social problems such as alcoholism and violent abuse of women. At our instigation, the community mobilised against an exploitative landlord. My understanding of what Christian faith meant, especially in relation to the world – an often unjust world – was growing.

Conscription into the South African Defence Force (SADF), which every white South African male had to face at that time, was looming for me after university. The SADF was a pillar upholding apartheid, so this was a hugely difficult problem. South African forces were active against several liberation movements in southern African countries, and were waging a war against the South West African People's Organisation (SWAPO) in South West Africa (now Namibia) and Angola. South Africa was then a highly militarised society. The state was showing no sign of retreat from its brutal apartheid policies and was using white SADF troops in the black townships to quell the resistance to apartheid that the June '76 uprising had ignited. Some friends and I resolved to be conscientious objectors because, according to the 'just war' theory, which most mainstream Christian churches hold to, it was clear the SADF was involved in an unjust war.

We became involved in the Conscientious Objectors' Support Group (COSG), which met at the Quaker meeting-house and at the home of Rob Robertson, a Presbyterian minister in Johannesburg. Two conscientious objectors, Richard Steele and Peter Moll, were incarcerated at the time for refusing to obey their military call-up.

I met Richard Steele when he was released from incarceration. He was a vegetarian as well as a pacifist. "How can I eat my brothers and sisters?" he used to say. His vegetarianism was part of his commitment to nonviolence. I was challenged and my youthful inclination towards vegetarianism resurfaced. My own commitment to nonviolence seemed to lack integrity as long as I continued to eat meat. While I criticised the Church for an inadequate understanding of nonviolence, my own commitment was deficient as long as I failed to complement nonviolence toward people with nonviolence toward animals.

On the day I had to report for military training, I reported but declared myself an objector. After a court martial I was imprisoned for ten months. The number of those objecting was increasing. Many left the country to avoid the call-up. While imprisonment was hardly pleasant, I was not traumatised. I found it exhilarating to stand against violence, domination and injustice, and for what I believe was the truth.

Years later in post-apartheid South Africa, when I was principal of a Catholic school in Soweto, I was a guest at the jubilee anniversary of a nearby state school. I found myself sitting next to a man in military uniform. I introduced myself as Neil, and he introduced himself as Siphiwe. I told him I was not fond of armies and had spent much of my life as a peace activist opposing militarisation. He was interested, so I told him my story. He turned out to be Siphiwe Nyanda, Chief of the South African National Defence Force. He was a past pupil of the celebrating school. I told him I hoped he would be out of a job soon, because I wanted to live in a world without armies. He just laughed, a little awkwardly.

All this time I was eating meat. No doubt I was in denial, but whenever I was in the company of vegetarians my conscience would be troubled. I once helped a friend, John McCormick, who is vegetarian and a Quaker, to move some heavy furniture. We enlisted the help of some students from a nearby school where a friend is a boarding master. Boys at boarding school are always hungry, so at my suggestion we took them to a hamburger joint to thank them. John ordered a veggie burger and when asked by the youngsters about his choice, said he wanted a world with less violence. With a hamburger clasped in my hands, I felt ashamed and hypocritical. Why am I eating meat if I claim to be a pacifist committed to nonviolence? I asked myself. Shouldn't nonviolence and compassion extend to animals? I knew I had to stop eating meat. I was later to understand how we entrench the culture of meat-eating through customs such as celebrating the accomplishment of a task with eating meat. I was helping to embed this association in these youngsters' minds.

I was at this time studying theology at a Catholic university. In a course I did on The Dignity of the Human Person, I was disappointed that a view of the human person as superior to and disconnected from all other creatures prevailed. Of almost one hundred selected course readings covering twenty-five centuries of philosophical thought, I don't think one presented humankind as an interdependent part of a much greater web of life, or raised the possibility that killing animals for food violated the dignity of both humans and animals.

During these theological studies, after much prayer and assistance in discernment by a spiritual director, I joined the Order of Preachers, a religious order of the Catholic Church popularly known as the Dominicans. This decision arose from a desire to live out more radically my commitment to the gospel of Jesus Christ. Continuing my theological studies during the year of Dominican postulancy, I wrote a paper about the ambivalence of the Catholic Church's position on war and nonviolence. In defining violence, I included the violence against animals practised by the meat, fishing, egg and dairy industries, and violence against the environment. My supervisor scratched this out, and wrote, "You are losing focus here." Ironically, such non-receptivity toward animals was helping the serious shortcomings of Christian theology to come into sharp focus for me.

I was urged to take a holiday before my novitiate year with the Dominicans. I decided to visit an old friend from university days, Eugene Risi, and his family, who now live outside Verona in Italy. Eugene is a committed vegan who had long been sending out e-mails encouraging people to "Be veg, go green, save the planet." He is a devotee of Supreme Master Ching Hai, who has done much to spread the vegan message worldwide. I was hoping my visit would give me the final impetus to embrace veganism. And indeed it did. We had many discussions and I ate vegan meals with the family. My liberation from consuming animal products was happening at last.

Eugene had a copy of *The World Peace Diet* by Will Tuttle. I read it avidly but reflectively, feeling like a bright sun was dispersing my mists of ignorance and denial. There was no reason to continue eating meat, and many good reasons to stop, starting with the notion, problematic to say the least, that we can kill animals for food. Then there was the cruelty and suffering inflicted on helpless animals; the devastation of the environment and the global warming the meat industry causes; the dishonouring of our place in the web of life; the spiritual woundedness we bring about in ourselves and society through slaughtering billions of animals; and the injustice caused to the poor through the meat diet being one of the structures of world domination.

I had little idea that eating meat, milk, eggs and other animal products had such serious ramifications. I had little idea of the trauma of cattle in feedlots and abattoirs, of the living hell of pigs and battery hens in close confinement, of the widespread use of antibiotics and artificial growth hormones to ready animals for slaughter, of fishing methods which pull fish up from the ocean depths so quickly that their internal organs burst, or of the 'by-catch' of turtles, dolphins and sea birds that is thrown back into the ocean dead or wounded. So low was my level of consciousness that my food choices had been about little else than my selfish desires. I felt profound sadness that the meat industry has reduced the relationship between humans and animals to one where animals are mere commodities for human use, an attitude that allows us to herd, confine, manipulate, abuse, kill and eat animals, and be oblivious to their magnificence. Behind it all is the mentality of domination, the mentality, as Will Tuttle puts it, "That starts on our plates and reverberates through our various cultural institutions as authoritarianism, oppression and violence."

I decided that in future I would make responsible food choices based on compassion and on what is good for the planet, not on what society has told us about the food chain or about Christmas not being Christmas without roast turkey.

Back home I signed up for the *World Peace Diet* facilitator training program to deepen my understanding of the ideas in *The World Peace Diet*. I made friends and interacted with kindred spirits all over the world, a community of caring, reflective, thoughtful people who do not see themselves as above or apart from the Earth and its inhabitants, but seek to coexist peacefully with all life. I have become much more conscious of how the Earth vibrates with magnificent energy. Even when out enjoying a walk now I am much more mindful of the teeming animal life around me and appreciative of the need to share this planet with all creatures. From the window of my room I love observing the trees changing with the seasons, watching birds in flight and listening to their song. The training also helped me see

I must integrate pacifism, veganism, social justice and environmental awareness within a spirituality of compassion and respect for all life.

The road to spiritual maturity requires divesting ourselves of ego and reaching a point where we derive no pleasure from triumphing over other people or animals, but simply want the common good. Veganism and pacifism are elements of such spiritual maturity. They are channels of healing that our misshapen culture sorely needs, leading to higher consciousness and freedom from the delusion of being a discrete self.

Foundational to this misshapen culture is the belief, prevalent amongst many raised in the Judeo-Christian tradition, that we have a God-given right to dominate animals, and kill them and eat them for food. Many quote the Bible – Genesis 1:28 – in this regard. But those who believe this need to read on, for in the next verse, 1:29, God specifically excludes the eating of animal flesh from this dominion over animals. This is a foundational principle in the spiritual history of humankind, but most people pass it by. In God's ideal world, represented metaphorically by the Garden of Eden, there was no suffering, domination or violence. The writers of the creation myths in Genesis understood the creator God to be one who intended not only humans, but all animals, to eat plants and only plants for their food (Genesis 1:30). In these myths, God gives humans not animals to eat but seed-bearing plants and trees that have fruit with seed in it (Genesis 1:29). Calling these Genesis stories myths does not devalue them; it simply identifies the biblical literary genre they belong to. The authors are doing theology, not writing history. The truth we extract from these myths is that humans are intended to be cooperators, not dominators, of nature by dispersing the seeds enclosed within the delicious, edible fruit. The provision of plants, not animals, as people's food recurs in the second account of creation (Genesis 2:16).

After the 'Fall', violence entered the world, of people's making. People waged war and ate meat as part of their fallen state. According to the Genesis narrative, after God's attempt to purge the earth of human wickedness through the flood, God 'relented' and allowed humans to eat meat, but this comes at a dreadful price for animals. Humans become "*the terror and the dread* of all the wild beasts, birds, crawling things and fish" because humans would now treat animals as food (Genesis 9:2-3). We are meant to understand that rather than animals being naturally 'red in tooth and claw', and that humans simply follow nature in this savagery, it is the other way round. Just as God anticipated, humans put terror and dread into animals, with our hunting spears, poisons, knives, rifles, gin traps, snares, factory farms, dairies, battery hen cages, fishing nets, abattoirs, butcher shops and all the rest. We destroyed the peace between humankind and animals when we insisted on eating their meat. We caused the alienation, such that animals now flee when they see us coming. Theophilus, Bishop of Antioch (150 CE), put it, "When man diverted from the path of goodness the animals followed him ... If man now would rise to his original nature and would do evil no longer, then the animals too would return to their original gentle nature." In eastern and esoteric thought the violence of nature is ascribed to us and our influence on nature through our violent thought patterns. Let us remember that the account of creation in Genesis stipulates animals were also to eat only plants (1:30). Their 'original gentle nature' would have precluded preying on one another.

Over the whole sweep of the Hebrew Scriptures, as the understanding of God's true nature develops, there is a gradual shedding of violence, such that God is by degrees extricated from involvement in human violence. God's aversion to animal sacrifice becomes a persistent theme of the prophets. God wants justice, mercy, defence of widows and orphans, clean hands and a 'humble and contrite spirit', not holocaust and sacrifice. Isaiah envisages a peaceable kingdom where *shalom* prevails. People will beat their swords into ploughshares and study war no more. Each will enjoy their own vine and fig tree, which produce seed-bearing fruits. There is no domestication of animals for slaughter. People and animals live in harmony. "The wolf lives with the lamb, the leopard lies down with the kid ... the lion eats straw like the ox ... the infant plays near the cobra's hole ... they do no violence, no harm ... for the land is filled with the knowledge of Yahweh" (Is 11:6-9). Knowledge of Yahweh includes knowing it is not necessary to eat meat.

In the Judeo-Christian Scriptures, then, can be traced humankind's long journey from barbarity, violence, retaliation and a vengeful angry God to forgiveness, repentance, mercy and a loving nonviolent God.

Because they are ambivalent about nonviolence, today's mainstream Christian churches remain mired in the way of domination and complicit in the violence that goes with it. The *Catechism of the Catholic Church* reduces animals to beings that exist primarily for human use, "Animals, like plants and inanimate beings, are by nature destined for the common good of past, present and future humanity" (2415). The *Compendium of the Social Doctrine of the Church*, even in its chapter on Safeguarding the Environment, is full of the language of domination. It denounces perspectives that see all living beings as part of a "biotic unity of undifferentiated value" where "man's superior responsibility can be eliminated in favour of an egalitarian consideration of the 'dignity' of all living beings."

This rather arrogant anthropocentrism produces a disconnected spirituality, where the compass of compassion extends only to human beings, and even there it is deficient in that it is not pacifist. This circumscribed worldview is also at work in the liturgy of the Catholic Church. Hymns and liturgical prayers are mostly confined to the relationship between God and humankind. Consciousness of our connectedness to nature is not entirely absent – there is some awareness of it in the offering of bread and wine as the fruits of the earth and the vine – but it is mostly missing. Our redemption is seldom seen in terms of discovering our true relationships within the cosmos.

Completely outside the Church's 'moral law' are animal husbandry practices, which manipulate reproduction in animals, such as castration, artificial insemination and embryo transfer. So too are the removal of a cow's calf soon after it is born, the human use of the milk intended for the calf, the chaining of the calf in a small crate and its subsequent slaughter for veal. The Church does not see such brutal intrusions into the life-giving and nurturing functions of animals as a terrible desecration of life or a violation of the dignity and bodily integrity of animals. It regards human in-vitro fertilisation as morally unacceptable, because it wants human life to be the result of an act of committed love and because embryos are discarded in the process, but humans may interfere with and manipulate the reproductive functions of animals – and exploit the uteruses and udders of cows in the process – as much as they like, and for profit.

Just as the Catholic Church, by its support of 'just war', has condemned humankind to enslavement to the violence of war, so by its demeaning view of animals it has condemned them to enslavement to the violence of slaughter.

However, things are changing. The churches' long indifference towards creation is opening up as some theologians explore a new cosmology, what some are calling 'the new universe story'. More and more it is being understood that the universe is a community of beings bound together in an inseparable relationship. The realisation is dawning that each being of planet Earth is profoundly implicated in the existence and functioning of every other being. The progressive alienation of the human from the natural world is being traced in the advent of village life, the rise of agriculture, the domestication of animals, the rise of civilisations and cities, industrialisation, the violent plundering of the Earth's resources, and the alteration of the functioning of Earth through the effects of human activity. The disastrous consequences of the loss of consciousness of the Earth's unfathomable mysteries are at last being acknowledged.

But, somehow, our most intimate connection with nature – the food we eat – is still a blind spot. The new awakening, welcome as it is, will not have any hope of reaching spiritual maturity as long as animals are treated as property for human use, as 'dumb' creatures with no intrinsic value or interests of their own. Until we admit our culturally-determined eating habits are numbing us to the suffering we cause to animals and to the damage we do to ourselves, our spiritual growth will remain stunted.

My youthful experiences planted in me a longing for a transformed world. Spontaneous love from Anna and Daniel (I never knew their African names), which gave the lie to the faked white supremacy of apartheid; the wonder of new life when our pet birds, caged though they were, had their young; and coercion by uncritical teachers, functionaries of the system of domination and supremacy, trying to indoctrinate me into it all helped to evoke for me a world where discrimination, anthropocentricism, competitiveness, suffering and greed are replaced by equality, appreciation of the interconnectedness of all life, cooperation, compassion toward all beings, sharing and magnanimity; where relationships based on domination and subjugation are transformed into relationships based on serving one another and love; where the individual does not set out to rise above others but we all move forward together; where things are also looked at from the point of view of the poor and the powerless, and where the magnificence of animals is appreciated. I am grateful for all the exposure and experiences I have had in my life that have enabled me to liberate myself from harmful indoctrination. But I am a very long way from 'complete'. I will always be seeking and learning and open to new insights, which will enlighten me along the journey of life.

Probably the Dominican Order's most beloved saint is Martin de Porres. The child of a Spanish grandee adventurer and his concubine, a freed Panamanian slave woman of African descent, Martin was a vegetarian and a healer learnt in the healing properties of herbs. His love and care were all embracing, shown equally to humans and to animals. He opened a home for orphans and abandoned children, and also a shelter for sick and injured animals, a pioneering thing to do in the sixteenth century. In the Dominican priory in Lima where he was a lay brother, he was the almoner, caring for the poor. He befriended and fed the priory rats, considered vermin by most people, and is reputed to have fed a dog, a cat and a mouse together from the same bowl without the three fighting among themselves. A *mulatto* who knew discrimination, he defended victims of racial injustice. In the spirit of Martin de Porres, I intend, wherever I can but especially in the church, to champion a consistent and compassionate ethic of life which weaves pacifism (nonviolence toward humans), veganism (nonviolence toward animals), social justice (nonviolence toward the poor) and environmental concern (nonviolence toward nature) together as threads in a seamless garment. My mission is to have a world free of the structures and mindsets of violence and domination of one group by another, a world without armies and abattoirs.

CHAPTER 10

The World in Change

▶ Paul Seymour and his 'darling girl' Rascal.

Rascal and her brother George were found, as puppies, in a wheelie bin. They were taken to Monika's Doggie Rescues, a wonderful establishment that has re-homed over ten thousand dogs. Paul found the two puppies there, and they have been together for eleven years now.

"All life wants to live. All life feels. All animals, including humans, need to be treated equally, with compassion. It's part of our evolution. Pythagoras, Da Vinci, Ben Franklin, Edison, Einstein and many others all said the same: Vegetarianism is the evolutionary future of mankind and until we stop killing animals we'll continue to kill each other." ■

—Paul Seymour, musician, songwriter, activist.

■ THE GIFT OF COMPASSION
Mark Hawthorne

"The fate of animals is of greater importance to me than the fear of appearing ridiculous." ■

—Emile Zola.

▶ Mark Hawthorne.

Mark Hawthorne is the author of two books on animal rights, *Bleating Hearts: The Hidden World of Animal Suffering*, which examines the many ways humans exploit nonhumans, and *Striking at the Roots: A Practical Guide to Animal Activism* (both from Changemakers Books), which empowers people around the world to get active for animals. He stopped eating meat after an encounter with one of India's many cows in 1992 and became an ethical vegan a decade later. His writing has also been featured in *Vegan's Daily Companion* (Quarry Books) and in the anthologies *Uncaged: Top Activists Share Their Wisdom on Effective Farm Animal Advocacy* (Ben Davidow) and *Stories to Live By: Wisdom to Help You Make the Most of Every Day* (Travelers' Tales). Mark and his wife Lauren live in California. You'll find him tweeting @markhawthorne... ■

Running with the bulls in Pamplona may seem like an unusual setting for an epiphany. But there I was in 1992, amid the roar of thousands of partygoers, celebrating my thirtieth birthday with two friends, and I left a different person.

In fairness, I should confess that my transformation was years in the making, and by the time I had reached Spain, my conscience was probably overdue for a reckoning. I was always a sensitive kid – always trying to rescue animals and insects in my neighbourhood. When my father and grandfather took me fishing for the first time on California's Big Bear Lake around 1971, I was appalled to see a rainbow trout thrashing at the end of my line. After congratulating me, my grandfather threaded a length of fishing line through the fish's mouth and his gills and let him struggle just beneath the surface by the side of the boat, keeping him alive until later. I sat stunned, no longer interested in the 'sport' of fishing. Oh, how I wanted to liberate that fish. And how I kick myself to this day for not speaking out against the cruelty I had a hand in. Of course, like most people, I was ignorant of what went on in factory farms, research labs, and the many other industries that exploit non-human animals for the pleasure and profit of humans. Yes, I loved cats and dogs; I still do. And yes, I ate cows, pigs, chickens, sheep, turkeys – and sometimes even fish; I know better now. I also visited circuses, zoos, and other businesses that imprison animals. And though I'd never watched a blood sport, I had no objection to participating in the revelry that is Pamplona's *Fiesta de San Fermín*.

As I sprinted up Pamplona's Estafeta Street, the six bulls easily galloped past, and I was awed by how graceful they were. Yet I could see fear and confusion in their eyes. These animals would die in the afternoon bullfights. After the run I felt ashamed, not only of my participation, but ashamed I was part of a species that exploited these noble animals. I was reluctant to change my eating habits, though, and I went on as before but with one difference: for the first time, I was thinking about what – or rather *who* – I was eating. Suddenly, there was a nagging little voice reminding me I could do better.

A few months later, I stuffed some clothes into a backpack and travelled to India, where I lived with a Buddhist family in the Himalayas. It was a sublime experience hiking among the centuries-old monasteries and stupas on mountain peaks and spending time with local monks and Tibetans who had fled their Chinese-occupied homeland to settle in Ladakh, an Indian region where the culture and traditions closely resemble those in Tibet. There was a serenity about the Tibetans and Ladakhis that was remarkable and inspiring. How much of their placid demeanor, I wondered, was owed to the First Precept, that Buddhist proscription against taking a life? They evidently didn't have an ethical problem with eating animals – just a logistical one: few people seemed to raise animals for food, and there was little meat in the community. Indeed, almost everything I ate was grown in the family's garden in the front yard. As a result, my diet was vegan, and I'd never felt physically or spiritually fitter in my life. Even living at 12,000 feet above sea level, I could walk for miles while hardly raising my heart rate.

Two months passed in an instant, and winter arrived. Before the snows came, Norboo and Yangchan, my Ladakhi hosts, dug a large hole in the yard and buried what remained of the cabbage, potatoes, and other vegetables for safekeeping. What happened next changed my life. Yangchan's mother lived across the road, and she kept two cows so that the extended family could drink butter tea – a delicacy that is an acquired taste, to say the least. Yangchan brought one of the cows into the garden so that she could graze on the remaining stalks and stems. I was only a few feet away, and as I watched this beautiful bovine tuck into the plants, she raised her head and met my gaze. Curious why this animal would be studying me, I became transfixed. I moved closer, and her brown eyes followed me. In those eyes I saw so much life, so much understanding, so much sentience. It was clear she had as much right – and as much will – to live as I did. I knew I could never eat another cow.

It's been more than twenty years since that moment, and hardly a week goes by that I don't marvel at it. I marvel, too, that it took me another decade to become a vegan, which was thanks to learning about the cruelties inherent in egg and dairy production and meeting some animals rescued from these industries at a sanctuary. Upon returning to the US, I began writing for an NGO working for Tibetan independence, but as I moved deeper into ethical veganism, I devoted more of my time to writing about animal rights, eventually contributing to magazines like *VegNews* and *Satya*. I yearned to be more actively involved in the movement, but found a dearth of information. It appeared that animal advocates either worked for an organisation like PETA, or they got advice from friends on how to be an activist.

What the movement needed, I thought, was a guidebook for the person who wants to make a difference without necessarily working for a group, so I wrote *Striking at the Roots: A Practical Guide to Animal Activism*, published by Change-makers Books in 2007. The book is the voices of the one hundred and twenty-plus activists I interviewed from around the world – their best practices on how to be an effective advocate. We all approach activism from a different angle, but the one thing activists share is the universal struggle to avoid getting burned out. We are faced not just with the sights and sounds of animal exploitation, but with the hubris and corporate hegemony that keep animals oppressed. They slaughter helpless animals, cut them into pieces, risk life-threatening diseases by eating them – and then call veganism strange. They give animals drugs, kill them while they're still young, package body parts to be unrecognisable – then call animal rights extreme.

Those who become involved in the effort to help animals do so with the best intentions, often ignoring their own health and happiness, and frequently without the ability to handle the trauma, and that can lead to burnout. Burnout is the result of prolonged exposure to suffering and injustice. It feels a lot like depression. In fact, some say burnout *is* depression. However you define it, a bad case of burnout can push you out of the movement altogether.

The symptoms of burnout are really the symptoms of stress:

- Headaches
- Fatigue
- Boredom
- Abusing drugs or alcohol
- Trouble sleeping – too little or too much
- Loss of appetite or overeating
- Difficulty in relationships.

I'm not saying that if you suffer from one or more of these symptoms you're burned out, or even stressed out. All I'm suggesting is we maintain an awareness about our physical, emotional, mental, and even spiritual wellbeing – if you have a spiritual practice – because burnout occurs when we ignore the warning signs of an impending emotional meltdown and continue to push ourselves too hard.

Eating well and getting plenty of rest can go a long way toward preventing burnout, but I offer here two sets of additional advice for animal activists.

The first set has four steps.

1. **Find a Good Fit.** One of the best ways to avoid burning out is to match your style of campaigning with your interests and strengths, creating activism that nourishes you.
2. **Include Achievable Goals.** Make sure your strategic plans include not only long-term aims, but also achievable, short-term goals that can be acknowledged and celebrated when they are met.

3. **Make Time for Yourself.** Resist the temptation to turn every hobby or interest outside the movement into an opportunity to help animals. I know an activist who felt she was on the verge of burning out, so she took up jogging. And, being a natural leader, she organised a bunch of her friends, and together they would go running through the neighborhood. Well, one day her activist gene kicked in. She looked around at all the blank T-shirts her fellow runners were wearing, and she said, "Hey, let's use that space for some pro-animal messages." Perhaps you can see where this is going. Before long, she was the leader of a *vegan* running group, and she was burdened with many of the stresses she was trying to avoid in the first place. The good news is she is still very active in the movement, maybe because she followed this next piece of advice:

4. **Make a Change.** If you pursue your life's work for animals, yet still experience the stress and overwork that can lead to burnout, it may be time to try something else. This isn't giving up – it's simply adjusting your campaigning style. It's having the courage to say, "What I'm doing is not working for me, and it's probably not working for the animals, either."

Finally, here's what I call the ACTIVE Approach to Avoiding Burnout. I call it the Active Approach because it's a six-step process, and each letter in the word ACTIVE stands for one of the steps.

A   Allow yourself to be human. Hard as we try, we are *not* superheroes, and we are not going to win every battle. So take a real vacation. Enjoy time with friends. Try to have fun and not feel guilty.

C   Create something tangible to remind you of your victories. This could be a scrapbook covering campaigns you've worked on, a website, a folder – anything you can refer to that reminds you you're fighting the good fight.

T   Talk to someone you trust. If you have *one* person with whom you can dare to be yourself, that is a gift. Animal activism is an emotionally loaded endeavour, and as activists it's important that we're able to unburden ourselves. If you don't have someone you trust, speak to a therapist.

I   Ignore upsetting text and images. When you feel guilt, grief, frustration, fear, or outrage come over you, that's probably not the best time to get out that DVD of *Earthlings* to watch with Uncle Fred. Give yourself some time away from it. I know there are activists who argue that we 'owe it to the animals' to view graphic images. Well, I don't necessarily believe that. I agree we should be educated about the issues, but that doesn't mean we need to torture ourselves in order to feel empathy for those who are tortured.

V   Visit an animal sanctuary. 'V' could also stand for Volunteer at an animal sanctuary. I have spent a lot of time at sanctuaries, and I am constantly amazed by how many *activists* have never rubbed a pig's belly, or whistled to a turkey to hear him gobble back, or watched a hen take a dust bath. Get some face time with the faces you're working so hard to protect. Volunteering at an animal sanctuary is also a great way to work up a sweat, which leads me to my final point …

E   Exercise. Walk, run, ride, hike, swim, do yoga – whatever you can do, do it. I like to go to the gym, but when I first got involved in activism, I stopped working out. I thought, "How can I devout this time to something selfish when I should be protesting a circus or writing letters to editors?" Big mistake. I lost energy, I lost focus, and I quickly realised I could no longer drink as much beer and still fit into my pants.

I became transfixed. I moved closer, and her brown eyes followed me. In those eyes I saw so much life, so much understanding, so much sentience. It was clear she had as much right – and as much will – to live as I did.   ◼

One of the gifts – or burdens, some might say – of being a compassionate person is that once you learn about suffering, you're likely to become an agent of change. That's the reason I became an activist, and it's why I wrote *Striking at the Roots*. It's also why I wrote *Bleating Hearts: The Hidden World of Animal Suffering* (Changemakers Books, 2013), which examines cruelties that get little mainstream media attention. Among many other abuses, there's a section that explores things you probably never knew about bullfighting, and readers will find a lengthy meditation on the 'sport' of fishing. Naturally, throughout the years I worked on *Bleating Hearts*, I spent plenty of time staying ACTIVE.

Link:
www.markhawthorne.com

■ NOT SO UNPOPULAR
Dan Cudahy

▶ Dan Cudahy and Sancho.

Dan Cudahy is the author of the blog *Unpopular Vegan Essays* (no longer available to the public, except as "UVE" archives). He performs financial statement audits of Colorado cities, towns, districts and nonprofit organisations as a partner with the accounting firm McMahan and Associates. He enjoys a wide variety of activities, including climbing and skiing adventures in Colorado's mountains, reading, running, and gourmet vegan dinners with his partner, Sue. Dan and Sue care for two lovely adopted dogs, Peter and Sancho... ■

It was on or about June 1, 2003. I was surfing the Web and stumbled on profoundly disturbing information about the lives of dairy cows and layer hens. I learnt how the veal industry was directly linked to the dairy industry; how the cows were forcibly and repeatedly impregnated; and how, after they were 'spent' and drained of so much nutrition, they were 'thanked' by being sent to a brutal slaughter. I learnt how male chicks are disposed of by being thrown alive into wood chippers or garbage dumpsters, to starve or suffocate to death; how hens live in the stench of the ammonia of their urine and disease-ridden filth, overcrowded in cages or sheds. I learnt that dairy and eggs were products of far greater cruelty than meat. This was appalling to me. I thought welfare laws regulated the use of animals. I was deeply disgusted and outraged by the time I had finished reading that day. While I wanted to and would verify and corroborate this information over the next few weeks, I was going vegan *immediately*, no matter how difficult it would be.

Within three months of going vegan, I read Peter Singer's *Animal Liberation*, Tom Regan's *The Case for Animal Rights* and Gary Francione's *Introduction to Animal Rights* in that order. The latter two each made more sense, and Francione's book was the overwhelmingly predominant influence on my views and remains so to this day. It was after I read Regan's work, and especially Francione's, that I fully realised we owe animals far more than our compassion; we owe them the basic justice of not using them unnecessarily, and that 99.9% of our uses are unnecessary. I may have gone vegan out of disgust, but by the time I had finished Francione's book, I had deeply internalised veganism as nothing more than basic moral decency. Veganism wasn't the most we could do; it was the least we could do.

Gary Francione's identification of non-human animals as legal property, economic commodities and things as an insurmountable barrier to any meaningful protection also made perfect sense to me at this time. It corresponded perfectly with slave history and my knowledge of the implications of basic legal theory and basic economics. Welfare laws are trumped by property rights, especially in a society that regards property rights as among the most important rights there are. But as Francione maintains, before we can change the legal property and economic commodities status of non-humans, we must first change their moral status. And there is no changing their moral status while the vast majority of us are consuming and exploiting them. It was therefore obvious that ethical veganism – rejecting all animal use – is both a moral *and practical* imperative.

Going vegan opened up a whole new world of experimentation, discovery and creativity relished by my partner, a trained chef. We have enjoyed some of the most delicious food we've had in our lives as vegans, and it is clear in looking at some of the vegan food blogs today that others are taking equally great pleasure in vegan cooking and eating.

As a long distance runner, mountain climber and backcountry skier, being vegan seems to have helped my performance and recovery times on and after long, difficult runs and climbs. If I were to guess why, I'd say it is likely due to reduced lactic acid build up during long or intense effort, resulting from the elimination of dairy from my diet. Combining the good results I've noticed in endurance activities with the healthy feeling and great blood test results Sue and I have had, it is evident being vegan has been beneficial to our health as well.

"My vision is for a future where everyone is aware of the mistreatment of all beings, and we put an end to war on our soils, on our plates and in our own families. I envision all beings achieving harmony and being treated with dignity and respect, where we relearn our connection with wild weeds and foods that nature has provided not only for meals but for medicine to keep our natural systems in balance."

—Ameena Jabour, Massage Therapist.

◼ YOU CAN'T BE A MEAT EATING ENVIRONMENTALIST
Cathryn Ross

▶ Cathryn Ross and calf friend.

Cathryn Ross is a Fine Arts student in Western Australia... ◼

The choice to become vegetarian was almost completely motivated by a poster I saw at an event that stated, "You can't be a meat-eating environmentalist." I'd been concerned about the state of the environment and my impact upon it for some time, and when I saw the poster my reaction was something like: "Of course! How could I not be vegetarian?" I began to phase meat out of my diet from that point on and as I already had a few vegetarian and vegan friends, my decision was never challenged or made fun of.

Another turning point occurred when my friend, Kerryanne, decided to become vegan and began to blog about it on *Livejournal.com*. I was forced to think about what her choices meant.

I didn't want to be so radically different from the rest of my friends and family but I could not continue eating animal products and feel guilty about it. I had two choices: I either had to stop caring about animals and their suffering – or stop eating them and their by-products. I chose the latter option.

Since becoming vegan, I've also become much more aware of and interested in my health. I joined a gym within a month of becoming vegan, and became much more interested in balanced eating as well as incorporating physical activity into my daily routine. As a result, my health has greatly improved. For the majority of my teen years, before I was vegan, I had a constant mild cold – a slightly runny nose that resulted in my always needing a few tissues tucked into my pockets or in my bag. Once I gave up dairy and started eating vegan, it cleared up completely. I also felt so much lighter and cleaner and right now I would say I'm the healthiest I've ever been in my life.

One thing that fills me with enthusiasm for vegan cooking and baking is blogging. I don't run a blog myself, but I regularly check up on my favourite blogs run by other vegans from all over the world. Reading these blogs makes me feel confident in my decision to be vegan and reminds me that it is a healthy diet and just as mouth-watering as any non-vegan creamy pasta dish or flaky pastry. It reminds me I'm a part of a community of caring, enthusiastic individuals who think outside the box. Sometimes, veganism can be a bit lonesome. I have great vegan and vegetarian friends and family, but when the majority of society eat meat and defend their choice to eat it so insistently, it's easy to feel discouraged and as if what I do doesn't matter. But it does, I know it does. One person being vegan may not change the world or stop animal cruelty forever, but I know that every time I buy vegan and cruelty free products, my money *isn't* supporting the slaughter and abuse of animals. For me, veganism is about doing what *I* can – many others may be supporting animal cruelty, but I'm not and that's what matters.

■ TURNING POINT FOR A LONG-TERM VEGAN PIONEER
Butterflies Katz

▶ Butterflies Katz.

My concern for animals began with our family cats. It was obvious to me they were conscious friends with whom I could communicate. I knew they deserved respect and therefore all animals equally deserved my respect. However, I did not connect that respect with the animals I ate until my turning point moment at the age of twelve. I was at the dinner table with my family and 'tongue' was the main course. There it was, undisguised, the tongue of a cow as the centerpiece on the table. My brother (who wanted my portion of dinner) told me that 'meat' is a dead animal. Although his motives were not pure and he did get my dinner, he educated me, and from that moment on I never ate animals again. Interestingly, my brother later became vegan himself.

My vegan turning point moment occurred years later when I read a copy of *Ahimsa*, the magazine of the American Vegan Society. I was reluctant to read it because some part of me recognised I would have to change, as in never again consume ice cream or cheese, which I lived on. However, when I read about the horrific cruelty inherent in the dairy industry, eloquently expressed by H Jay Dinshah, founder of the society, I was deeply moved to become a vegan at that moment. I did not want to be complicit in these crimes against non-humanity. It was as simple as that. I realised that becoming vegan is just extending to other species of animals the basic respect I was taught to extend to humans. I emptied my closet of leather and stopped buying products that were derived from exploiting animals.

For three and a half decades I've been optimally sustained by eating completely free of animal products along with exposure to sunshine. I feel the health benefits were even more profound because I began at an early age. It felt a little difficult to let go of my cheese and dairy addiction initially, but the overwhelming feeling of calm that came with the knowing that I don't participate in the unjust exploitation of other animals, supersedes any perceptions I had of giving up what I enjoy.

Along the way, I learned the importance of preparing scrumptious plant-pow-ered cuisine to get others to see the light. So I became a vegan chef. I co-authored *Incredibly Delicious; Recipes for a New Paradigm* by Gentle World. Many of the rec-ipes from the book were taken from Gentle World's restaurant that was on Maui, Hawaii, The Vegan, where I was one of the head chefs. We had customers from all walks of life come to the restaurant and say they would be happy to eat this way if the food was available or if they could learn how to make it.

The greatest difficulty I've encountered being vegan through the decades is being a part of a society that socially accepts the unnecessary violence inflicted on conscious animals. I have always found it easy to be vegan because I genuinely grasp the philosophy. I understand with all my soul that all animals have the right to live without being persecuted by humans. I have always believed that under-standing is all one needs to be vegan.

We can rise above our speciesist indoctrination and learn to live in harmony with the other inhabitants of Earth, and usher in a more civilised culture. We can use our purchasing power to protest cruelty. It is unnecessary to use ani-mals for food, clothing, toiletries, cleaning products, vivisection, circuses, zoos, entertainment or any other use of animals by humans, exemplified by myself and other long term vegans. Anyone sentient – human or nonhuman – has the fundamental right to live without being sexually assaulted, enslaved, objectified, having their newborn kidnapped from them, violently abused and killed by hu-mans. It seems so easy to see this is unethical. If we can live without exploiting animals, surely it is a moral imperative to do so. I never grew out of the knowing I had when I was an innocent twelve-year-old girl who knew eating other ani-mals was wrong.

Links:

http://www.thevegantruth.blogspot.com

http://www.veganpoet.com

■ ENVISAGING PEACE
Thuya Barbe

Thuya Barbe is a University graduate from Rotterdam, The Netherlands...   ■

▶ Thuya Barbe.

Reading *The World Peace Diet* did two important things for me. Firstly, it connected my spiritual journey with what I was eating and it made me feel less like a freak and more like a thoughtful, compassionate person. Secondly, and even more importantly, I saw there were hundreds of people who understood and had made the choice.

The wider vegan picture? I would very much like to see peace. Seriously, at the risk of sounding like a hippy, I think there is too much violence in the world. It hurts me a lot that we are using the Earth and her inhabitants in this way. I just don't get it. I never did. I used to get upset and yell: even a little kid can see this isn't sustainable. How come grown-ups, smart ones, are making these choices?

Money was the argument. But even that I couldn't understand. Who wants money when we can't breathe or eat anymore? Sheesh, I get upset again even thinking about it.

From not understanding, I found myself getting angry. How can we be doing this? It needs to stop. But how? I give a lot of my money to charity, I'm eating vegan foods, I recycle, do charity work, cycle, and live as green as possible. But will that save the last whale? I don't know. What I do know is that these small steps are crucial. Getting everyone involved in what is happening to the Earth as a result of their food choices will encourage them to look at all the other stuff that is happening, and if I have to cook delicious vegan food to help, well by golly, I will! All the other things I can contribute will become clear in their own time.

■ THE VERY BEST WE CAN BE
Angel Flinn

Angel Flinn is Director of Outreach for Gentle World...   ■

▶ Angel Flinn with Poof the Magic Rabbit.

My personal journey to veganism began with a number of twists and turns. When I first learnt of the concept, I asked questions of the people I knew who called themselves 'vegan'. What I found was, there was a sliding scale of dedication, and I'm saddened by the fact that my personal commitment was greatly influenced by this. Once I got on the right track, however, not only have I never looked back, but I continue to look forward with hopefulness about the opportunities for enhanced clarity, deeper understanding and a greater sense of inner peace than I knew was possible in this troubled world.

When I was nineteen, at a Millennium festival in New Zealand, I attended a workshop facilitated by the founders of a long-time vegan community called Gentle World. They described veganism as 'the keystone' in the foundation of their belief system, and pointed to their commitment to shared principles as a reason for the group's longevity, because they were still living and working cooperatively long after many of the communes from that same time had been left in the dust of disappearing sixties ideals. Even after nearly fourteen years of being a part of this vegan-intentional family myself, I distinctly remember my impression of these two inspiring figures at our first encounter, "They belong to a place where they feel safe. I want to go where they come from."

A few months later, I visited Shangri-La, Gentle World's four hundred and fifty four acre secluded haven in the Far North. This visit turned out to be the precursor to my decision to join the community – a move I made around six months later.

I didn't realise it at first, but at the time of my visit, the fields and rivers had only recently been liberated from shackles of barbed wire fencing. This was a reminder of the land's former life as witness to an (albeit bucolic) animal slavery operation, and it had all been lovingly removed, one post at a time, and the barbed wire banished in a gigantic burial.

I was beginning to learn that this remarkable band of dedicated and hard-working individuals was deeply committed to the ideal of nonviolence. I was told that along with the miles of barbed wire, they had also made it a top priority to dismantle the structures left over from the land's animal harming past. By the time I had the chance to lay my eyes on the sites where they once stood, 'The Wool Shed' and 'The Not-OK Corral' had been transformed into orderly piles of re-useable lumber; scraps of 'life-as-it-once-was' that might one day be used to help build 'life-as-it-should-be'. Some of the finest pieces had been used to construct a simple but beautiful fireplace mantle in the communal house – a fitting symbol of the hope to be found in somehow exorcising the terrible history of these materials by using them at the centre of something so new and promising. My mind was beginning to open up to the idea that there just might be a better way to live; not only in my imagination, but in reality.

At the end of the same year, I found myself visiting Gentle World again, this time at their educational centre in Hawaii. I was part of the volunteer team for an event where one of the founders was delivering a powerful presentation, and I remember clearly that I felt my perception change in an instant. She said one thing I will always remember the essence of. "I can't stop the animal industry from killing and torturing and enslaving animals – but I can stop myself from being a part of it. *"They're not doing it for me."* And all of a sudden, something in me shifted. The false beliefs I had been holding on to, that I already understood who animals really are, that I already knew what veganism was and that I had already reached the understanding I needed – it all just dropped away, to be replaced by a feeling of such relief, freedom and gratitude for the realisation that I actually had the power to liberate myself from the guilt and confusion that had been stopping me from moving forward.

Since that day, I have been more committed to the goal of building a vegan world than I have ever been to anything. As the years go by, I continue to be humbled by new realisations that allow my understanding to deepen and expand, and with every day that passes with the animals still in captivity, my determination gets even stronger to do the very best I can to help bring about their liberation.

It remains a tremendous privilege to spend my time and energy helping others to have the Gentle World experience, whether in person or through our online portal, through which we try to open the minds and hearts of all who might find themselves wandering through.

As we look into the future, impatient and anxious, yet always hoping emancipation might be closer than we think, my wish for those of us who call ourselves vegan is that we are able to somehow become even better at reaching out to those who are yet to be convinced, yet to be awakened to the profound truth of what veganism really means – for us, for the animals, and for life as we know it. I believe we must always be striving to reach the next turning point, the next new horizon in our world-view, for so many are depending on us. And for them, for the sake of the innocent beings who remain unrecognised by a world blind to their true value, we must be the very best we can be. Only then will we be capable of doing the very best we can do.

■ STRIVING FOR A VEGAN PLANET
Trisha Roberts

Trisha Roberts is an abolitionist vegan who created *LiveVegan*, an abolitionist vegan page on Facebook in 2009. She has a blog *"Veganism Is Nonviolence"*. . .   ■

▶ Trisha Roberts.

I grew up in the 1960s in South-East Queensland, Australia, in an environment rich in animal life. My relationship to non-humans was a significant aspect of my childhood. After leaving home, I lived in a number of communal houses, sharing with like-minded people. Social justice issues and activism were important to me. I was quite unaware of my own speciesism, being vegetarian at various times, and not at all consistent in applying moral concern for animals.

In the mid 1990s, I was influenced by Tibetan Buddhism with its principles of nonviolence and non-harm toward *all* sentient beings, including insects, but sadly Buddhist teachers promoted moral confusion by eating and wearing animal products in their daily lives.

My first real epiphany happened in early 2005, when I came across information on the reality of the dairy industry. I remember feeling horrified that this was seen as acceptable. After further investigation, my partner Dede and I realised we had to reject all forms of animal use and we became ethical vegans overnight, and although we knew little about veganism, we did our best to eliminate animal use from our lives.

After becoming vegan, I felt it was important to do whatever I could to assist in abolishing societal animal exploitation. We discovered a number of 'animal organisations' online, attended some protests, but we were disturbed by the fact that many protesters were clearly not vegan, and the 'solutions' to 'inhumane' treatment were just a slightly different form of torture. We distanced ourselves from these campaigns and organisations.

We then very naively decided to approach and lobby local government by setting up a small not-for-profit group. We quickly recognised the whole process of dealing with government was essentially a co-option, where animal advocates pushed for minor change, and in the process supported and reinforced it was morally acceptable to exploit animals as long as it was 'humane'. A watershed for us was when we were asked to make comment on the draft policy for the treatment of pigs. All animal groups were advocating for slightly bigger cages, slightly 'better' conditions, than the draft policy suggested, but all we could see in this policy and its recommendations was torture. We could not, in good conscience, recommend welfare reform, so we commenced our submission by stating we opposed animal use, and that the natural requirement for a herd of pigs was several square miles of forest understorey. Thankfully, our venture into this territory was short-lived, and in disgust, we ended any participation in lobbying government for welfare 'improvement'. We could not support something which – if applied to humans – would be considered torture and where the baseline position was the assumption that animals are property.

Our next venture, in mid 2006, was to introduce veganism to a large international Tibetan Buddhist organisation. The name, 'Liberation of Our Brother and Sister Animals' (LOBSA), was chosen for our group by the spiritual director. In an attempt to back up my position, I discovered many texts in which Shakyamuni Buddha said we should do our best to avoid harming non-human animals, including insects and invertebrates, and said we should avoid eating and wearing and using animal products which were the result of intentional killing and harm. However, speciesism is pervasive and there was much more resistance than I expected, which only increased when it was thought our vegan advocacy would reflect badly upon some of their teachers, including His Holiness the Dalai Lama who was non-vegan. Sadly after a year, we decided to end our association with their organisation. We then tried working through the Karmapa and Drukpa traditions and while it was more positive, we still could not find teachers who would advocate veganism.

I then decided my vegan advocacy would have a much greater reach online, and that my abolitionist advocacy would be secular in nature from a position of justice and nonviolence, so I started *LiveVegan* on social media sites, including YouTube and Facebook. In mid-2009, I came across Professor Gary L Francione online. I had heard of him before, but his work had been misrepresented. I observed his explanations to others and his ideas resonated immediately. In fact it was a relief to finally hear such clarity. Until this time, I had not felt the confidence to fully articulate my thoughts about speciesism and 'reform'. His explanations made a great deal of sense and I decided this was definitely the way to proceed. I was also impressed with the way he connected veganism to other social justice issues.

The disturbing thing about speciesism is that we are so heavily indoctrinated – that it is in plain sight and yet invisible. We mistakenly think we are doing our best to lead nonviolent lives and yet we live unconsciously each and every day as we eat, wear and use animals. Although I'm fortunate to live in a beautiful rural area in Tasmania, it is difficult to truly enjoy this while seeing non-human slaves in the fields, and with the awareness that we torture and murder well over one trillion land and aquatic animals globally each year, mostly for our palate's pleasure.

I spend as much time as I can doing vegan education. There's no financial gain at all from my efforts. It's been encouraging to see how many continue to join my abolitionist page *LiveVegan*. In early 2014 it had more than fifty-five thousand members, growing at a few thousand each month. This demonstrates an ever-increasing nonviolent, grassroots, vegan movement and the effectiveness of a morally consistent vegan message. In addition to online activism, my partner Dede and I have hosted several local events where we have provided free delicious vegan cakes and taken the opportunity to talk about veganism.

The disturbing thing about speciesism is that we are so heavily indoctrinated – that it is in plain sight and yet invisible. We mistakenly think we are doing our best to lead nonviolent lives and yet we live unconsciously each and every day as we eat, wear and use animals. ▓

I strive to incorporate *Ahimsa* into every aspect of my life; my thoughts, words and actions. I don't know how successful I am, but I try. I find that veganism has had a wonderfully profound and far-reaching effect on all aspects of my life, much more than I ever imagined, and through veganism I have a much better understanding about my own place in the world. It makes me grateful I did not leave the world before becoming vegan, and I hope to share this understanding with as many as possible before I do. It's clear to me now that enslaving and exploiting non-humans in any way is as morally unjustifiable and wrong as the exploitation and enslavement of children. It is also clear to me that we are all interconnected, and as long as we engage in violence and injustice by eating, wearing and using other animals for any reason, we will never know peace. Veganism will solve many of the world's problems. It is at the heart of nonviolence. Striving for a vegan planet is not 'idealistic', it is achievable and it starts with each of us. Becoming vegan is a moral imperative.

▓ CONTEMPLATING THE PRECIOUS LIFE OF ANIMALS
Vera Cristofani

▶ Vera Cristofani with Maggy and Luana.

"Compassionate exploitation *is the most contradictory combination of words I have ever heard!*" ▓

—Vera Cristofani

In 1995 I was sitting in a Buddhist monastery for the first time in California listening to a lecture on the five precepts. When it was said that the precept 'Do Not Kill' should be extended to all sentient beings, I had an epiphany. That apparently simple and obvious information suddenly brought me a series of recollections on what I had been doing in my life until that moment. After leaving the lecture room, my mind was utterly uneasy. I experienced thoughts that provoked mixed states of amazement, happiness, shame and sadness for many hours. I wondered how I could have been so uninformed and naive to the fact that other sentient beings had to suffer unnecessarily and die to satisfy my hunger? How did I fail to see that the animals I ate such as cows, pigs, chickens and fish were no different from the many beloved dogs and cats who have always been part of my life?

Several thoughts kept coming and going. On one hand, it was extremely sad I was thirty-three before I came to this realisation. On the other hand, it was nice to have had the opportunity to hear and understand the sublime teaching in that moment. When my emotions settled down, things started to fall into place quickly. The next day there was no doubt about what to do: I had to stop eating non-human animals immediately; and that was what I did without reflecting on any effects this decision would have on the people who surrounded me. It did not mean I was disrespecting them. It was just that there was an urgent need to include non-human animals into my realm of moral consideration. For three days I did not feel the desire to eat anything so I relied on nuts, raisins and lots of inner joy.

As with everyone in my culture, I was also indoctrinated with anthropocentrism, and there was little chance of encountering veganism in the 70s and 80s in Brazil. Although I have always had a strong connection with nature and all its creatures and had cried many times in front of the TV hearing about seal slaughter during Greenpeace actions, the process of investigating animal issues would only happen later. My attention was centered, for many years to come, on politics and its disastrous policies, which in my view were responsible for the increasing inequalities among people and the notion that problems could be solved only under fairer kinds of government. Since changing the world alone has never been an easy task, my choice was to try to understand it better first. So in order to undermine my inner growing rebellion, my focus shifted mainly to philosophy as an attempt to explain logically why we tend to make many destructive and irrational choices, often to protect our individuality, when all evidence shows that interconnectedness is more than a fact and should be part of every decision we make.

I discovered a booklet in Portuguese called *Animal Rights: The Abolitionist Approach,* with a collection of essays written by Professor Gary L Francione. On the second page I read, "There is no distinction between meat and dairy. To say that you do not eat meat but that you eat dairy or eggs is like saying that you eat large cows but not small cows. There is as much if not more suffering in a glass of milk than in a pound of steak and all of these animals end up in the same slaughterhouse after which we eat them anyway."

The impact of Professor Francione's message on me was profound. It was not the first time I had heard the term, however previous messages seemed to fail in some aspects of a conceptual, moral or even strategic nature in relation to animal rights. Most were loaded with welfarism conveying the idea of 'compassionate' exploitation, such as 'happy' meat, 'happy' cage-free eggs, 'happy' dairy. These failed to offer any meaningful protection to non-human animals considering that all animals value their lives, and if we reflect just a minute about them, we will certainly see they do not want to be exploited and killed. 'Compassionate exploitation' is the most contradictory combination of words I have ever heard!

In 2010, I participated in a workshop given by Professor Francione called 'A Revolution of the Heart', which has borne a lot of good fruit in my advocacy. The first step was the construction of a site called *Veganos pela Abolição* (Vegans for Abolition) with the intention to have one more channel to spread the abolitionist approach; and together with my partner Luis Martini, we started a reading group called *GeFRAN* that focuses on the study of Professor Francione's theory. In addition, inspired by PAN's Vegan Pledge, a project called *Apoio Vegano* (Vegan Support) was born to support new vegans and people who want to become vegan.

I can truly say that going vegan was one of the best things I have done in my life, and although I still walk around wondering about existence and its mystery, this crucial piece to the life puzzle that decreases violence and increases justice towards non-humans has been solved, leading to a more peaceful and fair relationship with all animals. If I could humbly leave one piece of advice I would say we have to consider that all we have in life is just this moment, and this exact moment is perfect for anyone to go vegan and speak on behalf of non-human animals.

Resources

Further information on adopting a well-balanced plant based diet.

Caldwell B. Esselstyn, Jr. MD. Prevent and Reverse Heart Disease. http://www. dresselstyn.com/

Joel Fuhrman MD. Smart Nutrition, Superior Health. http://www.drfuhrman. com/

Dr McDougall's Health and Medical Center. https://www.drmcdougall.com/ index.php

Michael Gregor, MD. http://www.drgreger.org/

Michael Klaper, MD. Physician, Consultant and Educator in Medicine and Applied Nutrition. http://doctorklaper.com/

Physicians Committee For Responsible Medicine. http//www.pcrm.org/

Documentaries.

A Sacred Duty. Co-producer Richard Schwartz.

Blackfish. Directed by Gabriela Cowperthwaite. 2013.

Cowspiracy: The Sustainability Secret.

Earthlings. Directed by Shaun Monson. Released in 2005.

Forks Over Knives. Directed by Lee Fulkerson. Released in 2011.

Got the Facts on Milk. Directed by Shira Lane. Released in 2011.

Our Diet – Leading to a Sustainable Future, Or Killing Our Planet? //www. vivalavegan.net/.

Peaceable Kingdom, the Journey Home. Directed by Jenny Stein 2009.

Skin Trade. Directed by Shannon Keith.

The Animals Film. Directed by Victor Schonfeld and Myriam Alaux. First released in 1981. DVD Released in 2007.

The Cove. http://www.thecovemovie.com/ Released in 2009.

The Ghosts in our Machine. http://www.theghostsinourmachine.com/about/ Released in 2013

Vegucated. A Filmbluff Presentation 2010.

Selected Bibliography.

Balcombe J (2006). *Pleasurable Kingdom: Animals and the Nature of Feeling Good.* Macmillan.

Balcombe J (2010). *Second Nature: The Inner Lives of Animals.* Palgrave Macmillan.

Balcombe J (2011). *The Exultant Ark: A Pictorial Tour of Animal Pleasure.* University of California Press.

Barnard Neal D (1993). Food Is a Wonder Medicine: The Power to Heal Is on Your Plate. Magni Publishing.

Barnard Neal D (1999). Foods that Fight Pain. Harmony Books.

Barnard Neal D (2009). A Nutrition Guide for Clinicians. 2nd ed. PCRM.

Barnard Neal D (2009). The Cancer Survivor's Guide. Book Publishing Company.

Barnard Neal D (2010). The Get Healthy, Go Vegan Cookbook. Da Capo Lifelong Books.

Barnard Neal D (2010). The Reverse Diabetes Diet. Rodale Books.

Barnard Neal D (2010). Turn Off the Fat Genes: The Revolutionary Guide to Losing Weight. Random House.

Barnard Neal D (2011). The 21-Day Weight Loss Kickstart. Da Capo Lifelong Books.

Barnard Neal D (2013). Power Foods for the Brain. Grand Central Life & Style.

Barnard Neal D and Jennifer Raymond (1993). Food for Life: How the New Four Food Groups Can Save your life. Harmony Books.

Barnard Neal D, Judy Brown and Dorothy R Bates (1995). Foods That Cause You to Lose Weight: The Negative Calorie Effect. Book Publishing Company.

Bauer Gene (2008). *Farm Sanctuary: Changing Hearts and Minds About Animals and Food.* Touchstone.

Bekoff M (2002). *Minding animals: Awareness, emotions and heart.* Oxford University Press, New York.

Bekoff M (2007). *The emotional lives of animals.* New World Library, Novato, California.

Bekoff M (2010). *The animal manifesto: Six reasons for expanding our compassion footprint.* New World Library, Novato, California.

Bekoff M (2013). *Why dogs hump and bees get depressed: The fascinating science of animal intelligence, emotions, friendship, and conservation.* New World Library, Novato, California.

Bekoff M (2014). *Rewilding our hearts: Building pathways of compassion and coexistence.* New World Library, Novato, California.

Bekoff M and Jessica Pierce (2009). *Wild justice: The moral lives of animals.* University of Chicago Press, Chicago.

Campbell T Colin and Thomas M Campbell (2005). *The China Study.* BenBella Books.

Carman Judy (1999). *Born to Be Blessed: Seven Keys to Joyful Living.*

Carman Judy (2003). *Peace to All Beings: Veggie Soup for the Chicken's Soul.* Lantern Books.

Carman Judy and Tina Volpe (2009). *The Missing Peace: The Hidden Power of Our Kinship with Animals.* Dreamriver Press.

Divine Kathy (2011). *Forever 21: The Empowering Guide to Reclaiming your Youth, Beauty, Health, Happiness and Spirituality.* Vivid Publishing.

Divine Kathy (2013). *Plant-powered Men.* Createspace.

Divine Kathy (2013). *Vegans are Cool.* 2nd edition. Createspace.

Divine Kathy (2014). *Plant-powered women.* Createspace.

Francione Gary L (1995). *Animals, Property, and the Law.*

Francione Gary L (1996). *Rain Without Thunder: The Ideology of the Animal Rights Movement*

Francione Gary L (2000). *Introduction to Animal Rights: Your Child or the Dog?*

Francione Gary L (2008). *Animals as Persons: Essays on the Abolition of Animal Exploitation.*

Francione Gary L and Anna E Charlton (1992). *Vivisection and Dissection in the Classroom: A Guide to Conscientious Objection.*

Francione Gary L and Anna E Charlton (2013). *Eat Like You Care: An Examination of the Morality of Eating Animals.*

Gentle World (2003). *Incredibly Delicious: Recipes for a New Paradigm.* Gentle World.

Hawthorne Mark (2007). *Striking at the Roots: A Practical Guide to Animal Activism.* Changemakers Books.

Hawthorne Mark (2013). *Bleating Hearts: The Hidden World of Animal Suffering.* Changemakers Books.

Iacobbo Michael and Karen (2006). *Vegetarians and Vegans in America Today.* Praeger Publishers.

Joy Melanie (2008). *Strategic Action for Animals.* Lantern Books.

Joy Melanie (2010). *Why We Love Dogs, Eat Pigs, and Wear Cows.* Conari Press.

Knight Andrew (2011). *The Costs and Benefits of Animal Experiments.* Palgrave Macmillan.

Linzey Andrew (1999). Animal Gospel. Westminster John Knox Press.

Linzey Andrew (2009). Creatures of the Same God. Lantern Books.

Lyman Harold and Glen Merzer (2001). Mad Cowboy: Plain Truth from the Cattle Rancher Who Won't Eat Meat. Scribner Publishing.

Patrick-Goudreau C (2007). *The Joy of Vegan Baking.* Rockport Publishing.

Patrick-Goudreau C (2011). *The 30-Day Vegan Challenge, Color Me Vegan.* Rockport Publishing.

Patrick-Goudreau C (2011). *Vegan's Daily Companion: 365 Days of Inspiration for Cooking, Eating, and Living Compassionately.* Rockport Publishing.

Phelps Norm (2002). *The Dominion of Love.* Lantern Books.

Phelps Norm (2004). *The Great Compassion: Buddhism and Animal Rights.* Lantern Books.

Phelps Norm (2007). *The Longest Struggle: Animal Advocacy from Pythagoras to Peta.* Lantern Books.

Regan Tom (1983). *The Case for Animal Rights.* University of California Press.

Rifkin Jeremy (1992). *Beyond Beef: The Rise and Fall of the Cattle Culture.* Plume.

Rifkin Jeremy (1998). *The Biotech Century.* Victor Gollancz.

Robbins John (2012). *No Happy Cows.*

Robbins John (1998). *A Diet for a New America.*

Roth Ruby (2009). *That's Why We Don't Eat Animals: A Book About Vegans, Vegetarians and All Living Things.* North Atlantic Books.

Roth Ruby (2012). *Vegan Is Love: Having Heart and Taking Action.* North Atlantic Books.

Roth Ruby (2013). *V is for Vegan: The Abcs of Being Kind.* North Atlantic Books.

Schwartz Richard H (1994). *Judaism and Global Survival.* Lantern Books.

Schwartz Richard H (1998). *Mathematics and Global Survival:* Scarcity, Hunger, Population Growth, Pollution, Waste. Ginn Press.

Schwartz Richard H (2001). *Judaism and Vegetarianism.* Lantern Books.

Schwartz Richard H and Yonassan Gershom (2011). *Who Stole My Religion: Revitalising Judaism and Applying Jewish Values to Help Heal our Imperiled Planet.* Lulu Press.

Scully Matthew (2011). *Dominion: The Power of Man, the Suffering of Animals, and the Call to Mercy.* Souvenir Press.

Sears David (2003). *The Vision of Eden: Animal Welfare and Vegetarianism in Jewish Law and Mysticism.* Spring Valley NY. Orot.

Sheridan J and Kim Sheridan (1991). *UnCooking with Jameth and Kim*

Sheridan Kim (2006). *Animals and the Afterlife: True Stories of Our Best Friends' Journey Beyond Death.* Hay House.

Singer, Peter (1975). *Animal Liberation: Towards an End to Man's Inhumanity to Animals.* HarperCollins.

Stanger Janice (2009). *The Perfect Formula Diet.* Perfect Planet Solutions.

Supreme Master Ching Hai (1991). *The Key of Immediate Enlightenment.* Supreme Master Ching Hai.

Tuttle W (2005). *The World Peace Diet.* Lantern Books.

Wulff G (2011). *I Love Animals.* SpiritWings Publications.

Wulff G (2011). *There's a Polar Bear in the Fridge.* SpiritWings Publications.

Wulff G (2011). *Uncle Edgar and the Lady with the Hat.* Published by Gypsy Wulff.

Young Richard A (1998). *Is God A Vegetarian?* Open Court Publishing Company.

Wagman Bruce A (2010). *Growing Up With Animal Law: From Courtrooms to Casebooks,* Journal of Legal Education, Vol. 60, No. 2 Nov. 2010.

Organisations/Advocacy groups.

Animal Justice Party of Australia. //www.animaljusticeparty.org/

Animal Liberation Victoria. //www.alv.org.au/

Animal Outreach of Kansas. //www/amimaloutreach-ks.org/

Animal Rescue Media Organisation.//www.arme.tv/
Animal Welfare Party, UK. //www.animalwelfareparty.org/
Billie Dean International Deep Peace Organisation. //www.billiedean.com/
Carnism Awareness and Action Network (CAAN). //www.carnism.org/
Companion Rabbit Advocates. //www.rabbitadvocates.org/
Cowspiracy: The Sustainability Secret. http://cowspiracy.com/
Evolve! Campaigns. http://evolvecampaigns.org.uk/evolve/default.aspx
Extreme Vegan Sporting Association. //www.extremevegansports.org/
Farmkind – Harold Brown. //www.farmkind.org/
Food Empowerment Project. //www.foodispower.org/
Free from Harm. //www.freefromharm.org/
Gentle World, New Zealand and Hawaii. //www.gentleworld.org/
Help International Plant Protein Organisation (HIPPO). //www.ivu.org/hippo/
Humane Research Australia http://www.humaneresearch.org.au/
Humane Society University. //www.humanesocietyuniversity.org/
In Defense of Animals. //www.idausa.org/
Matilda's Promise, Animal Rights & Vegan Education Centre, Ireland.
Matilda's Promise. //www.matildaspromise.org/
Mother Nature Network. //www.mnn.com/
Openrescue. //www.openrescue.org/
People for the Ethical Treatment of Animals (PETA). //www.peta.org/
Physicians' Committee for Responsible Medicine (PCRM). //www.pcrm.org/
Quaker Concern for Animals. //www/quaker-animals.co.uk/
Roots & Shoots. www/rootsandshoots.org/
Sea Shepherd Conservation Society. //www.seashepherd.org/
The Thinking Vegan. //www.thethinkingvegan.com/
Visakha Society for the Protection and Care of Animals India.//www.vspca.org/
Winsome Constance Kindness Australia. http://www.kindnesstrust.com/

For further information on animal treatment in Australia visit Animals Australia.

www.animalsaustralia.org.
A vast array of information and resources are available including Fact Sheets on:
Animal Experimentation
Animal Exploitation
Broiler Chickens
Companion Animals
Dairy Cows
Dissection
Duck Shooting and others.

Addendum

■ MEAT MAKES THE RICH ILL AND THE POOR HUNGRY
From Feed The World by Viva![1]

Introduction by Jeremy Rifkin

When representatives meet at the World Food Summit they supposedly focus on how to get food into the mouths of nearly one billion people who are currently undernourished. However, at all the dinners they attend you can expect to see the consumption of large quantities of meat. And herein lies the contradiction.

People go hungry because much arable land is used to grow feed grain for animals rather than people. In the US, one hundred and fifty seven million tons of cereals, legumes and vegetable protein – all suitable for human consumption – is fed to livestock to produce just twenty-eight million tons of animal protein in the form of meat.

In developing countries, using land to create an artificial food chain has resulted in misery for hundreds of millions of people. An acre of cereal produces five times more protein than an acre used for meat production; legumes such as beans, peas and lentils can produce ten times more protein and, in the case of soya, thirty times more.

Global corporations which supply the seeds, chemicals and cattle and which control the slaughterhouses, marketing and distribution of beef, eagerly promote grain-fed livestock. They equate it with a country's prestige, and climbing the 'protein ladder' becomes the mark of success.

Enlarging their meat supply is the first step for all developing countries. They start with chicken and egg production and, as their economies grow, climb the protein ladder to pork, milk and dairy products, then to grass-fed beef and finally to grain-fed beef. Encouraging this process advances the interests of agribusinesses and two-thirds of the grain exported from the USA goes to feed livestock. The process really got underway when 'green revolution' technology produced grain surpluses in the 1970s. The United Nations Food and Agricultural Organisation encouraged it and the USA government linked its food aid programme to the producing of feed grain and gave low-interest loans to establish grain-fed poultry operations. Many nations have attempted to remain high on the protein ladder long after the grain surpluses disappeared.

Human consequences of the shift from food to feed were dramatically illustrated during the Ethiopian famine in 1984. While people starved, Ethiopia was growing linseed cake, cottonseed cake and rapeseed meal for European livestock.

241

Millions of acres of land in the developing world are used for this purpose. Tragically, eighty percent of the world's hungry children live in countries with food surpluses, which are fed to animals for consumption by the affluent.

The irony is that millions of consumers in the first world are dying from diseases of affluence such as heart attacks, strokes, diabetes and cancer, brought on by eating animal products, while the world's poor are dying from diseases of poverty. We are long overdue for a global discussion on how to promote a diversified, high-protein, vegetarian diet for the human race.

Jeremy Rifkin is the author of Beyond Beef: The Rise and Fall of the Cattle Culture (Plume, 1992), and The Biotech Century (Victor Gollancz, 1998). He is also the president of the Foundation on Economic Trends in Washington DC, USA.

Despite the rich diversity of foods found all over the world, one-third of its population does not have enough to eat. Today, hunger is a massive problem in many parts of Africa, Asia and South America and the future is not looking good. The global population is set to rise from 6.5 billion (2006) to 9.3 billion by 2050[2] and Worldwatch reports[3] forecast severe global food shortages leading to famine on an unprecedented scale.

This misery is partly a direct result of our desire to eat meat. Children in the developing world starve next to fields of food destined for export as animal feed, to support the meat-hungry cultures of the rich world. While millions die, one-third of the world's grain production is fed to farmed animals in rich countries[4].

If animal farming were to stop and we were to use the land to grow grain to feed ourselves, we could feed every single person on this planet. Consuming crops directly – rather than feeding them to animals and then eating animals – is a far more efficient way to feed the world.

The problem today

The land in poor countries is still largely not owned by the people who work on it, and rents are high. Huge areas are owned by large companies based in the West. It is common for people to be thrown off the land, often going to the towns where there is little other work. About one hundred and sixty thousand people move from rural areas to cities every day[5]. Many migrants are forced to settle in shanty-towns and squatter settlements.

The sad irony is that the world produces more than enough plant food to meet the needs of all its six billion people. If people used land to grow crops to feed themselves, rather than feeding crops to animals, then there would be enough to provide everyone with the average of two thousand three hundred and sixty calories needed for good health[6].

Breeding animals means starving people

Breeding animals is an incredibly inefficient way to try and feed the world's growing population. Yet after food rationing during the Second World War, intensive animal farming was actively encouraged as a way of ensuring our future 'food security'.

Most meat in Western Europe is now produced in factory farms which, as the name implies, are production lines for animals. To meet the large demand for meat, billions of animals are kept in cramped, filthy conditions, often unable to move properly and not allowed fresh air or even natural light. Unable to feed outdoors naturally, they are fed grain, oil seeds, soya feed, fishmeal and sometimes the remains of other animals. High quality land is used to grow grains and soya beans – land that could be used to grow crops for humans.

The grain fed to animals does not convert directly into meat to feed people. The vast majority is either excreted or used as 'fuel' to keep the animal alive and functioning. For every ten kilograms of soya protein fed to America's cattle only one kilogram is converted to meat. Almost the entire population of India and China, nearly two billion people, could be fed on the protein consumed and largely wasted by the United States' beef herd[7].

Because of the demand for animal feed, a Western meat-based diet uses four and a half times more land than is necessary for a vegan diet and two and a quarter times more than for a vegetarian diet[8].

Where does the animal feed come from?

The amount of land used to grow animal feed in Western countries is not enough to meet their own needs and more is imported from developing countries. Land in some developing countries, such as India, is also used to grow grain for animals who are reared and killed for export.

Currently, farmed animals eat one-third of the world's cereal production. In the industrialised world, two-thirds of the agricultural land produces cereals for animal feed. The EU imports forty-five per cent of its oilseeds (soya) and, overall, imports seventy percent of its protein for animal feed (1995-96). As the European Commission admits, "Europe's agriculture is capable of feeding Europe's people but not of feeding Europe's animals"[4]. The European Union (EU) also imports cattle feed such as peanuts or soya because it is cheaper than buying animal feed grown in Europe.

At the height of the Ethiopian famine in 1984-85, Britain imported one and a half million pounds worth of linseed cake, cottonseed cake and rape seed meal. Good quality farmland was being used to grow animal feed for rich countries when it could have been used to grow food for Ethiopians.

In the United States, farmed animals, mostly cattle, consume almost twice as much grain as is eaten by the entire US population[9]. Seventy percent of all the wheat, corn and other grain produced goes to feeding animals[10]. More than one hundred million acres of US agricultural land is used to grow grain for animals[9] and still more is imported.

In Central and South America, ever-increasing amounts of land are being used to grow soya beans and grain for export – to be used as animal feed. In Brazil, twenty-three percent of the cultivated land is currently used to produce soya beans, of which nearly half are for export[9]. The Oxfam Poverty Report explains that the subsidised expansion of the EU's dairy and livestock industry has created a huge demand for high protein animal feedstuffs, and the demand has in part been met through the expansion of large-scale, mechanised soya production in Brazil. Smallholder producers of beans and staple foods in the southern part of the country have been displaced to make way for giant soya estates. Soya has now become the country's major agricultural export, "however, it is a trading arrangement which had proved considerably more efficient at feeding European cattle than with maintaining the livelihoods of poor Brazilians"[11].

Twenty-five years ago, livestock consumed less than six percent of Mexico's grain. Today, at least one-third of the grain produced in that country is being fed to animals. At the same time, millions of people living in the country are chronically undernourished[9].

It's not surprising that the World Health Organisation has called for a shift away from meat production so people can consume crops directly. It says:

"Farming policies that do not require intensive animal production systems would reduce the world demand for cereals. Use of land could be reappraised since cereal consumption for direct consumption by the population is much more efficient and cheaper than dedicating large areas to growing feed for meat production and dairying. Policies should be geared to the growing of plant foods and to limiting the promotion of meat and dairy."[12]

Governments worldwide have ignored this advice. Instead of promoting the growing of plant foods for human consumption, they offer subsidy payments and financial incentives to livestock farmers, thereby actively encouraging meat production.

Who is hungry?

About six billion people share the planet, one quarter in the rich north and three quarters in the poor south. While people in rich countries diet because they eat too much, many in the developing world do not have enough food simply to ensure their bodies work properly and stay alive.

Eight hundred and twenty-six million people around the world are seriously undernourished – seven hundred and ninety-two million people in developing countries and another thirty-four million in industrialised countries[13]. Two billion people – one-third of the global population – lack food security, defined by the Food and Agriculture Organisation (FAO) as a "state of affairs where all people at all times have access to safe and nutritious food to maintain a healthy and active life"[5].

Today, some twelve million children die annually of nutrition-related diseases. The Food and Agriculture Organisation says, "Doubtless, far more are chronically ill"[14].

There are more chronically hungry people in Asia and the Pacific, but the depth of hunger is greatest in sub-Saharan Africa. In forty-six percent of countries there, the undernourished have an average deficit of more than three hundred kilocalories per day[14]. In 1996-98, twenty-eight percent of the population on the African continent were chronically undernourished (one hundred and ninety-two million people)[15].

Access to food is a basic right, enshrined in a number of human rights instruments to which states around the world have committed themselves. At the 1996 World Food Summit, leaders from one hundred and eighty-five countries and the European Community reaffirmed, in the Rome Declaration on Food Security, "the right of everyone to have access to safe and nutritious food, consistent with the right to adequate food and the fundamental right of everyone to be free from hunger." They pledged to cut the number of the world's hungry people in half by 2015[16].

Starvation does not occur because of a world food shortage. If everyone ate a vegetarian, or better still a vegan diet, there would be enough food for everyone. The only sane way forward is to grow food for humans rather than to feed it to farmed animals.

Much of the aid given to developing world countries has been 'tied aid' – this means the countries that receive it have to buy goods and services from the countries that give it. In this way, most of the money is simply returned to those who gave it.

During the 1970s, the US only gave aid to Nicaragua in exchange for the production of beef, causing the loss of one thousand square kilometres of rainforest per year. By 1979, Nicaragua was Latin America's biggest supplier of beef to the US.

Falling harvests

Reasons for falling grain harvests include poorer soil, lack of water and climate change but the message is clear – unless we change our diet to one not centred on animals we will force millions more people into starvation throughout the world. Whilst grain harvests are falling, the demand for grain is rising. The Worldwatch Institute states that, "Grain production is unlikely to rise fast enough to satisfy projected demand for both food and feed"[17]. If global grain production does not rise fast enough, there will not be enough grain to satisfy demand and grain prices will rise. But livestock farmers would still be able to sell their meat to the wealthy, and so would be able to outbid the poor in the market for scarce grain.

Human starvation will worsen whilst animals will continue to be fed so rich people can continue to eat meat.

The green revolution

The 'green revolution' of the late 1960s and early 1970s was billed as the solution to world hunger. Productivity was increased through farm machinery, pesticides and fertilisers, irrigation and the replacement of traditional crops with high-yielding varieties.

It failed to benefit those who needed it. This 'revolution' focused on boosting the yields of a narrow base of cereals – corn, wheat and rice. The gains in cereal production often came at the expense of cultivation of more nutritious legumes, root crops and other grains. This resulted in reduced dietary diversity and contributed to widespread nutritional deficiencies as well as depletion of the soil and wildlife loss.

The 'revolution' also favoured wealthier farmers because they were the ones who could afford to invest in the new technologies. The United Nations Population Fund states that, "Landlessness among former subsistence farmers and impoverishment have been unlooked-for consequences of the Green Revolution"[5].

The livestock revolution

Many countries in Asia and Africa have traditionally based their diets around rice, beans, pulses and vegetables, either following a wholly vegetarian diet or only including low amounts of meat and fish. This is exactly the type of nutritious diet that is now being promoted by health officials in the West in an attempt to combat diseases such as obesity, heart disease and cancer – low in animal fats and high in fibre, vegetable protein and essential vitamins. Yet developing countries, keen to copy Western lifestyles, increasingly perceive meat eating as a sign of wealth and progress. This shift towards meat consumption is being described as the Livestock Revolution.

The insanity of factory farming

This increase in factory farming is creating huge problems. In Bangladesh, for example, which is one of the world's poorest countries, battery hen systems have become widespread. The country has massive shortages of food, many unemployed people and very little money to spare. Factory farming needs money for equipment, creates hardly any jobs and uses up much valuable plant food that could be fed to people.

Factory farming does not meet the needs of these people but it does benefit people in Western countries where much of the equipment needed, such as tractors and building materials, is made. When developing countries buy them they then become dependent on the suppliers for spare parts and repairs.

Poultry World magazine highlighted "the great scope for expansion" in Africa. It emphasised how African countries are largely dependent on Western countries for breeding stock, feed and pharmaceuticals[18].

China has seen an enormous rise in pork production over the past decade and hence an enormous increase in its need for animal feed. The country has transformed from being an exporter of eight million tonnes of grain in 1993 to becoming a net importer of sixteen million tonnes by 1995[19].

If developing countries look to consuming the same quantity of meat per head as the average American, food shortages will become desperate. Yet rather than switch to vegetarianism, livestock scientists advocate boosting the 'feed efficiency' of animals. A modern intensively raised chicken will put on three kilograms from the same amount of feed that in 1957 only yielded two kilograms. US scientists have discovered that pigs can be made to grow forty percent faster on twenty-five percent less feed if they are injected with DNA encoding a modified, long-lasting releasing factor for growth hormones[17]. In livestock science, animals are perceived as unfeeling, unthinking, protein-making machines that can be tweaked and manipulated for our own benefit.

Factory farming means exporting the overuse of antibiotics and the increased risks of food poisoning and diseases such as cancer and heart disease which are associated with increased consumption of meat. It also means exporting the environmental damage caused by intensive farming systems, including the overuse of water and land degradation to provide the massive amount of crops these poor creatures are fed. If we act now, we could still stop this cycle of insanity and move towards agricultural systems, which would genuinely feed the world.

Malnutrition and obesity

For the first time in history, we have reached a situation where the number of overweight people rivals the number who are underweight, both estimated at 1.1 billion[20].

As countries grow wealthier, meat consumption tends to rise. Hunger problems are reduced but hospitals begin to see more cases involving illnesses such as obesity, cardiovascular disease, diabetes and cancer – all of which are linked to diets high in animal produce. China is at the forefront of the 'livestock revolution'. The share of adults who are overweight jumped from nine percent to fifteen percent between 1989 and 1992.

The number of diabetics worldwide whose condition results from overeating is projected to double between 1998 and 2025, with more than three quarters of this growth occurring in the developing world. Some countries will be battling hunger and obesity at the same time.

In a nutshell: countries whose people are starving are using their land to grow grain for export to feed the West's farmed animals. Nutritionally valuable food is being fed to animals to produce meat, on which Western countries are literally gorging themselves to death.

Send a Cow

Charities have been set up in the UK with the specific aim of promoting livestock farming in the developing world – claiming they are working to alleviate poverty. Some projects receive funding from the Department for International Development (DFID).

Send a Cow was set up by a group of Christian farmers in 1988. Most of Uganda's dairy cows had died during the civil war and the farmers literally began sending live cows from England to Africa. The charity has now set up a breeding programme within Africa[21].

Farm Africa also promotes livestock farming. Its promotional literature states, "The sort of poverty we see in the developing world is simply unacceptable. Our moral imperative must be to do everything in our power to overcome it"[22].

The point to be grasped is that whilst encouraging animal farming may temporarily alleviate the poverty of individual families, it can only contribute towards poverty in the long run. Promoting meat production can never be a solution to world hunger because it means promoting a diet, which drains valuable grain stocks and devastates the environment.

HIPPO

A welcome antidote to these charities is HIPPO – or Help International Plant Protein Organisation. It provides emergency relief for the hungry in the less developed world but just as importantly it encourages people to grow their own food – not meat or dairy but plant protein.

HIPPO's logic is simple: why wastefully feed millions of tons of soya to animals when it could feed far more people directly? It has nearly fifty percent high-quality protein, is rich in iron and calcium and all kinds of other vitamins and minerals, keeps without refrigeration, has low fat, no waste, no food poisoning bugs and doesn't cause suffering to animals[23]. Textured Vegetable Protein (TVP) – made from soya – can feed sixty people from the same amount of land that would feed two people on meat – and much more healthily.

Currently, HIPPO is supporting projects in various parts of Africa and one in Europe. At Keyevunze, they are supporting the training of one hundred and twenty health workers who are showing people how to improve their diets by growing soya. Results are already beginning to show with a reduction in kwashiorkor – a disease of poor nutrition.

In Malawi, HIPPO is working with the regional agricultural department to introduce soya as a crop to local villagers. They are helping to construct a small reservoir for irrigation and providing a soya mill to process the beans.

HIPPO was set up by Neville Heath Fowler after a trip to Ethiopia in 1992. Says Fowler, "If only some of the cotton fields could be devoted to soya, we dreamed, and if people could learn to value it as the miracle of nutrition that it is, then saplings such as those which the goats routinely destroyed could grow into spreading trees. Perhaps Ethiopia could then begin to recover the forests it had lost, climate change would be reversed and soil erosion arrested. And this could happen all over the world. If only we could deliver the antidote to the diseased Western idea that progress is synonymous with meat." HIPPO can be contacted at: Llangynog, Carmarthen.

E: hippocharity@aol.com

Global water shortage

The massive quantities of grain required to sustain a meat-based diet are not the only problem. The meat production process uses up vast quantities of water in a world where water is in short supply. It takes one thousand litres to produce one kilogram of wheat and one hundred thousand litres to produce one kilogram of beef[24]. About three quarters of the water we use goes on growing food[25] but vegetarians need less than a third as much water to sustain their diet as meat eaters[9]. Living in the West, it's easy to imagine that our water supplies are unlimited but globally, our fresh water supplies are being used up so fast that almost half a billion people already depend on non-renewable sources[26]. Seven percent of the world's population has not enough water, and by 2050 this will be seventy percent[25]. The situation is so dire that battles over water supplies are predicted to become a major source of conflict.

Worldwatch Institute chairman Lester Brown states, "In consumption terms, four hundred and eighty million of the world's six billion people are being fed with food produced with the unsustainable use of water. We are already using up the water which belongs to our children"[26]. The International Water Management Institute predicts that by 2025 about 2.7 billion people – a third of the world's population – will live in regions faced by regular and severe water scarcity. Asia and sub-Saharan Africa will be hit the hardest[47].

It's hard to imagine a scenario more sickening than a rich elite gorging itself on meat while the poorest third of the world's population literally dehydrate. A shift away from meat consumption must become a global priority if we are to have a hope of meeting the basic needs of the world's six billion inhabitants.

The solution is in our hands

The fast growth of the world's population is a serious problem because it means there are more mouths to feed, resulting in more pressure on water, land, wildlife and so on. By 2050, the forty-nine least-developed countries will nearly triple in size, from six hundred and sixty-eight million to 1.86 billion people[2]. By 2050, today's developing countries will account for more than eighty-five percent of the world's population[2].

However, although this makes the hunger problem worse, it does not actually cause it. It is the growth of incomes and demand for 'luxury' items in rich countries that have triggered the hunger crisis. The world is a much wealthier place today than it was forty years ago and as wages have risen they have encouraged large-scale meat eating in richer countries, heightening the competition for cereals between animals and humans.

A huge 'consumption gap' exists between industrialised and developing countries. The world's richest countries, with twenty percent of global population, account for eighty-six percent of total private consumption, whereas the poorest twenty percent of the world's people account for just 1.3 percent.

A child born today in an industrialised country will add more to consumption and pollution over his or her lifetime than thirty to fifty children born in developing countries[5].

The decline in world fish stocks, the erosion of agricultural land and the limits of technology to boost grain yields mean we are fast approaching the limit of resources and the Earth's carrying capacity. We need to rethink the way limited supplies of plant food are distributed and start feeding the world.

Eating meat is not the only reason for world hunger but it is a major cause. We must drastically change our eating habits if we are to feed the world adequately. People are going hungry while ever-increasing numbers of animals are fed huge amounts of food in a hopelessly inefficient system.

By not using animals as meat-producing machines, this food could be freed to help those who need it most. Vegetarianism, and even more, veganism, by using up far less of the world's resources of food, land water and energy, are positive steps we can all easily take to help feed people in poorer countries.

Endnotes:

1. Excerpt from Viva! www.viva.org.uk/guides/feedtheworld.htm
2. World Population Prospects: The 2000 Revision. United Nations Population Division.
3. Brown, L, Full House, Worldwatch Inst. 1994.
4. D'Silva, J, Factory Farming and Developing Countries, Compassion in World Farming Trust Briefing, January 2000.
5. Footprints and Milestones: Population and Environmental Change, United Nations Population Fund, 2001.
6. Tickell, C, speaking at the British Association for the Advancement of Science, 26 August 1991, reported in The Independent, 27 August 1991.
7. Gellatley, J, The Silent Ark. Thorsons 1996.
8. Spedding, C.R.W, Food for the 90's: The Impact of Organic Foods and Vegetarianism, 1990, pp. 231-41.
9. Rifkin, J, Beyond Beef, Penguin Books, 1992.
10. Ayres, E, Will We Still Eat Meat? Time, 08 November 1999.
11. Oxfam Poverty report, Oxfam, June 1995.
12. World Health Organisation, Geneva, 1991. Diet, Nutrition and the Prevention of Chronic Diseases, Technical Report Series 797.
13. The state of food insecurity in the world: www.fao.org/FOCUS/E?SOF100).
14. Balancing Interests and Resolving Conflicts: www.fao.org
15. Perspectives on Hunger, Poverty and Agriculture in Africa, Keynote Address by Jacques Diouf, Director-General, FAO, at the National Gathering on Africa, Washington DC, USA, 23.06.01: www.fao.org.
16. Food: a Fundamental Right: www.fao.org
17. Protein at a Price, New Scientist, 18 March 2001.
18. World Poultry, February 1989. In: The Meat Business – Devouring a Hungry Planet. Ed. Tansey, G. & D'Silva, J., Earthscan Publications, 1999.
19. Brown, L.R., Facing Food Scarcity, Worldwatch, November/December 1995.
20. Escaping Hunger, Escaping Excess, World Watch, July/August 2000.
21. How it Began: Send a Cow information sheet.
22. Farm Africa Annual Review 2000/2001.
23. Lane, T., Hip Hip Hippo, Viva!Life, Autumn/Winter 2001.
24. Dinyar, G., The No Nonsense Guide to Climate Change, N.I., 2001.
25. Water, Water Everywhere – But Only 0.8% to Drink, Observer, 19 December 1999.
26. Global Water Supply central issue at Stockholm Conference, www.cnn.com, 14 August 2000.
27. Scientists Search for a Way to Avert World Water Crisis, The Independent, 14 August 2001. Edited version of Feed the World published with permission by Viva!

SpiritWings Humane Education Inc. is a non-profit organisation creating a kinder world for animals and humans. It produces publications that show how our choices impact on animals and their well being. The organisation grew from a desire to reveal animals as sentient beings with unique intelligence and capacities, rather than as property and objects to be used for human purposes.

SpiritWings board members Gypsy Wulff and Fran Chambers both have extensive teaching backgrounds that span primary, secondary and tertiary education. They have worked together to compile *Turning Points in Compassion*, which profiles stories and philosophies from advocates around the world.

The organisation has also produced the *I Love Animals* series of books and activities for young children, designed to promote cruelty-free living with animals in an age-appropriate way.

All proceeds from the sale of *Turning Points in Compassion* and the *I Love Animals* series go to animal sanctuaries and rescue groups.

For more information visit: www.spiritwingspubs.com.au or www.turningpointsincompassion.info

Other publications from SpiritWings Humane Education Inc.

For Children

The I Love Animals Series contains three storybooks with accompanying activity books. These can be purchased separately or as a set. Suitable for 5-8 year olds. (And all those young at heart)

Great Uncle Edgar and the Lady With the Hat.

The Lady With the Hat is no ordinary Lady and Edgar is no ordinary pig! Together they team up to teach others to see what only a waking heart can know: that inside every pig is a being who would much rather be our friend than our food.

There's a Polar Bear in the Fridge.

Why would a polar bear want to live in your fridge? Find out what message this special bear has for children living in the suburbs.

I Love Animals.

What is there to love about animals? Lots of things! What do animals love about us? Find out in this delightfully illustrated book for younger children.

For Orders:
www.spiritwingspubs.com.au

CPSIA information can be obtained at www.ICGtesting.com
Printed in the USA
LVOW05s0222290815

452030LV00022B/79/P